Front Cover Photo

Veteran B&O historian and master model builder Edwin Kirstatter captured a freshly-painted I-5Dm C-2011 at Akron Junction, Ohio, in August 1961. The cab had been painted at the Du Bois, Pennsylvania, shops.

Rear Cover Photos

From top to bottom: Ed Kirstatter photographed two former I-16 cabooses renumbered as X-4197 and X-4194 for non-revenue MofW service in 1963 at Indianapolis. The C-2244 is shown on display at Somerset, Pennsylvania, on September 6, 1959, after being painted at the shops there. On December 30, 1966, the C-2177 is shown at Washington DC wearing a Brunswick, Maryland, paint scheme. The Brunswick shops also painted the C-2086 shown on the caboose track there on August 24, 1969. The class I-5 cab C-2245 was last painted at the Chillicothe, Ohio, shops and is shown with some minor wreck damage in August 1972. *Four images collection of Dwight Jones* C-1986, C-1912 and C-2082 are shown on the caboose track at Cowen, West Virginia, on November 29, 1974. *Dwight Jones*

Encyclopedia of B&O Cabooses
Volume 4
I-5 and I-16 Cars

Copyright © 2016 by Dwight Jones

All photos by Dwight Jones unless otherwise noted

Library of Congress Control Number: 2016915627
International Standard Book Number 978-0-9966798-1-7

Published by

Columbus, Ohio

Printed by
Walsworth Publishing Co.
Marceline, MO 64658

Contents

In the Next Volume . . .

We continue our journey back into B&O caboose history prior to the era described in this book, covering cars built in the 1920s and earlier. In Volume 5, readers will be informed by our extensive coverage of the I-10 cabooses, acquired from the BR&P, as well as first-generation B&O system-standard cabooses, classes I-1, I-1A, I-2, I-3 and some smaller classes. We will also cover B&OCT, Alton/GM&O, SIRT, and some smaller lines with ex B&O cabs. Stay tuned for the publication announcement.

Do You Have Any Photos?

We are still trying to document I-18 cabooses that were repainted during 1971-1972 into the solid blue scheme with yellow side lettering and yellow side stripe (the same scheme that the C-26 cars were delivered wearing). If you have photos showing this (caboose series B&O C-3000 to C-3045), please contact us. During 2016 thanks to the generosity of readers, we have added several hundred additional B&O caboose images to our collection—images that will help us with future coverage. If you would like to help by sending us scans of your images, or loaning us your originals to scan, please let us know.

Introduction

Welcome to the B&O Caboose Encyclopedia, Volume 4. If you have the previous volumes, you know that our format is starting with the modern cars and working our way backwards in time. In this volume we focus mainly on the popular I-5 family cars, the last group of cabooses built by the B&O with cupolas, and the I-16 cars, which had to be bumped from the previous volume due to space limitations.

To dash or not to dash. We prefer the dash (-) between the "C" and the caboose number. So that is our preferred method of referring to caboose numbers in this and our other books. B&O was inconsistent in their use of the dash—some shops used it at various times and others did not. We have never seen any official documentation from B&O officers indicating a preference either way. As historian John P. Hankey has observed "the B&O was consistently inconsistent".

Thanks to the generosity of other fans, modelers and history students we have been blessed with more and more unsolicited B&O caboose images coming our way. It is obvious that others appreciate the extensive coverage we are giving B&O cabooses and they are willing to help us by sharing their photography. Since our last volume we have received several large collections. These are great for research and use in books so please continue to help us if you can. Some fans have donated their originals while others, who have scanners, have copied their originals and sent to us digital reproductions. Even though we cannot use them all they all help with the historical documentation that we are doing.

Records and data also help. Years ago the Cincinnati Railroad Club was given a substantial collection of B&O files from the Division Offices for the Western Region of the B&O. Faced with vacating their storage venue in a Cincinnati warehouse, the records were scheduled for the dumpster. Knowing of our interest in cabooses and other B&O history, member Jim Corbett contacted us to see if any of the material was of interest to us. Thanks to Jim we were able to locate several very interesting files on B&O cabooses and their assignments as well as other files on B&O subjects. Hating to see all of the other records go in the local landfill, we made arrangements for the balance of the Ohio records to be saved by the Ohio Historical Society at Columbus. A total of six full pallet loads were saved as well as the 10 or so bankers boxes we salvaged to support our projects.

You will see the term neoletter (or neo-style letter) used in this edition. We use this term because it is the term used by the B&O Mechanical Department. What is a neoletter? In today's vernacular it would simply be a letter with a standard format so whatever information is in the letter, all such letters would have the same "look" or format.

Feedback received from earlier volumes indicates readers appreciate the reproduction of official B&O letters conveying key information of interest to modelers and historians. So we have continued that practice with this volume. These give a definite B&O flavor to the work and provide key background information on specific caboose changes and upgrades.

This volume is heavy on I-5 family cupola car coverage, but some cars are not covered (SIRT and B&OCT I-5 cars) as they will appear in a future volume when cars of those roads are presented. So if you wonder about a specific car that had an oddball modification and you do not find it herein that may explain its omission for now.

Class I-10, originally scheduled for inclusion in this volume, must be moved back to volume 5 due to space limitations, even though we added additional pages to this volume. Apologies to my fellow "I-10 Historical Society" members.

In this volume we have continued our extensive rosters which has taken literally decades to compile from many different sources both within and outside. The railroad's official files were maintained by many different departments.

We also have continued our previous practice of supplying information on assignments for those discriminating modelers who want to model specific cars used in their area of concentration. This information comes wholly from company documents. We have specifically stayed away from using photo caption information for these tabulations.

Updates / Corrections for Previous Volumes

Our goal is to present information that is as historically correct as possible. When mistakes slip through or new information is uncovered after publication, we want to make sure to present that to our readers. It is important to document and correct errors so they do not become established fact. An obvious misspelling of a word is not considered by us to be an error and hence any are not included in this review.

Corrections and Updates for Previous Volumes

Volume 2, Cover photo of caboose C-2877 (other I-17/17A caboose photos inside):

A question has been posed about the lightning bolt emblem that appears on the caboose that is pictured on the cover of volume 2. The graphic shows just above the journal repack stencil.

This lightning bolt emblem is a symbol that indicated that the axles had been inspected with ultrasound, a non-destructive test which could pick up defects such as cracks and other undesirable imperfections in the metal. The device for this inspection was called a Reflectoscope. On the C&O there were several small motorized vehicles (about the size of a golf cart) where inspectors could simply motor up to a freight car and use a probe against the end of the axle without getting out of their cart which had the needed gages to show good or defective condition of the inspected axle.

This inspection using the Reflectoscope started in 1954 on the C&O and was used at various shops. There is a color photo on the outside rear cover of my C&O steel caboose book which shows recently painted C&O 90187 at the Raceland shops with the lightning bolt emblem painted on a small panel mounted just above the right truck. Alongside the lightning bolt emblem was the shop code (station symbol) and month and year of testing.

We assume this testing was done not only at Raceland but also at other C&O key shops (Grand Rapids, Huntington, etc).

It is interesting on the B&O that it only appears on the I-17/17A cabooses shopped at Du Bois in 1970-1971. Perhaps this was done as a testing experiment or because the axles on those cars were older and suspect. It did also appear on an I-12 car processed through Du Bois and painted in the solid blue scheme (cab C-2814 pictured on page 131 of volume 3).

If the process was successful one would have thought it would have continued but we do not see it on C&O cabooses shopped in the late 1960s. Perhaps an improved inspection method was later developed.

Volume 2, Page 64: CABOOSE POOLING. Susan Yosten has sent us information indicating that the pooling of cabooses on the Buffalo Division went into effect on May 15, 1967.

Volume 3, Page 50: The caption for the top photo should indicate the I-5BA class designation was created in 1940 instead of 1942.

Volume 3, Page 61 and 63: CLASS CONFUSION. More on that subject to clarify our point:

B&O diagram sheets show class I-5B and class I-5BA both as weighing 38,600 pounds, with the only difference being the increased wheelbase (from 15 feet to 19 feet). The B&O neo-style letter reproduced in this section confirms that class I-5BA covers cars with this increased wheelbase only. Certain cars from this group also were ballasted to increase their weight. When this was done with I-5C cars they then became class I-5D. But the I-5BA cars received no such class change when ballast was added. Our point is that an I-5BA car that was ballasted meets neither the class I-5B or class I-5BA specifications. The neo-style letters issued (see a sample on page 83) specifically listed I-5BA cars that had been ballasted so officers obviously felt this was important to know. But there never was a new class created for an I-5BA car that had been ballasted.

Volume 3, Page 119: "S of E" in the table heading stands for "Summary of Equipment", a pocket-sized book published by the B&O on a periodic basis, mostly yearly, from 1912 to 1960 which listed all rolling stock along with certain specifications.

Volume 3, Page 144: The caption for the middle photo should read "...after January 1, 1970."

Volume 3, Page 146: Harry Meem corrects the spelling of the town to Corriganville.

Supplementary Photos for Volume 3

Who would have believed it—a single shark unit in helper service! Visibility for the backup move must have been difficult. Of course photos can be misleading. This may be a local with only two cars ahead of the caboose, or it could be a train that stalled with the dispatcher pulling a unit off a following train to assist, or it could be a unit fresh from the shops being broken in for a day as a helper. Caboose C-2460 gets the assist this day in the early 1950s. *S.K. Bolton, Jr, Rail Photo Service*

A rare I-13 is shoved past WD Tower at Fairmont, West Virginia, in June of 1956 by 0-8-0 1819 in this H. Reid photo. The C-1811 escaped the lenses of most photographers until this image surfaced. The I-13 class was covered in volume 3.

Baltimore, Md., December 3, 1940.

102 - Caboose Cars - Classification of Altered I-5 Caboose Cars -

Messrs.
W.S.Everly   W.F.Harris   J.T.Connelly   A.J.Larrick
W.B.Porterfield   J.P.Hines   E.Stimson,Jr.   F.J.Crockett
F.L.Hall   W.H.Longwell   J.S.Major   H.A.Harris
C.W.Esch   J.W.Schad   W.A.Bender   W.P.Hollen
J.R.Groue   H.M.Sherrard   E.B.Cox   E.H.Meckstroth
L.L.Harper   C.H.Spence   A.H.Keys

      To properly identify Caboose Cars of the I-5 classes which have been altered, it has been decided to reclassify these cars as follows:

I-5c -- I-5 Caboose Cars with 19'-0" Truck Centers.

I-5d -- I-5 Caboose Cars with 19'-0" Truck Centers and Weight Increased by Addition of Cement and Scrap.

I-5ba- I-5b With 19'-0" Truck Center.

      All I-5 cars should be checked, and if any of them have been or are changed as mentioned above, they should be reclassified and stencilled accordingly.

      Report all changes to this office on Form 2404-A.

[signature]

Cy. Messrs.
G.H.Emerson   C.M.House   H.J.Burkley   W.S.Galloway
J.J.Tatum   H.Rees   W.W.Calder   E.W.Walther
G.F.Malone   F.A.Baldinger   W.H.Gordon   H.Shoemaker
E.J.McSweeney   H.W.Brewer   H.A.Lockhart

hlh-ers

Group 102 -

New Classes Established

The B&O neo-style letter reproduced above documents the creation of new classes for cabooses with increased weight and longer wheelbase modifications in order to qualify the modified cars for heavy duty pusher service.

The 1940 date of this letter corrects our "1942" date mentioned in the top photo caption on page 50 of volume 3.

These memos, which the B&O referred to as "neo-style letters" were the primary communication method used to quickly relay information from the mechanical offices in Baltimore to employees in the field. Many times they would be sent with attached blueprints when that was appropriate to better explain a new change.

Car formen are typically listed on the top of the letter with copied staff officers listed on the bottom.

Even though class I-12 cars were of steel construction, that did not help much in certain situations, such as this November 26, 1947, wreck at Kingmont, West Virginia, near Fairmont. Full details of the story surrounding this wreck can be found in Terry Arbogast's excellent book *Old Main Line, Volume One, West of Cumberland,* on page 108. Needless to say, the damage to caboose C-2450 was a little more than the skilled craftsmen at the Keyser shops could repair; <u>the cab became the first wagon-top caboose to be retired</u>—in February 1948. *O.V. Nelson photos, courtesy of Terry E. Arbogast*

More on the M-26 Boxcar Conversions

The above memo from A. W. Johnston, General Manager of the Western Region focuses more light on the interesting M-26 boxcar conversions to cabooses (referred to officially on the railroad as "rider cars"). The three states these cars were used in (Ohio, Indiana and Illinois) all had laws on the books relating to caboose construction and all three required that cabooses have a platform of a specific dimension on each end of the car. There were other requirements as well but it is likely that the one glaring problem with the M-26 conversions was the lack of the end platforms. That probably explains why they were referred to as "rider cars" and not cabooses and why they were retired from caboose service so quickly (the above memo alludes to the fact that the cars are being removed from caboose service due to these state laws). General Manager Johnston must have been under some real pressure to replace these cars with qualified cabooses as he makes his point clear by stating it three times in this short memo! The date of this memo is just a little over one year after the last of the 18 M-26 family cars was released from the Chillicothe shops. This memo is one of the interesting finds in the Cincinnati records salvaged by the author. The memo covers 10 of the original 18 cars. XM900 (XM3021) is the car mentioned by the General Manager as the bunk car located at Sandusky, Ohio.

Photos of B&O's first bay-window caboose, C-2500, in its pool colors, are rare. So we are pleased to present this image of the car at Sterling, Ohio, taken by Charles Laird, Sr. in the 1970s, probably not long before it was destroyed.

courtesy of David P. Oroszi

The listing at right, of B&O's very first bay-window caboose, was tabulated from the caboose location files of the Western Region discussed in the records chapter next in this book from the archives of the Cincinnati Railroad Club. They supplement the assignment information published in volume 3 which covers the history of the C-2500.

Cab #	Date	Assignment
C-2500	10-31-62	Chillicothe, OH, pool service
C-2500	2-12-63	Chillicothe, OH, pool service
C-2500	5-30-63	Chillicothe, OH, pool service
C-2500	6-14-63	Chillicothe, OH, pool service
C-2500	2-10-64	Chillicothe; painted DU 4-62
C-2500	7-15-64	Chillicothe, OH, freight pool
C-2500	3-1-65	Chillicothe, OH, freight pool
C-2500	6-1-65	Chillicothe, OH, freight pool
C-2500	6-1-65	Chillicothe, OH, freight pool
C-2500	12-1-65	Chillicothe, OH, freight pool
C-2500	3-1-66	Chillicothe, OH, freight pool
C-2500	4-23-66	Chillicothe, OH, freight pool
C-2500	6-1-66	Chillicothe, OH, freight pool
C-2500	6-30-66	Chillicothe, OH, freight pool
C-2500	7-21-66	Portsmouth to Jackson turnaround
C-2500	9-10-66	Portsmouth to Jackson turnaround
C-2500	1-5-67	Portsmouth to Jackson turnaround

Below is listed more assignment information for the interesting M-26 family caboose conversions (or Rider Cars in B&O lingo) which has been extracted from the newly-researched Cincinnati Railroad Club B&O Western Division files.

Cab #	Date	Assignment
XM900	7-25-64	Chillicothe released from shop
XM901	7-25-64	Chillicothe released from shop
XM907	9-25-64	Seymour, IN, switcher
XM913	9-8-65	Washington CH, OH, district run
XM913	3-22-66	Newark, OH, sent to Chillicothe
XM914	12-1-65	Cincinnati, outside transfer
XM915	12-1-65	Oakley, OH (Cincinnati)
XM916	12-1-65	Storrs (Cin) to Sedamsville, OH
XM2114	7-25-61	North Vernon, IN, extra service
XM2114	10-23-64	Cone, East St. Louis, IN
XM2120	10-23-64	Cone, East St. Louis, IN
XM3021	10-23-64	Newark Division
XM3021	3-22-66	Newark, OH, rider car unassigned

Cab #	Date	Assignment
XM3021	6-15-66	Sandusky, OH, crew quarters
XM3021	1-8-69	Sandusky, OH, crew quarters
XM3022	10-23-64	Cincinnati, OH
XM3023	10-23-64	Dayton, OH
XM3024	10-23-64	Lima, OH
XM3025	10-23-64	Newark Division
XM3025	3-22-66	Columbus, OH, rider car, yard
XM3027	10-23-64	Cincinnati, OH
XM3028	10-23-64	Newark Division
XM3028	3-22-66	Columbus, OH, rider car, yard
XM3028	6-15-66	Newark, OH, unassigned
XM3028	1-8-69	Newark, OH, MofW department
XM3029	10-23-64	Cone, East St. Louis, IN

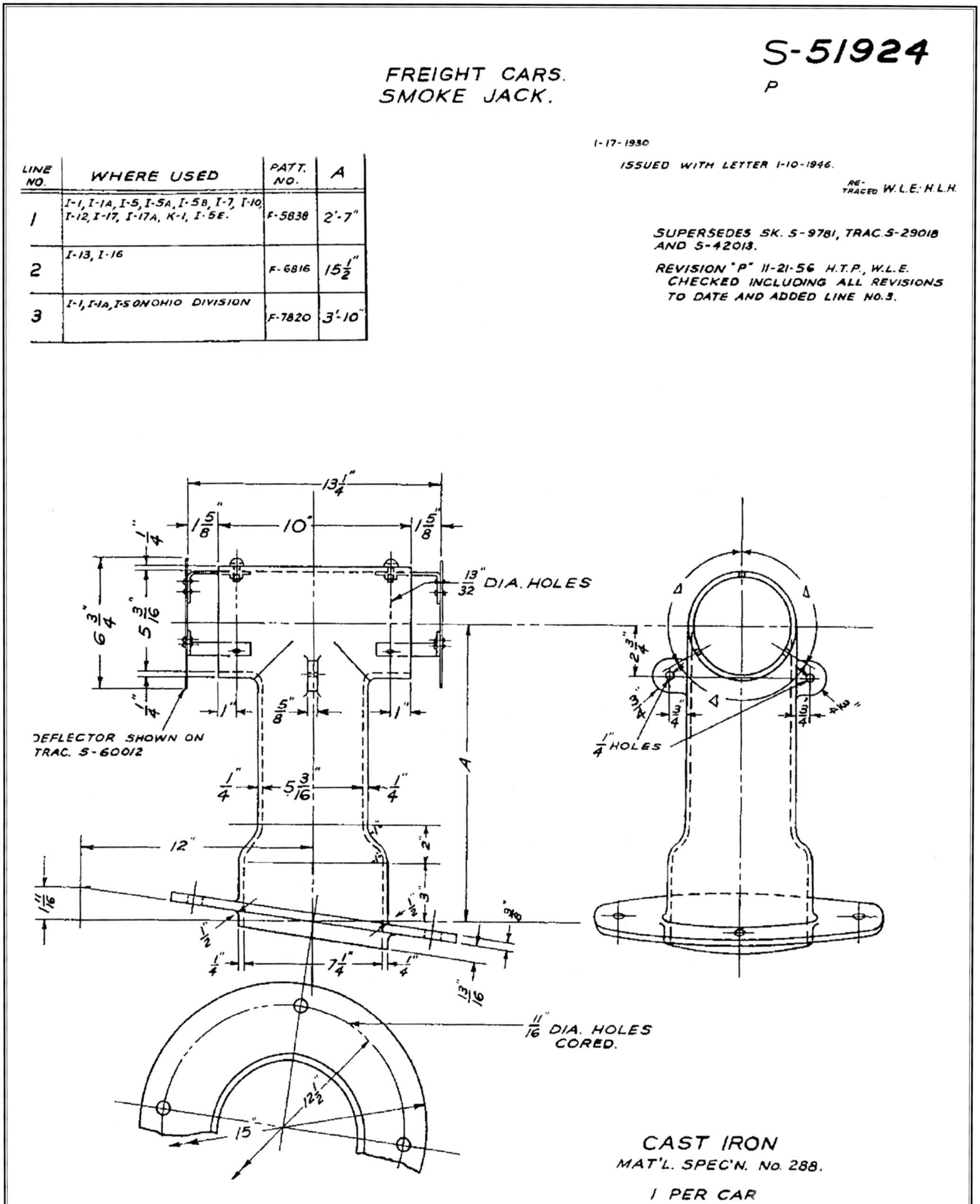

FREIGHT CARS.
SMOKE JACK.

LINE NO.	WHERE USED	PATT. NO.	A
1	I-1, I-1A, I-5, I-5A, I-5B, I-7, I-10, I-12, I-17, I-17A, K-1, I-5E.	F-5838	2'-7"
2	I-13, I-16	F-6816	15 1/2"
3	I-1, I-1A, I-5 ON OHIO DIVISION	F-7820	3'-10"

1-17-1930
ISSUED WITH LETTER 1-10-1946.
RE-TRACED W.L.E. H.L.H.

SUPERSEDES SK. S-9781, TRAC. S-29018 AND S-42013.

REVISION "P" 11-21-56 H.T.P., W.L.E.
CHECKED INCLUDING ALL REVISIONS TO DATE AND ADDED LINE No. 3.

13/32" DIA. HOLES

DEFLECTOR SHOWN ON TRAC. S-60012

1/4 HOLES

11/16" DIA. HOLES CORED.

CAST IRON
MAT'L. SPEC'N. No. 288.

1 PER CAR

This B&O caboose stack drawing from 1930 (updated to 1956) has some interesting information of interest to fans and modelers. First, it documents the "shorty" stack used on the I-13 and I-16 cabooses. More interesting is the fact that a different size stack was specified for cupola cabooses used on the Ohio Division. From our coverage of the I-12 cars in a previous volume it was shown that officers wanted standardization on caboose stacks. So what was so special about the Ohio Division that allowed for a unique size only in that territory?

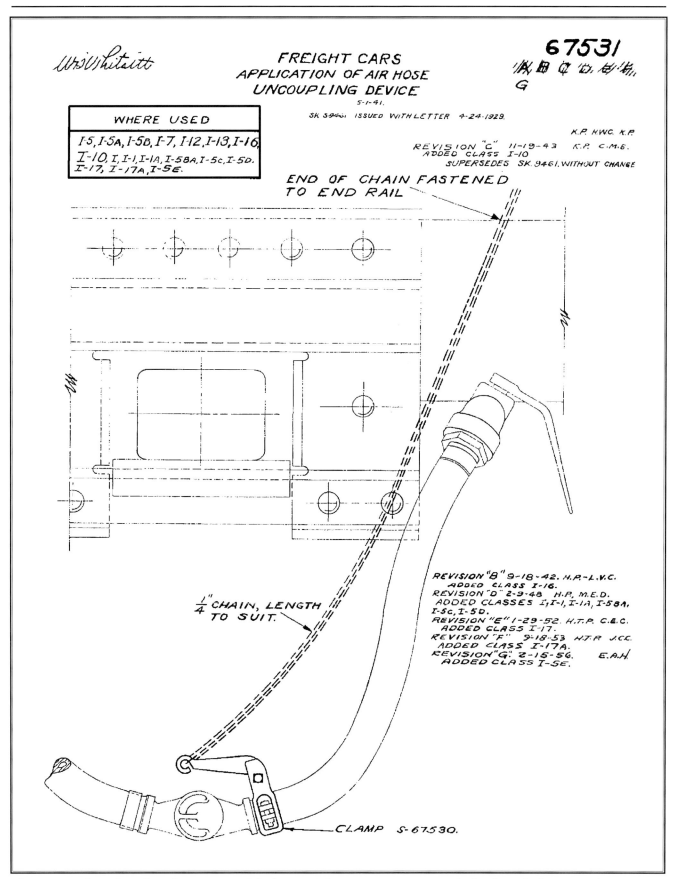

Wm U Whitsitt

FREIGHT CARS
APPLICATION OF AIR HOSE
UNCOUPLING DEVICE
5-1-41.

SK 5946 ISSUED WITH LETTER 4-24-1929.

67531

A, B, C, D, E, F,
G

K.P. H.W.C. K.P.
REVISION "C" 11-19-43 K.P. C.M.E.
ADDED CLASS I-10
SUPERSEDES SK.9461.WITHOUT CHANGE

WHERE USED

I-5, I-5a, I-5b, I-7, I-12, I-13, I-16,
I-10, I, I-1, I-1A, I-58A, I-5c, I-5D.
I-17, I-17A, I-5E.

END OF CHAIN FASTENED
TO END RAIL

¼" CHAIN, LENGTH
TO SUIT.

REVISION "B" 9-18-42. H.P.~L.V.C.
ADDED CLASS I-16.
REVISION "D" 2-9-48. H.P. M.E.D.
ADDED CLASSES I, I-1, I-1A, I-58A,
I-5c, I-5D.
REVISION "E" 1-29-52. H.T.P. C.E.C.
ADDED CLASS I-17.
REVISION "F" 9-18-53. H.T.P. J.C.C.
ADDED CLASS I-17A.
REVISION "G" 2-15-56. E.A.H
ADDED CLASS I-5E.

CLAMP S-67530.

One question that has been posed is how airhoses were uncoupled when helper engines were behind cabooses. Two chains were on the rear platform of many cabooses—one pulled the pin on the coupler and the other, shown by this B&O drawing, could uncouple the air hose.

Three class I-12 wagon-top cabooses are shown on the rear of this passenger train at Terra Alta, West Virginia, circa 1950. This scene likely shows extra crews from Keyser or Cumberland being deadheaded back to Grafton, West Virginia. *collection of the Rowlesburg, West Virginia, museum*

Recall 193 To Shops

The economic picture for Du-Bois received a bright spot with the announcement today by the Baltimore & Ohio that nearly 200 men will be recalled to the DuBois car shops.

The announcement said that 193 will return to their jobs on Wed., Jan. 4. Added to the 66 now employed, this will give a work force here of 259.

This recall constitutes 3½ work units who will concentrate on the repairing of open top coal cars. The remaining 35 employes will make heavy repairs to caboose cars.

The majority of the men recalled have been furloughed since Sept. 7.

This article appeared in the *Du Bois Courier Express* of December 30, 1960, announcing the recall of the shop workers who would work the cabooses that this author calls I-5Dm as well as their I-10 counterparts. That program started in January 1961.

Questions have been posed about the mail slot located in caboose doors. The drawing on the following page likely would give B&O carpenters a headache! Caboose doors were a lot more complicated than one would imagine. This particular B&O drawing, from 1935, specified a caboose door to be made from poplar. The mail slot can be seen just under the window and centered on the door. Not just a slot straight through the door, the mail slot was angled upward at a 30 degree angle, likely to prevent someone from looking into the caboose. Later drawings showed the mail slot angled downward. When crews were sleeping in their caboose at away from home terminals clerks could slip messages into the caboose without bothering the crew. At home terminals crews could find messages in their caboose upon reporting for duty.

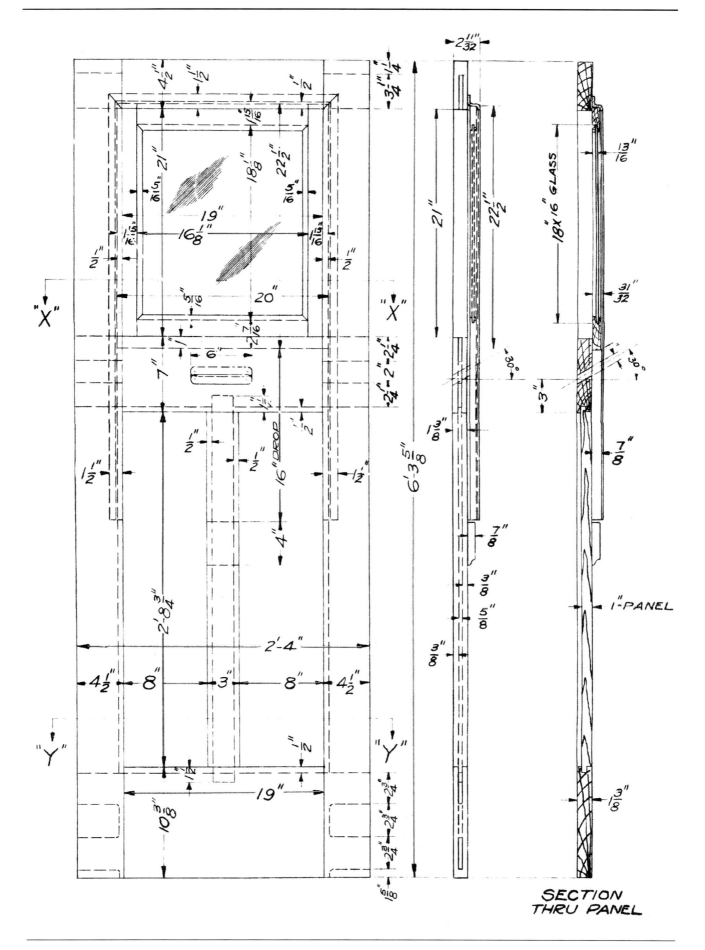

SECTION
THRU PANEL

CHAPTER 1

Research, Records & Rosters

The subject of this chapter first appeared in volume 1 of this series and positive feedback was received from readers on the coverage. We are happy to provide more information in this edition.

About 1986 the old B&O offices in Cincinnati were being cleaned out and a number of old files were offered to the Cincinnati Railroad Club. These files had been stored in what was known either as the B&O Freight House, or the O&M Freight House, depending on your preference. These records covered files for the Western Region of the B&O (old St. Louis Division, Toledo-Indianapolis Division and Ohio-Newark Division). The records covered depot construction and modifications, track additions, retirements and contracts, dispatcher sheets, Superintendent bulletins, local assignments, and just about any other subject imaginable. Oh ... and caboose information!

One of the members of the club had spent considerable effort in 1996 making an index of the files in each box, which then were identified with an orange box number. The index was arranged by location and not by subject, so for us looking for caboose files was like looking for a needle in a haystack.

These records, which filled around 200 or so banker boxes were stored by the Cincinnati group on the sixth floor of an old warehouse (known locally as the Shoney's warehouse) one block north of the Cincinnati Union terminal.

Cincinnati Railroad Club member Jim Corbett was familiar with our work on cabooses, and we saw Jim periodically at the Columbus railroad show. Jim mentioned to us in early 2014 that the club was discussing parting with all those records and perhaps we might want to come to Cincinnati to review them and see if there were any that we could use in our research. Jim was aware that our interest was B&O caboose history, but also the history of the Portsmouth Sub-division, which we grew up watching in our home town in southern Ohio and which we affectionately refer to as "the most ignored line on the B&O system".

We finally agreed on a date when both of us could meet at the records storage room, and on June 28, 2014, we made the trip to Cincinnati. Jim had warned us that the room would be extremely hot in the summer and extremely cold in the winter. Boy,

This Jim Corbett photo from April 2016 shows some of the 200+ boxes of Western Region B&O records as they were stored in the 6th floor of a Cincinnati warehouse.

By early April Cincinnati Railroad Club members had cleaned out the 6th floor storage room and moved the records to the loading dock area of the warehouse. On April 9 Jim Corbett, right, and the author review boxes of records looking for caboose files and any pertaining to the Portsmouth Sub-division. Any records left were dumpster-bound.

was he right! Using the group's index we had identified a number of boxes that we wanted to review. After a couple of hours of research the heat was too great to continue and we had to abort the work. The good news was that we had located enough material to fill four bankers boxes.

At the December 2015 Columbus railroad show Jim indicated that the records were now definitely in jeopardy and might have to be thrown away. In early 2016 Jim contacted us and advised that the Cincinnati group had to be out of the warehouse and all records were scheduled for disposal. If we wanted to finish the rest of our review we needed to return soon.

We returned to the records room with Jim on March 25 and again on April 9 to look for information on cabooses and the Portsmouth Sub. Five more boxes of interesting records were located on these trips.

Jim indicated that April 16 was the drop dead date that they had to have the records out of the warehouse. He had been given the unenviable job of ordering a large dumpster to throw the records into. Most disappointing. Jim indicated the records had been offered to three railroad historical societies and all three had turned them down.

Upon return home we decided we would check with the Ohio Historical Society to

see if they might be interested in saving the records. A positive reply was received from Matt Benz, Manuscripts Curator. We made arrangements to meet Matt at the Ohio Historical Society center and show him samples of the records we had saved.

A decision was made that they would save any of the records pertaining to Ohio. On April 14 we were able to load almost all of the Ohio records into their box truck for transportation back to Columbus. A few boxes had to be left behind as the truck was maxed out. They did not want the Illinois and Indiana records. One of the Cincinnati club members had made arrangements to pass Indiana records on to the Indiana Historical Society. It is unclear exactly what happened to the Illinois records. Fortunately there were not many for that state. It is believed those were tossed in the dumpster since no home for them could be located.

Curator Benz did indicate that they would be open to

On April 14 the author helps Matt Benz and an assistant, Kevin Latta, from the Ohio Historical Society load a box truck with Ohio B&O records.

This two-inch file, which was located in the Cincinnati records stash, contains 10 years of caboose assignments for the Western Region of the B&O. Fascinating information for the caboose enthusiast! This information has been compiled and is a part of the assignment information listed in this publication.

passing the records on to the B&O Railroad Historical Society at some future date if the society was interested in them after securing more space in their new archives building near Baltimore.

Some of the caboose records, obtained in our early visit, appeared in volume 3 of this series. More of those records, particularly referring to caboose assignments, are listed in this volume including data on those interesting M-26 boxcar cabooses and some on first bay-window caboose C-2500.

The list of assignments on this page were tabulated from the files obtained from Cincinnati and relate to cabooses covered previously in volumes 2 and 3, supplementing the assignment data provided in those volumes.

Cab #	Date	Assignment
C-1808	1-13-64	Toledo-Indianapolis Division
C-1813	1-13-64	Toledo-Indianapolis Division
C-1817	1-13-64	Toledo-Indianapolis Division
C-1817	1-11-68	Columbus, OH, yard turn
C-1817	7-31-68	Newark, OH, bad ordered
C-1820	1-13-64	Toledo-Indianapolis Division
C-1824	1-13-64	St. Louis Division
C-1824	7-25-66	Washington, IN, to Cincinnati
C-1826	4-26-62	Newark, OH, pool service
C-1826	11-1-62	Newark, OH, pool service
C-1826	1-1-63	Newark Division pool service
C-1826	6-22-63	Willard to Benwood pool
C-1826	12-3-63	Newark Division pool service
C-1826	1-13-64	Ohio-Newark Division
C-1826	1-18-64	Newark, OH, pool service
C-1826	2-3-64	Newark, OH, pool service
C-1826	2-10-64	Newark, OH, needs heavy repairs
C-2412	8-31-61	Chillicothe, OH, freight pool
C-2412	10-31-62	Chillicothe, OH, pool service
C-2412	2-12-63	Chillicothe, OH, pool service
C-2801	10-31-62	Chillicothe, OH, pool service
C-2801	2-12-63	Chillicothe, OH, pool service
C-2801	5-30-63	Chillicothe pool
C-2801	6-14-63	Chillicothe pool
C-2856	10-31-62	Chillicothe, OH, pool service
C-2856	2-12-63	Chillicothe, OH, pool service
C-2856	5-30-63	Chillicothe pool
C-2856	6-14-63	Chillicothe pool
C-2864	10-31-62	Newark, OH, pool service
C-2864	1-1-63	Newark to Cincinnati pool
C-2864	4-17-63	Southwest Pool, Newark, OH
C-2864	5-30-63	Chillicothe pool
C-2864	6-14-63	Chillicothe pool
C-2864	6-22-63	Newark to Cincinnati pool

CHAPTER 2

General Caboose History

Condition of Caboose Cars (1948)

A. K. Galloway issued the following memo under date of September 4, 1948.

"On line of road this trip noticed several caboose cars that had been cleaned by use of some acid cleaner. The paint was taken off, evidently due to solution being too strong or it was left on too long.

"Where this happens the least that could be done would be to paint the caboose and not let it continue in service presenting an unsightly appearance.

"Arrange to have caboose cars checked and where this condition exists they should be painted."

On April 10, 1049, A. H. Keys issued the following memo:

"During the week of April 10th, Mr. Galloway and I covered a considerable portion of the railroad and we were very much disappointed in the appearance of our caboose cars. The outsides were very dirty. The majority of them can be cleaned by scrubbing instead of painting them.

"While I realize we cannot do very much scrubbing during the winter months, it will be necessary to get our caboose cars cleaned up promptly, repainting those in need of painting and scrubbing those that can be cleaned by scrubbing.

"Wish you would get behind this matter immediately at all points."

Guns and Cabooses (1950)

Superintendent H. D. Graffious, of the Buffalo Division, issued the following instructions on October 31, 1950.

"With the opening of hunting season, I want to remind you of what occurred on our territory a couple of years ago, when we had quite a serious accident due to flagman carrying his gun in caboose and he was out hunting when he should have been protecting his train.

"It will be necessary for you to caution all of your employees, as well as the supervision, that they will not do any hunting while on duty. Of course if on vacation they may do as they see fit, but you must make it plain to engine and train crews that there must be no guns carried on engines or cabooses during hunting season, as we do not want any recurrence of what happened a few years ago. Train masters should make check of cabooses and if they find a gun in the caboose or on an engine during hunting season, and the men have been cautioned, we have sufficient grounds for administering severe discipline.

"Want you to look after this personally so that nothing occurs in this respect."

P. L. Hofstetter issued the following to his Car Foremen with his memo of September 25, 1953.

"In connection with previous correspondence on the Board of Directors' Special, which will be on the Central Region some time the first part of October.

"In has been brought to my attention that the condition of our cabooses is such that it might result in some criticism from the directors. On the previous visit they had taken exceptions to the dirty appearance of these cabooses and to eliminate any possible complaint of this kind want you to get into this matter and see that cabooses are cleaned, both interior and exterior, and painted where necessary."

On April 20, 1955, W. C. Reister issued the following

memo:

Updating Caboose Trucks (1951)

"Effective at once you will set up a program to either wash or paint each and every caboose car assigned to your territory. It will be necessary that this be done during this campaign.

"In checking over a number of cabooses find they are in bad condition; many require repainting, while others recently painted require washing.

"We had started this program at some terminals with remarkable success while at others the matter has been badly overlooked. You will therefore see that this program is progressed at the earliest possible date and continued until each caboose car has been taken care of.

"In repainting caboose cars you will follow instructions in my letter of April 14, 1955, using large B&O initials, etc.

"It will be necessary that you furnish this office with weekly letter giving a list of caboose cars either washed or repainted, showing date and terminal doing work and on the caboose cars painted advise whether new large B&O initials applied."

A check of cabooses on the Central Region indicated that nine cabooses still were equipped with arch bar trucks. F. B. Rykoskey issued a memo indicating his displeasure over this situation.

"There is no excuse for these caboose cars running around with arch bar trucks inasmuch as we are dismantling box cars daily with 5 x 9 side truck frames under them.

"See that these cabooses have side truck frames applied immediately, advising me as each car is equipped."

The nine cabooses were listed as:

Buffalo Division	C-374
Pittsburgh Division	C-382
Chicago Division	C-1951
B&O CT	C-1892
Akron Division	C-319
"	C-182
"	C-158
"	C-258
"	C-2042

Baltimore, Md., November 1, 1963 JJG-ERS

Messrs.

W. S. Furlow	15	P. R. Lewis	5
B. J. Borgman	15	W. J. Baumiller	
K. F. Mewshaw	15	R. P. Mullen	
A. F. Pugh	15	H. M. Dowling	
G. B. Kirwan	15	W. A. Barrick	
		L. M. Schalk	

Requisition received in this office for approval, ordering coal burning caboose stoves has been cancelled.

With the number of cabooses now authorized for condemnation and currently being dismantled, there are sufficient coal stoves available from these cars to supply our needs.

Before requesting authority to purchase coal stoves, the stations needing stoves or parts should contact other General Zone Supervisors asking them to fill their requirements.

W. A. Mullen

Baltimore, Md., February 12, 1948.

Messrs. F. A. Baldinger
        H. Rees
        H. J. Burkley
        C. H. Spence
        J. S. Major
        G. W. Short

        The Trainmen's Committee have registered serious complaint concerning the condition of caboose cars, alleging that our people are not giving them the proper inspection or attention. They have called attention to loose fitting windows, permitting rain, snow and cold air to enter cabooses, leaky roofs, especially around the cupolas, defective interior equipment, including stoves, some of which they state are cracked, defective wheels, causing the cabooses to ride roughly, and, in some cases, called attention to the siding being loose due to nails working out.

        There is no excuse for our inspectors permitting caboose cars to operate in this condition. With periodic shop attention, cabooses should be maintained in first class condition by our operating forces at all points, and certification cards should be applied each trip at both ends of its run to indicate that a careful inspection is made and that the caboose is in first class condition. Cabooses that are in need of extensive repairs should be relieved from service and sent to designated shops where work can be properly performed.

        It was alleged that in many instances conductors made reports to trainmasters covering defective conditions and that nothing was done about it. We have requested that, in addition to making messages to the trainmasters, that the conductors or brakemen give a copy of their letter to the car foreman so that he will know about the complaint. This is especially true due to the inability of our people, in many cases, to enter the cabooses account being locked with private locks by the crews, and where interior repairs are needed, arrangements should be made by the car foreman with the crew to leave the caboose open or leave the keys in charge of some responsible foreman so that repairs can be made while they are off duty.

                                                A. K. Galloway

Smokestack Modifications (1954)

A B&O memo dated January 29, 1954, from East Salamanca, NY, indicated the following:

"I have again conducted investigation and the General Car Forman advises that train crews made complaint about smoke entering the cupola. In order to diffuse the smoke, it was decided to use Elbows fastened to the smoke jack above the roof. The 6" are preferred as they fit over the outside tee of the smoke Jack, however, 5" can also be used by fitting them on the inside tee of the cast iron Jack.

"During past six years we issued 78 of the elbows such as ordered on requisition Y-12339. You may cancel these on my requisition and will confine to ordering 5".

The Baltimore and Ohio Railroad Company

MOTIVE POWER DEPARTMENT

BALTIMORE, MD., February 15, 1926
(Folder 665)

CIRCULAR No. F-163-A
(Superseding Circular No. F-163)

MAINTENANCE OF CABOOSE CARS

Caboose cars will be maintained at all times in good serviceable condition; the interior and exterior must be in good repairs; roofs kept water-tight; doors and window sash in cupola and body of car must be kept tight, and well weather-stripped so that elements and drafts will not be admitted to insideof car.

Draft gear, running gear, foundation brake gear and safety appliances must be maintained in good operative condition, complying with requirements of the safety appliance laws at all times.

To insure these cars being in such condition, they will be scheduled through shop for classified repair as follows:

8-wheel steel underframe and steel center sill caboose cars, once each two years.
4 and 8-wheel all wood cabooses, once each twelve months.

When these cars are given classified repairs they will be repaired by the unit organization on the spot system which is assigned to rebuild box cars, and will go through the spots with box cars as they are being repaired. See limit cost of repairs, blue print U-38669.

As each of these cars are given classified repairs it will be reported to General Superintendent Car Department on Form 1150-A, with date repaired, the shop repairing it and date and shop in which it was previously given such repairs. For cars put in shop for classified repairs within a period less than that above mentioned, an explanation will be made as to why it was necessary to give such repairs before the scheduled time for it to receive repairs.

Between classified repairs, these cars will be kept in condition by the Operating force, the roofs tight so they will not leak and the doors and sash maintained tight and properly weather-stripped to exclude drafts and elements.

J. T. Carroll.

General Superintendent Motive Power and Equipment

INDEXING: C—Cabooses, maintenance.
M—Maintenance of cabooses.
R—Repairs to cabooses.
S—Shopping of cabooses.

GROUP No. 102.

Baltimore, Md., April 23, 1942.

102 – Caboose Cars)
127 – Safety Appliances) Side and End Handholds –
    SUPERSEDING LETTER OF 3-16-1942 (GROUP NOS. 122 & 127) FOR HANDHOLDS ONLY

Messrs. W.S.Eyerly   W.F.Harris   C.H.Spence   A.J.Larrick
        H.M.Sherrard   J.P.Hines   W.E.Lehr   F.J.Crockett
        C.W.Esch   W.H.Longwell   J.S.Major   H.A.Harris
        F.L.Hall   W.B.Nolan   W.A.Bender   W.P.Hollen
        F.M.Galloway   G.H.Rosenberg   E.B.Cox   E.H.Meckstroth
        L.R.Haase   E.Stimson,Jr.   R.B.Fisher   G.O.Prosser
        I.L.Harper   J.W.Schad   A.H.Keys

This letter supersedes instructions covering Side and End Handholds in letter of March 16, 1942, and includes all classes of Caboose Cars.

It has been decided to change the contour and eliminate the center support of the side curved handholds to be used at the four corners of Caboose Cars.

The combined horizontal and vertical handhold was also changed to improve clearance at the bolting brackets.

Copies of the following prints are attached covering the changes in the handholds:

S-68754-A – Side Handhold – Classes I-1, I-1a, I-3, I-5, I-5a, I-5ba, I-5c, I-5d, I-5b, I-7, I-12, I-13, K-1 – Superseding Prints S-6382 and S-68618.
S-68780-A – Application of Side Handhold – Classes I-1, I-1a, I-3, I-5, I-5c, I-5d, I-7, K-1.
S-68769-A – Application of Side Handhold – Classes I-5a, I-5b, I-5ba, I-12.
S-68776-A – Application of Side Handhold – Class I-13.
S-44773-L – Handhold Base – Classes I-5a, I-5b, I-5ba, I-12, I-13 – Superseding Print S-67448.
S-52628-G – Combined Vertical and Horizontal End Handhold – Classes I-1, I-1a, I-5, I-5a, I-5b, I-5ba, I-5c, I-5d, I-7, I-12, I-13.

Whenever the above Caboose Cars are on shop tracks for either light or heavy repairs, the side handholds, per print S-68754-A, should be applied, following the arrangement prints for the respective classes.

When cars are on shop tracks for heavy repairs or any repairs necessitating removal of inside end lining, the combined vertical and horizontal end handholds should be changed in accordance with print S-52628-G.

                                                    E.H.Einwaechter

                                APPROVED:
                                                    W.B.Whitsitt

Cy. Messrs.
    F.H.Becherer   H.Rees   W.W.Calder   H.Shoemaker
    H.L.Holland   F.A.Baldinger   W.S.Galloway   H.A.Lockhart
    E.J.McSweeney   H.J.Burkley   E.W.Walther   W.H.Gordon
    C.M.House   E.M.Scherch   R.W.Eves

P-ors
enc.
Groups 102, 127 –

Baltimore, Md., November 18, 1965   C/1

Mr. H. M. Dowling:

Let me know quickly the status of Caboose 2089 which is to be sent to Washington for use in connection with Christmas Mail. We must get this caboose to Washington no later than the 29th so that electricians can install the necessary lighting.

R. H. Minser

Cabooses sometimes were called on for special needs. Although we are not sure what the use was at Washington for the "Christmas Mail", the fact that special lighting was to be installed makes us wonder if it was for a Santa Claus display. The above memo was written by the Baltimore Division Superintendent (Minser) and was directed to the Shop Superintendent at Mount Clare (Dowling).

Caboose C-2089 was outshopped from the Du Bois shops as an I-5Dm car in March of 1962 and still was in great shape when photographed at Brunswick, Maryland, on June 23, 1963, a little over a year after leaving the Du Bois program and about two-and-a-half years before it was needed per the above memo. The caboose continued to be used out of Brunswick until sold as scrap from Mount Clare in May 1978. *collection of Dwight Jones*

Roster Interpretation

This book contains the most extensive rosters ever compiled for B&O cabooses. This information has been accumulated from many different sources, including, in the case of the paint dates, copying the information off the side of the cabooses. In this section we explain the various column categories and codes that are used.

ORIGINAL NUMBER = original caboose number
PHOTO = YES = an author photo; PHOTO indicates another's image
      On the I-5 roster, YES indicates a photo from any source
DATE BUILT = build date as recorded in railroad records
PAINT DATA = various columns to show paint scheme data
BUILT BY = builder name
PLACE, DATE RENUMBERED = shop code, date renumbered
ACI PLATE APPLIED = shop code, date ACI plate was applied
DATE RETIRED = official retirement date in company records
DISPOSITION = what happened to the caboose when retired
COMMENTS = various specialized data and clarifications

> On some roster listings you will see a comment that the car was retired because it could not be found on the system by agreement with E. J. Henshaw, General Manager of the Car Department. This indicates the car likely "disappeared" from the railroad years earlier but was not properly reported or recorded in company records.

In the DISPOSITION category we many times will state "see Volume III" (or whatever volume number). This refers to the books we have done on C&O/B&O dispositions (see the list of books at the end of this publication). These books provide photo evidence of the caboose disposition. In some cases we refer to volume V which, at the date of this writing, has not yet been published. Some of these volume V references may actually end up in a volume VI. Since volume V has not yet been laid out it is difficult to know for sure. A few may appear in the book we published on cabooses at the B&O Railroad Museum.

The DATE RETIRED refers to the date that the B&O caboose number was retired in company records. If a cab is relettered from B&O to CSXT that is handled as a retirement of the B&O number. In a future book on CSX cabooses we will pick up the new CSXT number and show in that book's rosters which CSXT numbers have been retired and which still are in active service.

The shop codes that we use in our rosters are, for the most part, the official station symbols used by B&O. A list of those used in this book, in alphabetical order, follows:

BD = Benwood, WV
BW = Brunswick, MD
BY = Barr Yard, Chicago, IL
CE = Chillicothe, OH
CU = Cumberland, MD
CV = Connellsville, PA
DU = Du Bois, PA
ES = East Salamanca, NY
FR = Fairmont, WV
GRF = Grafton, WV
GS = Gassaway, WV
GW = Glenwood, PA

HA = Hazelton, OH
KY = Keyser, WV
LO = Lorain, OH
MTC = Mt. Clare, MD
NE = Newark, OH
PV = Painesville, OH
RA = Raceland, KY
RUS = Russell, KY (C&O)
SO = Somerset, PA
YO = Youngstown, OH
WA = Washington, IN
WR = Willard, OH

> "System Accident"
> This term was used by the railroad on caboose record cards for those cars involved in wrecks, fires, etc. We have repeated that term in our rosters.

When we show a caboose sold to a scrap dealer, that is the best information we have at present. We consider our rosters to be living documents, constantly being updated and revised as new information might be discovered. Sometimes a scrap dealer will resell a caboose to a private owner. Over the years we have tried to keep in touch with the various scrappers used by the railroad in order to continue tracking caboose dispositions. But, some of the scrappers are small operations and do not keep detailed records. In some cases the railroad has directed individuals who desire to purchase a caboose to contact a scrapper. This eliminates the need for the railroad to process paperwork for a single car sales—they would rather sell several at one time.

Refer to the end of the I-5 roster for more definitions specific to that roster as well as Notes to further explain some listings.

Knowing the Players

Someone once wrote that you can't know the players without a program. Railroad employees changed jobs from time to time. Nevertheless here are titles as best we could find them for some of the key players mentioned in this book.

B. J. Borgman - Car Superintendent
O. C. Cromwell - Assistant to Chief, Motive Power & Equipment
H. M. Dowling - Superintendent, Mount Clare Shop
F. H. Einwaechter - Chief Engineer, Motive Power & Equipment
George Emerson - Chief, Motive Power & Equipment
A. K. Galloway - General Superintendent, Motive Power & Equipment
H. D. Graffious - Superintendent, Buffalo Division
E. F. Gross - General Car Forman
P. L. Horstetter - Division Master Mechanic
A. W. Johnston - General Manager, Western Region
A. H. Keys - Superintendent, Car Department
R. H. Minser - Superintendent, Baltimore Division
W. C. Reister - General Car Forman
F. B. Rykoskey - Supervisor, Shops
L. M. Schalk - Master Car Builder
E. Stimson - Superintendent, Motive Power
J. J. Tatum - General Superintendent, Car Department
C. W. Vanhorn - Vice President, Operations & Maintenance
W.B. Whitsitt - Mechanical Engineer

The C-2064 was photographed at Sandusky, Ohio, on February 6, 1965. The horn installation is an indication that this car is used in some sort of backup move. An electric light helps showcase the dual horns. An electric line runs from the right of the car to a junction box under the platform roof. Sometimes cabooses were used as an office in an out of the way location but the wheels are shiny on this car. The crew has probably found a way to hook up to electric power at their away from home layover point. This electricity was sometimes used to power interior lights, a fan, possibly an electric heating plate, etc. Note the dash (-) in the number on the end.
Eileen J. Wolford

Quick History

Original Numbers: C-1900 to C-2299		**Cars Built:**	**401**
New Numbers (1982): **none**		**In Service** (2015):	**0**
Year Built: 1924 to 1929		**Chessie Class:**	**C-6**
Weight: 40,500 lbs		**Preserved:**	**180** approximately
Built by: B&O Shops, Mt. Clare and Washington, IN			

The most ambitious caboose building program in the eight-wheel era was undertaken by the B&O in the mid-1920s. A newly-designed caboose was assigned class I-5 and a prototype car, numbered C-1900, was assembled at B&O's Mt. Clare shops in Baltimore. B&O's mechanical engineering department was located within walking distance and this gave car designers the ability to observe car construction and make drawing adjustments quickly.

This new class of caboose featured a steel frame as well as steel ends although tongue-and-groove wood still covered the sides.

Reportedly, prototype car C-1900 was circulated around the system for input from operating employees to review and for the company to collect feedback. This is borne out by the long construction date difference between that first caboose and the production cars that followed, as well as the following B&O quote:

"The design as well as the interior arrangement, was adopted after considerable study and after recommendations had been made by the Trainmen's Committee."

The C-1900 was built in January 1924, and the first production car, C-1901, was not built until 22 months later in November 1925.

The First Production Lot

The construction of the I-5 production cars was assigned to the car shops at Washington, Indiana. An AFE was issued for building 100 cars in the first batch of cabooses. Numbered C-1901 to C-2000, the cars were assembled starting in November 1925 and concluding in February 1926. Some minor revisions were incorporated on this first lot of 100 cars, as can be seen by comparing the photos on the next page.

Some railroads rostered some pretty ugly cabooses

B&O I-5 class cabooses were the first to feature additional steel in the framing as well as steel ends as exemplified by this photo. The cars also had metal roofs. *Dwight Jones*

Prototype I-5 caboose C-1900 is shown outside the Mt. Clare car shop as a new car in January 1924. The shading of this black-and-white photo shows an interesting yet undetermined contrast of colors. *B&O Photos, collection of Dwight Jones*

The photo of C-1995, below, shows the car upon completion at the Washington shops. Several refinements are visible: a color change is apparent, window shades have been enlarged on side windows and a shade has been added to the cupola side windows replacing the gutter on C-1900, side windows were lowered, smokestack baffles are gone, and step sides are changed with air slots added.

Another builder's photo of prototype caboose C-1900, photographed outside of the Mt. Clare car shops in 1924. As built, there was only a handhold at the top of the ladder on the latitudinal running boards. The painters have used extended-font numbers on the end of the caboose as normally would be found on passenger equipment. Just to the left of the right end window is one of the B&O's homemade whistles. The car shop building in the background now is a part of the campus of the B&O Railroad Museum. *B&O Photo, collection of Dwight Jones*

INTERIOR VIEW OF
CABOOSE CAR C-1900,
MT. CLARE, 1-28-1924.

INTERIOR VIEW
OF CABOOSE
CAR C-1900
MT. CLARE 1-28-1924

This April 1984 photo of C-1900 shows where the side windows were lowered by about nine inches (two arrows). Below, an announcement in *Baltimore & Ohio Magazine* regarding the completion of the first 100 production cabooses of the I-5 class.

The Last of the One Hundred

Washington Car Department has just completed building 100 new steel caboose cars, the first being completed on November 7, 1925 and the last on February 6.

The Car Department employes made a nice showing on these cabooses, the one hundred being completed in eighty working days by fifty-five men, with Sam McLemore directly supervising the work.

but B&O cabooses always had a very esthetically pleasing appearance. An example of this is that the side windows were lowered by about 9" after the prototype car was built. And that prototype car, C-1900, later was modified by lowering the side windows on it by that same amount!

The Second Production Lot

Beginning five months after the first batch of 100 cars was completed, the Washington shops started on the next 100 cars in July 1926, with construction continuing until September 1926.

As the last of the 100 cars was being finished up, one car (C-2094) was destroyed in a derailment. With sufficient material on hand a replacement car was completed at the Washington shops. Apparently originally numbered C-2100, it was renumbered to be C-2094 (2nd) to fill the vacant number of the destroyed car.

The Third Production Lot

After another gap of seven months, shop personnel at Washington began work on a third batch of 100 class I-5 cabooses. Beginning with road number C-2100 (2nd) in April 1927, the work continued until June of 1927, when car C-2199 was finished.

The Fourth Production Lot

Twenty-six months later the final group of 100 cars was started at the Washington shops. Beginning in August 1929 the work continued until November 1929 resulting in cars in series C-2200 to C-2299 being built.

A Special Car

One of the last I-5 cabooses was outshopped as a special car with an all-steel riveted body. Our speculation is that C-2297 was built with a steel body as a test case to document application costs.

The Pennsylvania already had completed a caboose with steel body in 1914, 15 years earlier. Subsequent B&O cabooses were built as steel bay-window cars (except for stock and boxcar conversions which retained their wood side and end configurations).

Building the I-5 Cabooses

The B&O hired a professional photographer from Cincinnati to travel to the Washington, Indiana, shops and photograph the step-by-step building of the last batch of I-5 cabooses in 1929.

A unit force consisting of 50 men were assigned to this project. Building of these last 100 cabooses commenced on August 1, 1929, with the first caboose completed one week later on August 7, 1929.

As can be seen from the aerial views of the Washington shops later in this book, four parallel tracks were located to the west of the main shop building where car construction could be staged and where these cars were built. The assembly work followed B&O's "spot" system where standard work was established at each spot which could be completed in one shift, all cars then moving ahead to the next spot on a subsequent shift. *all photos, collection of Dwight Jones*

Starting the construction process trucks are assembled at right in the left photo and couplers are being installed into the frame. Various hydraulic jacks and lift tables make the work easier and reduce the need for manpower.

Below, workers install components of the "K" brake system. In the background, on a parallel track, assembled frames show the metal construction of the I-5s.

Three men are required to assemble I-5 ends. Panels are placed on a fixture table which assures proper alignment of the various pieces. One man heats up the rivets and the other two assemble them. It appears a liberal coat of car cement is applied in the areas where rivets are installed. The metal framing pieces on the ground by the riveting machine are pre-formed to the angle of the roof to fit behind the top of the side panels.

Two men work at assembling the framework for the cupola. Temporary pins are used to locate the various pieces pending permanent attachment. A simple wood frame provides the fixturing to assure all cupola frames are virtually the same and will fit onto the caboose framework.

Below, side frames are assembled using the hot rivet method. At each operation a sign specifies the standard work at that point. Unit No. 4 identifies the group of 50 men assigned to the I-5 building project.

With the end panels and side framing completed, a small one-man, self-propelled shop crane lifts the parts into place. The assembly work can be completed with only three men at this spot. Note the dark discoloration around the edges of the ends where the rivet lines are located. A liberal amount of car cement is applied where parts are joined together to help deter future degradation of the metal at the joints. Note all of the assembled superstructures in the background.

The crane is lifting one of the pre-built side frames in the photo above. Note that a heavy chain on the crane is used to help stabilize the three-sided assembly while three carmen work on attaching the bottom of the side. With the framing firmly secured, the crew can work on assembly of the opposite side.

Assembly work continues at this spot with the pre-fabricated cupola now being swung into place. The worker inside the car has a pin in his hand, ready to temporarily lock the cupola into place. Note that he is standing on a narrow scaffold board placed across the car.

Two men are working on riveting the superstructure framework to the side sill while a third employee is working on the hand brake equipment on the end platform as well as the end railings and ladder installations.

Steps are another sub-assembly that are built "off-line" and stockpiled to have a supply ready when the superstructure shows up. In this view enough step assemblies have been fabricated to cover the next two cars that arrive while the two men work to assemble even more. The completed steps are staged so there is a supply ready at each end of the car, reducing the distance to move the steps to the caboose body. This work is nearing the far west end of the Washington shop complex.

The first step is being riveted to this car. These steps are heavy and it would be interesting to see just how they were lifted into place. The underbody tool box has been installed (visible to the right of the worker) and a stem-winder brake wheel also now is visible on the end platform.

Carpenters are now on the scene, installing the floor first, which provides a good working platform for installation of the wood studding on the sides. Hand saws and wrenches are the tools of the day.

A layer of black "building paper", according to B&O specifications, was to be applied under the side sheathing and shows on this car as carpenters nail the wood siding. Interesting is the fact that they install the siding from one end to the other rather than starting at the centerline of the car and working toward each end. The second car in the background already has one window cut into the siding.

In the photo above a painter is spraying on the first coat of paint. B&O specifications required three coats of paint on new wood. Below, the painter is applying the final coat of paint. Note that the window shades and safety grabirons have already been applied before final painting.

No electric tools here! Carpenters use hand saws and hand drills on the roof. The drill is being used to make a hole for attachment of the cupola handholds. Note all of the wood thrown inside the caboose. Farther down the line painting occurs.

Metal roof panels are ready for installation. At this operation safety appliances are also to be installed as well as running boards (note the running boards already are installed on the car the photographer is on). The car has been primered and final paint also is applied at this spot.

In the photo above a couple of carpenters are nailing interior lining boards to the ends. Trimming the boards for the door opening as well as the window openings will come as a last step. Boards that have excessive splits or other defects are rejected and are lying along the wall at the left. The lower photo shows that the interior marker light brackets have been installed above the right end window, and the metal heat shields for the stove area are in place.

Carpenters are busy finishing out the interior of this car. It's hammers, nails and hand saws at this labor-intensive era. Below, a look at the finished interior, showing the gravity-feed round water tank on the wall and conductor's desk on the right. Note that as built these cars did not have a false ceiling hiding the steel roof support beams. That would come later when the cars were upgraded with plywood interiors.

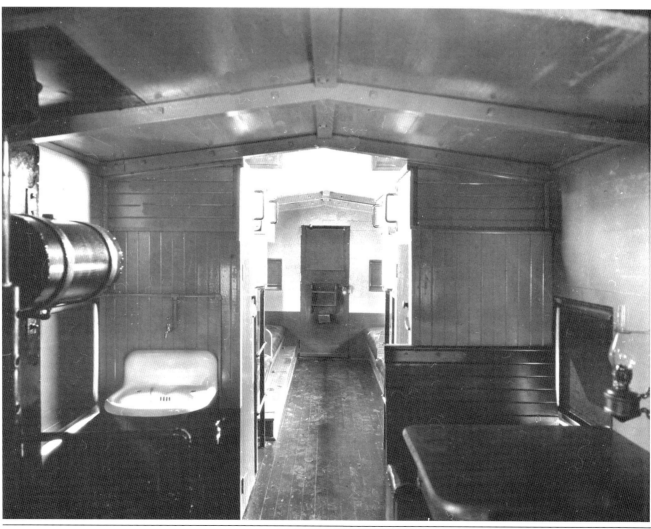

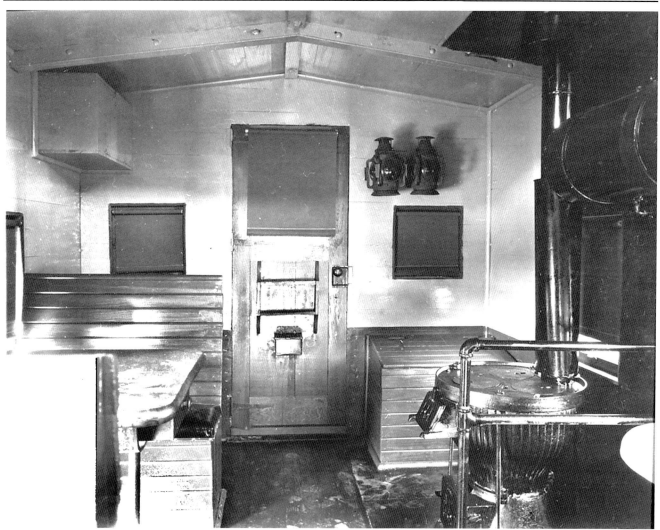

In the photo above the conductor's desk is shown on the left, with a box mounted on the wall above to hold various forms and other paperwork. Across the aisle is the coal box, round pot-belly stove and a partial view of the wash basin (seen better in the image on the previous page). The marker lights are the old style with four external cage brackets. The opposite end of the caboose (photo at right) had four bunks, two on each side separated with a raised partition. A chain box shows on the floor by the bunks on the left side.

A group of 25 cars have had their steel work completed and are ready for application of wood sheathing which shows as the light colored car toward the rear of this string. It appears that the carpenters cannot keep up with the metal workers!

This string of brand new I-5s is almost ready to release to service. It's pretty clear that the Washington shops was heavily involved in box car work at this era.

The sign at this spot states "Station Spot "F". Work to be Done: Final Inspection of Cars. Test and Adjust Brakes. Stencil and Ship Cars." The man kneeling at left is using an air gage to check the braking system (it is being charged from the opposite end air hose). At far right a man is using the "pouncing" method to stencil the car number. His stencil reads C224 with the last digit to be applied separately. The man on the platform has a hammer and appears to be adjusting the door (there's an old saying that if you can't fix it with a hammer you have an electrical problem!).

Comparing the above photo of C-2200 to the earlier view of the C-1995 shows that a small stencil has been added near the marker light on the right corner which is a PAINTED WA stencil with the applicable date. UNITED STATES SAFETY APPLIANCES STANDARD has been stencilled above the repack stencil.

The Cincinnati photographer was smart enough to know that to capture the full end details of the cupola he would have to shoot a long distance view. Comparing this car with the end photo of the C-1900 earlier in this chapter shows changes that were made to these cabooses between 1924 and 1929. Handholds from the ladder to the roof now are standard, the end profile of the steps has been changed, a mail slot has been added to the door and the horizontal ladder rungs have been slightly adjusted (lowered) so the roof grabirons have room to be attached to the vertical sides of the ladder.

One of the last I-5 cabooses, C-2297, was selected as a test case for application of all-steel sheathing as built at the Washington shops. The car lived a somewhat secluded life, apparently never venturing off the St. Louis Division/Cincinnati for 40 years until being dispatched to the Chillicothe shops where it was photographed April 24, 1970, in the Bone Yard. With broken windows and needing other repair work, it was retired

and sold to a private owner. No photos have ever surfaced showing the car in service except one partial view of it on the cab track at Cincinnati in the 1960s. It remained a short wheelbase I-5 all its life and was the only I-5 family car that never had the side grabirons changed. Attesting to its seclusion on the St. Louis Division, it last had its air reservoir serviced and stencilled by the K&IT at Louisville, Kentucky. This was B&O's first new steel-bodied caboose. *Dwight Jones*

It has always been a question whether C-2297 was built new with a steel-sheathed body or whether it was modified some time later. This question was answered in 1992 when a large FedEx box of drawings arrived at our house. CSX mechanical engineers had saved original drawings relating to cabooses when cleaning out their offices in Baltimore in preparation for moving to new offices in Jacksonville.

Included in the box was a drawing of the application of steel sheathing to caboose C-2297, showing that the caboose was given the steel body as originally built in 1929. B&O sketch W-9772 was dated 9-18-29 and was titled "Steel Sheathing, I-5 Caboose Car".

I-5 Roofs (1925)

Drawing U-44472, dated July 23, 1925, specified that the roofs for the I-5 cabooses were the "Improved Chicago Flexible Outside Metal Roof". Application of this type of roof can be seen in the construction

photos earlier in this chapter.

Ladder-to-Roof Handholds (1926)

Prototype caboose C-1900, as well as the first batch of 100 I-5 cars, were built without ladder-to-roof handholds.

The A.A.R. allowed the option of either using ladder-to-roof handholds or using a single handhold attached at the top of the roof and parallel to the ladder step treads. B&O opted for the latter option on these early cars. (see the photo on the bottom of page 59 of volume 3 for a down-on view of both types).

At some point officers changed their mind and decided that the ladder-to-roof handhold version was a safer alternative. Batch number two of the I-5s received the safer version. Surprisingly, there is little documentation that we have found for this improve-

The first steel caboose? Some believe that PRR 486751 is that car. Built at the PRR's Altoona, Pennsylvania, shops in 1914, it was stated at the time that the car had not been adopted as standard but would be thoroughly tested in different parts of the road. It would be 15 years later before B&O's first steel caboose was built in 1929. *collection of Dwight Jones*

The two B&O Railroad Company photos on this page illustrate opposite sides of new class I-5 cabooses. Both photos represent the "as-built" characteristics of this class. The car above has the
flat stock ladder-to-roof handholds (which measure 2" wide by 3/8" thick, the same as the ladder
sides) while the car below has the round-stock version. The photo below, with its background
whited out, was used in the railroad's book *The Catalogue of the Centenary Exhibition of the Baltimore & Ohio Railroad 1827 - 1927,* although it is unclear if the caboose actually participated in the
pageant. Several bolt heads appear between the two windows on the right side. They appear to
have recently been touched up with paint. Our speculation is that the caboose has been updated
with a different style of water tank, a round one, which was bolted to the wall with steel straps.

Caboose C-2113 was built in April 1927, but shows in this photo as being painted at Locust Point, Maryland, five months later. Perhaps the car was involved in some type of system accident that required repainting at this early age. Lettering on the right indicates UNITED STATES SAFETY APPLIANCES STANDARD. Paint colors are still unknown at this early era, but shades on this black-and-white print show the body painted one color, steps and end platforms painted a different shade and the window sash and window frames painted a third color. Not only is it interesting that the car was repainted at the age of five months, but also that the company photographer was called out to photograph it. *collection of Dwight Jones*

ment. B&O drawing Y-41424 was redrawn "including revisions to date" on March 20, 1928, and shows the ladder-to-roof handholds already added prior to that date. It is apparent that cars C-2000 to C-2299 were built with this safer version. Many drawings were redrawn in this same era, possibly because a Mt. Clare fire destroyed the originals.

However, the handhold style did vary. Some cars received them made out of flat stock (the same size as the vertical ladder posts) while most received them made from round stock. An analysis of photos leads us to conclude that cars in series C-2001 to C-2083 received the flat version. Subsequent cars received the round-stock version. Cars with damaged flat-stock versions were repaired using the more popular round stock style. One car showed a flat-stock version on one end and a round-stock version on the opposite end!

Interestingly C-2500 (built in 1930 at Mt. Clare) was built with the ladder-to-roof handhold version but C-2501 and C-2502, from the mid-1930s, received only the single handhold version (see the photos in volume 3).

Early I-5 cars later were retrofitted with the safer style. The vast majority of the C-1900-series cars received the round stock version.

Early Derailment Problems (1927)

A January 28, 1927, memo from A.K. Galloway indicated the following:

"We have experienced some derailments of caboose cars between M & K and Terra Alta, and it has been decided to try out a Pivot Coupler on the front end of locomotives that will not swing out as much as the present coupler, and, to accomplish this we have marked up blueprint S-45342-C.

"Wish you would have a new coupler taken from stock and made according to this print. After this has been done the coupler should be shipped to M&K Jct., and applied to a helper engine."

A June 8, 1927, report relative to the derailment of caboose C-1953 at Gans, Pennsylvania, on May 27, 1927, ended with the following conclusion:

"It is the opinion that the construction of the caboose is responsible for the derailment. The trucks being set too close together provides too much overhang between the truck bolster and coupler, which, together with the long, rigid wheel base of helper engines behind, results in caboose shoving sidewise, wearing the ends of brasses and bending couplers, which ulti-

The Newark, Ohio, shops painted the C-2031 in November 1939 and the car was photographed shortly thereafter. Cars painted in the 1920s and 1930s display a PAINTED stencil in the upper right corner as shown on this car which reads PAINTED NE 11-39. This stencil seems to duplicate the shop stencil in the bottom left corner. Perhaps that is the reason it was eliminated.
Paul Dunn collection / collection of Dwight Jones

mately results in caboose shoving off track."

It is interesting to note that since this report was issued in 1927, there was ample time to make changes to the I-5 cabooses before more were built in the late 1920s, but no such changes were made to those cars.

Trouble in the Mountains (1930)

A B&O memo dated April 15, 1930, indicated that cutting off cabooses at Hardman and M&K Junction and placing them behind helper engines was resulting in considerable delay to trains. An additional delay of 12-15 minutes at Tunnelton and 10 minutes at Terra Alta was occurring in order to remove helper and reattach caboose to rear of train.

On previous tests it was found that helpers would raise a caboose off the rails on an average of two or three times each 24-hour test period. The general feeling was that there was too much overhang between the couplers of the caboose and the trucks.

B&O's newest cabooses, the I-5 class, were approved only for "light" helper service. Caboose occupants were not interested in riding in the caboose with two Mallet locomotives coupled behind the caboose.

Officials observed that on the Pennsylvania Railroad they were using two and sometimes three locomotives as helpers, with the caboose on the train ahead of the helper engines.

B&O officials acquired diagrams of the Pennsylvania Railroad cabooses to compare their construction with that of the B&O cabooses.

Comparison of B&O and PRR cabooses showed that the B&O I-5 cars had a much stronger center sill construction than the PRR cabs but that the PRR cabs had a 19-foot truck center compared to 15 feet on the B&O.

B&O officers surveyed the cabooses of eight other railroads which showed that only the B&O and the Union Railroad had short truck centers. Almost all other railroads had cabooses with 19 feet between truck centerlines. The B&O officers paid particular attention to the PRR and Reading cabooses, both of which had 19-foot truck centers.

Colonel Emerson issued a message dated July 14, 1930, in which he indicated his feelings on redesigning B&O cabooses to have 19-foot truck distances:

"We should arrange to do this as soon as possible. We will then change one of our standard cabooses and test it out in helper service."

A September 23, 1930, memo indicated that caboose C-2119 had been modified at Mt. Clare to have 19-foot distance between truck centers. Instructions were issued on October 10 that the test caboose should be sent to the West End of the Cumberland Division.

Test caboose C-2119 was operated on several trains on the West End, with company officers riding the caboose and filing reports of their observations.

On October 14, two Mallet helpers were behind the caboose on a train with 55 loads. No problems were noted.

On Cranberry Grade it was observed that the caboose did not do so well, but it also was noted that helper engine 7209 had not been equipped with wedges to prevent excessive coupler swing. It was ordered that this helper not be used again until outfitted with the wedges.

On October 16 the caboose operated on an eastbound and it was noted that there was excessive vibration in the center of the caboose. Another eastbound run showed no problems with the caboose.

Some of the problem was no doubt psychological in nature as noted by this statement:

"Mr. Henry concludes his report by stating that the worst thing about the matter is the thoughts of what is behind you while you are in the caboose, or what might happen if the train had a burst air hose or a break-in-two near the head end or some other situation. However, in view of the reduced speed that the trains are making, the likelihood of any serious consequence is not apparent."

Another comment in this same report indicated the following:

"We had the 2119 weighed at Keyser and found that no additional weight had been given the caboose. It now weights 20-tons and it is our opinion that 20 tons weight should be added.

"There is some little feeling against this test on the West end, and it is felt that there has not been enough change made in the caboose to warrant it being tested out with men riding in the caboose. All feel that considerable additional weight should be added before we go any further with the test. I have talked to Liller and Henry, who rode this caboose up the grades last week, and they admit they felt very uneasy while making the trip. The additional weight referred to could be placed in the floor with concrete and scrap iron, and would reinforce the body as well as assist in holding the body down in case of shock."

These comments were signed by the Superintendent.

A November 15, 1930, report indicated the following: "Conductor and Flagman riding this caboose are still riding on the helper engine while ascending Newburg and Cranberry grades, claiming that they are afraid to ride inside the caboose with two Mallets shoving."

A March 6, 1931, memo indicated that the Mechanical Engineers had determined that adding increased weight to the I-5 cars would be accomplished with a mixture of one part cement, one-half part sand, and three parts boiler punchings. It was planned to do this by cutting holes in the floor and not disturbing any of the interior furnishings.

Baltimore, Md., May 21, 1936-TS.

Mr. W. B. Whitsitt:

        Please note attached memorandum from Mr. Calder of May 19th, with letter from Mr. E. P. Welshonce addressed to Mr. H. R. Laughlin of May 7th, and with return of same advise what you know about this question of spreading the trucks to a greater center space on our 8-wheel caboose cars than we now have.

        I didn't know anything of this sort was permitted by any instructions we have issued, and have no advice as to the necessity of doing it. Have you any such advice, and do you recommend that it be done?

                                                        J. J. Tatum.

In this memo J.J. Tatum is asking about the modification of I-5 cars with extended wheelbase.

A memo dated April 10, 1931, reported that caboose C-1981 had been modified with the increased wheelbase as well as increased weight under the floor and had been dispatched to the West End Cumberland Division for more testing.

Shop officials found that the extra weight bottomed out the original elliptic springs so they installed heavier springs which they happened to have on hand from an old camp car which the shop had dismantled.

An initial test run showed the caboose was satisfactory with the exception that the couplers pushed up against the head blocks on both ends. It was decided to equip caboose with National Draft Gears to prevent this.

A report of April 29, 1931, indicated that caboose C-1981 had been in service three weeks and no problems had been experienced in its use between Keyser and Fairmont.

Caboose C-2119 was being used between Keyser and Grafton and had been involved in three incidents one of which bent the coupler stems.

The report recommended that all cabooses on the West End be equipped the same as test caboose C-1981.

A Standard Estimate was prepared under date of May 25, 1931, to equip five cabooses with increased truck centers and weight under floor. Caboose C-1981, already converted, was considered as one of the five cars.

A September 9, 1931, memo indicated that the additional four cabooses would be converted at Keyser.

Later correspondence indicated that caboose C-1920 was completed on March 10, 1932, and that the

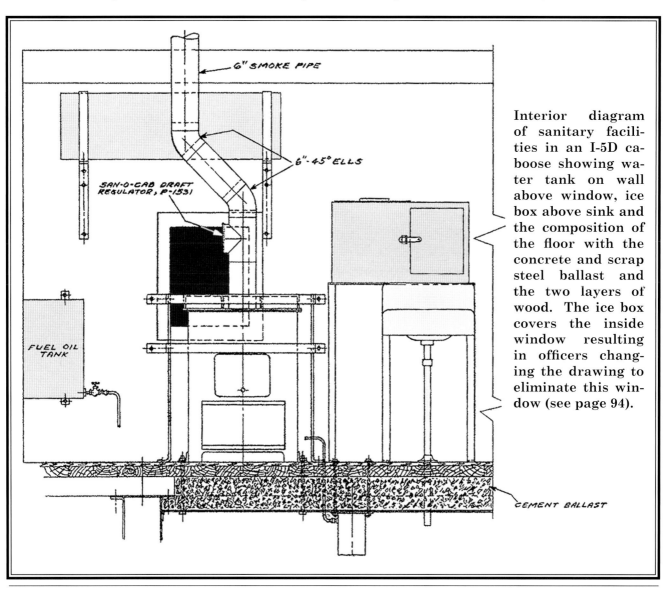

Interior diagram of sanitary facilities in an I-5D caboose showing water tank on wall above window, ice box above sink and the composition of the floor with the concrete and scrap steel ballast and the two layers of wood. The ice box covers the inside window resulting in officers changing the drawing to eliminate this window (see page 94).

These two photos reportedly identify Hot Shot train 118 above and 117 below at Pittsburgh. Actually it appears to us that both views show train 117 on arrival at Pittsburgh based on sun angle and the scene. B&O literature identified these trains as "Fast Merchandise Freights" which operated between Pittsburgh and Jersey City (New York) on a fast passenger train schedule (clocked as going as fast as 75 MPH). The older photo (above) shows the train operating with many C-15 express cars. These later were replaced with C-16 express box cars which were modified from M-53 box cars (and show in the later photo below). Cabooses C-2084 and C-2160, described in this chapter, were assigned to these fast trains. Some have made the case that they were ballasted due to the fast train speed. The photo above also shows they were modified to have the 19-foot truck centers. However the real reason may have been for helper service. The eastbound train received helpers only occasionally based on tonnage but the westbound counterpart always received helpers at Hyndman to the summit. Due to the fast schedule the extra time to switch the caboose behind the helpers may have been unacceptable.

additional three cars would not be converted due to insufficient forces to do the work.

On February 7, 1934, Standard Estimate 1931 was prepared to do a total of 10 cabooses with 19-foot wheelbase and extra weight under the floor.

Tool Boxes Removed (1931)

Mechanical engineers issued a B&O neo-style letter on March 14, 1931, indicating that under-body tool boxes were to be removed from cabooses when cars were on shop tracks for other work. See the neo-style letter in this chapter.

This decision came about as the engineers were planning to apply a concrete floor to one of the I-5 cabooses. The existing tool box would need to be removed and then modified for reattachment. Best to just eliminate them.

Trains 117/118 Cabooses (1935)

"Hot Shot" L.C.L trains 117/118 operating between New York and Pittsburgh (also described as operating between Pittsburgh and Philadelphia) were given two assigned cabooses (C-2084 and C-2160) which were each given concrete floors in August 1935. These trains operated at high speed (75 MPH) and some have reported that the increased weight was to allow the cars to track better in this high speed service.

These two photos document upgraded end platforms and steps for I-5 family cabooses. At left the end platform is of the Apex grating style with Morton-style steps. On the right the end platform is of the Super Diamond Plate style while the steps are of the Apex grating style. There was no requirement about not mixing and matching the various types. There were Morton-style end platforms too. *Dwight Jones*

During early operation of these weighted cabooses there was considerable problem with rough riding of the cars and constant breaking of the truck springs. Memos dated in February and March 1936 documented the problems. The cabooses had not been updated with larger springs when the extra weight was added. Replacement springs, which were stronger, solved the problem.

Caboose C-2084 was weighed on March 4, 1936, and was found to weigh 62,700 pounds. Mechanical Engineers reported that this was more than they anticipated the cars would weigh.

Although only two caboose numbers were mentioned, there must have been other backup cabooses that could be used in this service when one of these cars required a visit to the shop for routine repairs. We suspect that some of the other cabooses listed at the bottom of page 72 would have been the backups for this service.

The fact that only two caboose numbers were listed for this specific service makes one think that the cabooses may have operated throughout the whole 525-mile run without change. This would make sense since this was a time sensitive train and it would have taken time to change out cabooses at each crew terminal. If true, this would be an early use of the concept of caboose pooling. The use of these weighted cabooses for heavy pusher service may have given crews on the east end of the system the false impression that they had been weighted for their high speed service, not realizing that the real reason was for the heavy grades west of Cumberland that required helper locomotives.

Trains 117/118 reportedly existed from September 29, 1935, to April 25, 1941.

More Pusher Problems (1937)

On December 23, 1937, O.C. Cromwell issued the following memo to George Emerson:

"While on the FM&P Branch, in talking with the Road People, they state they have more or less trouble with the steel underframe cabooses in pushing service being pushed off the track sidewise and it is thought due to the overhanging of the bumper beyond the trucks.

"It looks to me, after making inspection of the caboose that the trucks could be easily moved towards the end of car and reduce the overhang."

Conversion of I-5 cabooses - lengthen truck centers and apply
ballast and new steps -

Lorain, Ohio, January 5, 1953.

Mr. B. B. Stuart:-

Instructions were issued on Nov. 24, 1952 by Mr. F. H. Einwaechter
on the above subject.

Check develops that on the Wheeling Division, there are 29 class
I-5 cabooses that require floor to be ballasted, 22 of which also have to have the
bolsters extended to 19 ft. centers. We expect to do 2 of these cars per month at
Lorain.

In order to ballast a car only, it will require the following
material:

1 car set of ballast pans - BP T-82124-A
7 tons of punchings.
12 sacks of cement.
3000 lbs. of sand.
4 stock #902 double elliptic springs - BP S-28446-U.

If car requires bolsters to be extended from 15 feet to 19 feet
it will be necessary that the steps be changed per blueprint and the following
material should be ordered.

2 steps complete as shown on BP T-66946-A
2   "   "   reverse "   "   "

Arrange to order at once on special requisition, as we expect
to start this work at Lorain as soon as material is recieved.

W. W. Manwell.

cc-Mr. H. W. Chew/
    Mr. F. H. Becherer.
    Mr. C. R. Wheeler.

The above memo is presented to document the bill of material need to convert I-5 and I-5C cabooses to class I-5D. Instructions in this memo indicated that most of the required parts were to be ordered on requisition. It is assumed that the punchings were to come from the Cumberland Bolt and Forge shop. Likely the steps would come from the Mt. Clare shops. It is interesting that the steps were to be ordered rather than have the shop at Lorain remove and modify the existing steps. Ballast pans were welded to the underframe and served to hold the cement and punchings when they were poured in through openings in the floor. Heavy duty elliptic springs for the trucks were required due to the increased weight of the I-5D cars.

For a look at a small section of an I-5D concrete floor, which was salvaged by the author, see the photo on the bottom of page 187.

Colonel Emerson hand-wrote the following message on the bottom of the memo directed to W.B. Whitsitt:

"This is the first report I have received of any complaint regarding new caboose cars."

Grabiron Changes (1942)

Side and end handholds were changed with a drawing revision of August 28, 1942. Individual cars would have been changed after that date as shop forces could work them in. This revision changed the side grabirons from the original style which had a third attachment point near the center of the grabiron to a full radius side grab that had only end point attachment feet. This safety enhancement prevented a train service employee from having his hand caught or injured by the attachment point near the center of the grabiron. Clearance was also improved for the end grabiron attachment feet.

"AB" Brakes (1948)

Class I-5 cabooses were built with type "K" brakes which were updated to type "AB" mostly in the early 1950s. Refer to our roster listings for the exact update for each caboose. A description of "AB" brakes can be found later in this chapter.

As is the case with many government-required updates to equipment, the deadline for equipping cars was moved back to accommodate the requests from the railroads. A B&O mechanical engineer letter dated December 11, 1952, indicated the following:

"Referring to first paragraph of Page 2 of general letter of November 5, 1951, regarding time limit for application of "AB" brakes to interchange freight cars-

"The Interstate Commerce Commission's latest order dated November 18, 1952, now requires all interchange cars be equipped with "AB" brakes on or before June 30, 1953."

Note that this information supplements that in our side bar on "AB" brakes found later in this chapter.

Plywood for Cabooses (1956)

In early 1956 B&O officials observed that the Great Northern was using plywood on the exterior and interior of their cabooses. Officers sent a letter to the GN under date of February 15, 1956, to learn more about the use of plywood on cabooses by the GN.

A January 31, 1956, memo indicated that the Keyser shops was to outfit a Baltimore Division class I-5 caboose with plywood, inside and outside, and send the cab to Baltimore for further inspection. There was no indication of the caboose number so modified.

For an early use of plywood on the interior of I-17 cabooses see Volume 2, page 14.

I-5D Modification Costs (1956)

A September 27, 1956, company memo documented the costs for modifying cabooses to class I-5D:

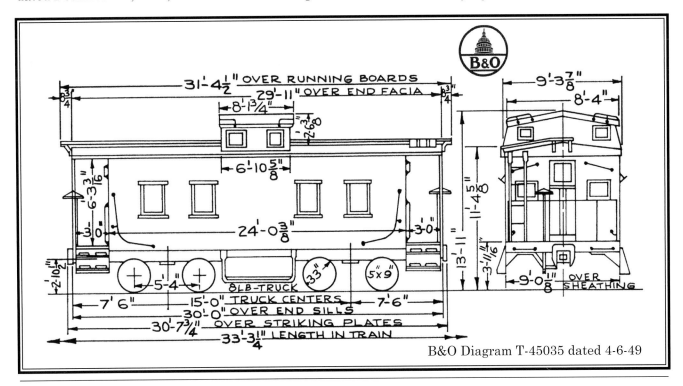

B&O Diagram T-45035 dated 4-6-49

Material	$859.92
Labor	$406.00
Stores Expense	$ 98.73
Shop Expense	$ 81.20
Total Cost	$1446.85

Class I-5E (1956)

B&O Mechanical Engineers invested considerable design work for a new caboose class to be identified as I-5E. From the many drawings that were updated it appears that I-5 family cupola cabooses were going to be modified to a style of cab mimicking that of the I-17A cars.

After all that work the idea was apparently quickly squashed. As an example, existing drawing T-85455 was revised on 1-10-56 to add class I-5E and it was revised again just four months later on May 15, 1956, to remove class I-5E.

Perhaps road numbers C-2910 to C-2924 were skipped to reserve these numbers for the proposed I-17A lookalikes.

Steps Modified

Steps underwent two types of changes over the years. Width and design was changed to accommodate changing the truck centers and upgrading the trucks while the treads were changed from wood coverings to metal.

Drawing T-89203, dated 2-2-61, documented the use of Apex Tri-Lok treads for steps.

Drawing T-89219, dated 2-23-61, documented the Morton type of metal steps.

See photos included in this chapter.

Window Eliminations (1960)

Perhaps the most-asked as well as the most-confusing question of the I-5 family cupola cars is in relation to the window eliminations. And there were many variations! Some cars had four windows per side, some three, some two, some one and some none! Further complicating the issue is that the windows that were eliminated also varied so two cars, each with one window eliminated on a side may not have had the same single window eliminated.

Supported by photos in this book, we provide the following review to attempt to clarify the window eliminations. To help modelers who want to model

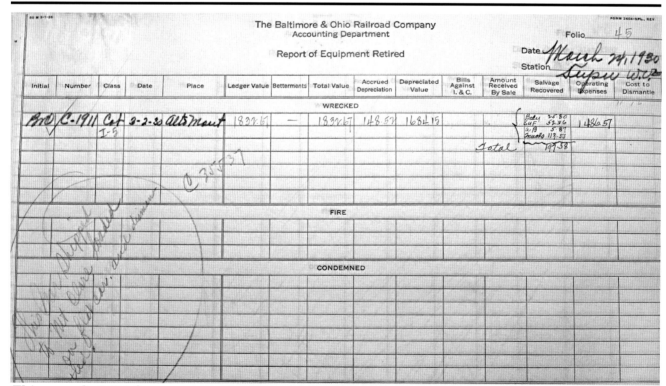

This sample 2404 form covers the disposition of class I-5 caboose C-1911 wrecked at Altamont, Maryland, on March 2, 1930. The 2404 form was completed at the Keyser, West Virginia, shops on March 24, 1930. Note the breakdown of the salvage recovered from this wrecked caboose, tabulated in the upper right corner. Also of interest is the hand-written comments on the left side of the form: "This car shipped to Mt. Clare loaded on flat car and dismantled."

An unusual modification is exhibited by the C-2215 which has the side cupola windows sheathed over. The photo does not reveal if the cupola end windows are still open. The two body windows nearest this end appear to have screens covering the windows. Still an original I-5 configuration with original three-point attachment side grabs, this photo likely was taken in the 1930s. *collection of Dwight Jones*

specific caboose numbers, we have compiled a table which addresses window eliminations on specific cabooses. The data in the table is based on examination of photos in our collection. We have images of over 90% of the I-5 fleet but not necessarily of both sides of each caboose, which would be needed to be more definitive. In general the following is true:

1. All I-5 cars were built with 4 side windows on each side.

2. Beginning in 1960 the first window eliminations are indicated in company files. Two memos in this chapter document that company officers determined that the inside window near the stove was blocked by installation of an interior ice box and should be eliminated as a practical measure. Drawing Y-88278 subsequently was revised to show this (revision "C" dated 9-6-60).

3. Drawing Y-88278 was further changed with revision "G" dated 8-3-61 to remove six of the eight side windows leaving the two adjacent to the conductor's desk. This covered the substantial number of I-5Dm cabooses outshopped from the Du Bois shops starting in January of 1961 when sanitary facilities were added to meet the state requirements of New York, Pennsylvania and Maryland.

4. The shops at Willard, Ohio, updated a number of cupola cabooses in the mid-1960s creating copy cat I-5Dm cars (at least on the exterior sides as these cars did not have all of the betterments that the cars from Du Bois received). The shops at Willard also did a number of the cupola cars that predated the I-5

family cabooses.

5. By the time of the 1970-1971 rehab program at the Chillicothe shops (when the cabs were painted C&O yellow), there seemed to be more of a "who cares" attitude with many cars receiving window eliminations when plywood was added. It was easier for the shops to just cover the windows. Also many cars were received at the shops in pretty poor condition and the shops at Chillicothe may not have had the ability to fabricate replacement sash. After all, the railroad was just trying to squeeze a few more years out of these veteran cabooses.

6. And finally this catch-all category to cover oddball window eliminations perhaps to customize certain cars based on their assignment (such as the urban jungles around the Chicago area where windows were just considered target practice).

We have provided a number of photos in this chapter to help document the categories listed above.

Truck Upgrades (1961)

Drawing U-89197, dated 1-30-61, showed the reduced width of steps when trucks were upgraded to size 5-1/2" x 10".

Cupolas Removed

Some I-5 cabooses had their cupolas removed at some point in their careers with cupolas being restored to some of these at a later date. The removal was likely due to a fire or some other in-service

Baltimore, Md., March 14, 1931.

102 - Caboose Cars - Removal of Tool Boxes -

Messrs.

T.R.Stewart	F.R.Gelhausen	J.H.Shay
H.T.Cromwell	M.A.Gleeson	C.G.Slagle
W.K.Gonnerman	W.F.Harris	R.A.Conner
F.L.Hall	J.P.Hines	D.M.Ambrose
G.C.McGuire	C.E.McCann	J.F.Powden
F.A.Baldinger	T.E.Mewshaw	W.A.Bender
H.J.Burkley	F.K.Moses	W.V.Calder
R.H.Cline	T.C.O'Brien	T.H.Hollen
F.C.Cooper	Harry Rees	E.B.Miller
J.H.Dawson	J.W.Schad	F.A.Teed

Whenever caboose cars are on shop tracks for repairs, the tool box now located under floor and on one side of car should be removed.

Any new cars built should have this box omitted.

hlh-ers

Cy -
G.H.Emerson	A.H.Hodges	H.Shoemaker
A.K.Galloway	W.D.Johnston	J.R.Orndorff
G.R.Galloway	W.B.Porterfield	A.L.Miller
J.J.Tatum	E.J.McSweeney	C.T.Rommel
F.H.Lee	J.J.Smith	
H.A.Blair	W.S.Galloway	
A.E.McMillan	B.W.Walther	

mishap.

Cars with cupolas removed (based on photos) include the following:

C1904
C1922
C1966 cupola later restored to this car
C2009
C2032 cupola later restored to this car
C2040
C2094 used on SIRT
C2136
C2207

On July 9, 1944, conductor Roy Bragg at Gassaway,

West Virginia, wrote the following to C. W. Van Horn, Vice President Operations and Maintenance:

"My regular caboose #2132, caboose that I have held for years, and can not say when it was last in shops for repairs, and it is now going in shops for General Repairs, July 12th at Gassaway, W. VA. and I am wondering if I would be asking too much of you to give Car Foreman, at Gassaway authority to leave Cupola off.

"And this why I ask, we now have all Stokers fired engines and we have from one to three helper engines on rear of train pushing and you could not ride cupola of caboose if you wanted to account of cinders and smoke, the cupola is a dirt harbor and by leaving

January 25th, 1934.

Mr. G. H. Emerson:

      Referring to your letter January 23rd, regarding General Superintendent Hoskins' recommendation that certain cabooses operating in through freight service on the West End Cumberland Division be reinforced similar to caboose No. C-1981.

      Note you state if we propose to use two Mallet engines as pushers behind cabooses on the mountain, the safest thing to do would be to weight some of the cabooses down. In this particular case, you probably observed from the General Superintendent's letter that there was only one Mallet helper on the rear of the train and when coupler broke, train buckled, applying the brakes in emergency, and when train came to rest an empty box car was raised up off its truck, body of the car riding west platform of caboose C-1981, caving in west end of body of the caboose about three feet.

      I feel these cabooses should be reinforced with concrete and scrap iron and will be glad if you will prepare Form 940 so authority may be secured to undertake the work.

                  C. W. Van Horn.

cupola off could have a much cleaner caboose, and would save very much on labor and material.

"If you can grant this request I will thank you a lot and if you can not I will still thank you.

"My run now is between Gassaway and Grafton, W. VA. and you started me in this R.R. game when you was at Clarksburg, W. VA."

On July 12, 1944, Vice President Van Horn acknowledged the conductor's letter indicating that the matter was being referred to the General Superintendent Motive Power and Equipment for his handling. However Van Horn sent A. K. Galloway the following comments on a blind copy of the letter:

"In view of the circumstances, I think it would be well to eliminate the cupola if it is possible to do so."

RIDER

STANDARD ESTIMATE NO. 1931

APPLICATION OF CEMENT UNDER FLOOR AND RELOCATING
TRUCKS - 10 CLASS I-5 CABOOSE CARS

PRESENT — In order to overcome objections of train
crews on the West End Cumberland Division,
the present caboose cars when used with
pusher or helper service are switched from
position in rear of trains to position back
of helper locomotives.

PROPOSED — So that this condition can be avoided and
resultant saving made it is proposed to
stabilize ten of our class I-5 caboose cars.
This will be done by respacing the trucks
and applying cement and iron weighting under
floor and by so doing increasing weight of
car about 17,000 pounds.

SAVINGS — This betterment will effect a saving of at
least 40 minutes per trip on our coal trains.
We are operating now an average of about nine
coal trains per day, so that the saving would
be six hours per day practically all of which
is on overtime, the overtime rate for the
train and engine crew being $6.27. With the
present amount of business, the saving would
amount to $37.62 per day, or about $14,000.00
per annum, which of course, would increase as
business increases.

A. K. Galloway replied to Van Horn with the following letter of August 12, 1944:

"General Car Foreman Hollen was instructed to remove the cupola from this caboose providing the laws of the States in which it operated did not prohibit operating cabooses without cupola. We are attaching letter from General Car Foreman Hollen which brings up the question of other trainmen having previously requested removal of cupola, and whose requests were denied. On receipt of Mr. Hollen's letter we wired him not to remove cupola from caboose C-2132 until further advised.

"We feel you should be acquainted with this situation before any action is taken. Will you kindly advise your wishes in the matter."

On August 17, Van Horn replied with this note:

continued on page 62

Baltimore, Md., October 27th, 1938.

102 – Caboose Cars – Application of Look-out Window – Class I-5 Caboose Cars –

Messrs.

W.S.Eyerly	J.P.Hines	H.L.Geidenberger	A.H.Keys
J.Howe	T.E.Mewshaw	J.S.Major	F.A.Teed
W.B.Porterfield	J.W.Schad	W.A.Bender	H.A.Harris
H.J.Burkley	H.M.Sherrard	W.W.Calder	V.P.Hollen
V.F.Harris	E.Stimson, Jr.	E.B.Cox	E.H.Meckstroth

    Whenever any of the class I-5 Caboose Cars, Series C-1900 to C-2299, go through shop for classified repairs, arrange to apply look-out windows as illustrated on the following prints copies attached:

    T-64485-A – Arrangement and Application of Look-out
           Window.

    T-64496-A – Details of Look-out Window.

    The windows are to be applied to side window openings nearest "B" end of car, both sides.

    The cupola now on cars will not be removed account of various State Laws.

hlh-ers
enc.

U.B.Whitsitt

Cy. Messrs.

G.H.Emerson	C.M.House	H.Rees	H.A.Lockhart
J.J.Tatum	H.A.Blair	V.S.Galloway	W.H.Gordon
G.R.Galloway	F.A.Baldinger	E.W.Walther	
E.J.McSweeney	H.W.Brewer	H.Shoemaker	

By 1938 the concept of the bay-window caboose had found enough acceptance on the B&O that an idea to quickly adapt the improved visibility provided by an extended side window was rolled out to the fleet of I-5 cupola cabooses. The memo on this page as well as the photos on the following page document how a fabricated side bay window could be attached to one of the existing I-5 side windows, specifically the windows closest to the "B" end of the car.

It is interesting that B&O drawings and the above neo-style letter do not indicate if the windows were to be made at local company shops or whether they were to be ordered from one of the better equipped larger company shops.

The window was constructed to have 18" x 22" side glass and 8-3/4" x 22" glass on each end. The lookout window was not intended to be easily removed. It was secured to the caboose window opening with a series of wood screws around the periphery of the window.

Caboose C-1922 is shown at the Keyser shops in 1937 with a test box installed on one of the windows as a way to adopt the benefits of a bay-window caboose to an older caboose. This concept did not see widespread use, perhaps used only on this car.

The car is stencilled as an I-5 but appears to have the extended wheelbase. The lack of a cupola suggests that it has been in a fire or wreck and has been rebuilt at Keyser with a new sectional metal roof, likely reclaimed from a dismantle box-car.

This car survived until 1974 on the B&O, when it was sold to Majestic Mining from Grafton. See another photo in the color section of this book.

Baltimore, Md., March 20th, 1946.

102 – Caboose Cars   )
122 – Brakes   ) Application of 5" x 9" Trucks –
129 – Trucks   )
                   (SUPERSEDING LETTER OF 1–31–1940.)

Messrs.

C.H.Spence	F.J.Rosenberg	R.B.Fisher
H.M.Sherrard	G.H.Rosenberg	A.J.Larrick
R.A.Conner	T.I.Schachtele	A.F.Pugh
J.T.Connelly	G.W.Short	H.A.Harris
F.L.Galloway	E.Stimson,Jr.	T.H.Hollen
L.R.Haase	F.C.Gimbel	E.H.Meckstroth
F.L.Hall	P.L.Hofstetter	H.A.Friebe
J.P.Hines	J.S.Major	B.J.Mangan
W.H.Longwell	E.B.Cox	G.O.Prosser
L.L.Robinson,Jr.	F.J.Crockett	W.C.Reister

This letter embodies previous instructions with revision to include changes in brake arrangement of Caboose Cars, when applying trucks with 5" x 9" journals and increasing truck centers from 15'–0" to 19'–0".

When Caboose Cars with 4–1/4" x 8" trucks, or 5" x 9" trucks with arch bars, are on shop tracks for repairs, arrange to apply 5" x 9" trucks with serviceable "T" or "L" section cast steel side frames, either integral box or Andrews type reclaimed from condemned cars.

The following prints   copies attached, cover Arrangement and Details of truck and alterations to foundation brake arrangement, account of change in truck brake levers:–

    W-65892-B – Arrangement of Truck with 5" x 9" Journals.
    Y-61256-B – Brake Arrangement.
    S-12663-H – Spring Seat.
    S-18680-Z – Truck Brake Levers.
    S-26300-Q – Rollers.
    S-28446-P – Double Elliptic Springs.
    S-38217-I – Side Bearing Shoe.
    T-43549-H – Roller Seat and Spring Cap.
    S-44738-O – Spring Plank.
    U-45297-Y-1 – Cylinder and Floating Lever.
    U-64589-M-1 – Brake Rods.
    S-65900-A – Spring Plate.

Trucks will have elliptic springs per print S-28446-P, applied as shown on print W-65892-B.

Roller seat, print T-43549-H, shows cut for clearance of elliptic springs, and print S-65900-A covers spring plate used with this seat.

Caboose C-2050 was photographed, probably in 1947, at Chillicothe. The car last was painted at Lima, Ohio, in August 1946. It appears the assigned conductor has framed his caboose number to customize the car. The new "13 states" emblem apparently has baffled the painters who did not fill in the stencil tabs (bridges).

A professional photographer covered the C-2050, and made good quality interior photos which follow. Good interior views of these cars are very rare, particularly from the 1940s. The below view shows an improved wall covering in the end of the caboose and cupola. An air gauge shows between the cupola windows.

continued from page 56

"Write Conductor Bragg and state that we have had our Mechanical people look in to the question of removing cupola from caboose 2132 and to do so means making changes in the superstructure of the caboose and it is not felt this should be done until sometime the caboose is shopped for general overhauling, at which time this will be given further consideration."

On August 24th conductor Bragg wrote the following to Mr. Van Horn:

"Mr. Vanhorn, this caboose is in the Gassaway shops at this time for a general overhauling, and the cupola is practically rottened off so to speak, and it will be a new cupola to build and it would cost far less to eliminate cupola. I have talked to Mr. Arrasmith our General Car Forman at Gassaway, and he said, it would save in material and labor, and for the next general overhauling I fear that you and I will not be working for the Baltimore and Ohio Railroad Company that is if the proper care is taken of caboose and it stays out of the shops just half as long as it has this time."

One final note from Mr. Galloway to Vice President Van Horn indicated the following:

The bunk end of a working caboose complete with coat hanging on the left and a collection of hangers on the right. Curious is the bed springs serving as a backing on one of the bunks on the right. The car is very clean and well kept. Perhaps they knew the photographer was coming. At least three different styles of bunk cushions are present. It is interesting that this end of the caboose does not have a false ceiling but that the opposite end of the caboose does.

Baltimore, June 30th, 1952

Mr. W. C. Baker:

Referring to conversation in connection with condition of caboose cars for pusher service. Called attention to the fact that use of the four unit diesel helpers had changed our situation to considerable extent, sofar as strength of caboose cars is concerned.

Arranged for the Engineering Department to make a survey of the entire caboose car situation, from standpoint of design and particularly strength of center sill. We have always had caboose cars that were not to be used in helper service. So that classification of our caboose cars would be brought up to date, attached print was prepared, classifying our ownership of 1105 cabooses into three categories. You will note 241 should not be used in pusher service;
    635 are satisfactory for light pusher service
    229 are satisfactory for heavy pusher service.
1105 - Total.

One class of caboose car, namely the I-5, of which we own 279, have been shown as satisfactory for light pusher service. These cars have 15-ft truck centers and could readily be modified by increasing truck centers to at least 19-ft.; which has already been done on some of this type. They would then be satisfactory for heavy pusher service. It will involve relocation of the bolster and some changes in underframe details. Estimated cost of doing this work per car is $580.00. Very little new material will be required, as the present body bolsters can be reused if in good condition.

By light pusher service, we consider a 3000 HP diesel locomotive of two units; for heavy pusher service, a 6000 HP diesel locomotive of four units, or steam locomotives of equivalent power.

As we view it, it will be necessary to set up program converting the class I-5 caboose cars to class I-5-D, which includes ballasting. This will give us better than 200 additional caboose cars for heavy pusher service.

Am giving copy of this letter to the General Managers, Superintendents Motive Power and Master Mechanics, in order that they may be familiar with the caboose car situation and review it on their territory. They should be certain caboose cars are assigned to service, to correspond with sttached statement, "Comparison of B&O caboose cars - Pusher Service".

A. K. Galloway.

Baltimore, Md., November 24, 1952

102 - Caboose Cars) Increasing Truck Centers and Applying Ballast,
131 - Underframes) changing Class I-5 Caboose Cars to Class I-5d -

Messrs.
		R.A.Gerrigus	G.F.Bissett
C.H.Spence	A.W.Gibson	H.W.Chew	L.R.Freeland
H.M.Sherrard	P.L.Hofstetter	R.W.Baldinger	E.F.Gross
L.R.Haase	F.J.Rosenberg	F.J.Crockett	W.W.Manwell
W.J.Baumiller	G.H.Rosenberg	R.B.Fisher	W.C.Reister
A.E.Beckman	T.I.Schachtele	A.L.Kerr	F.P.Ryan
E.L.Brown	G.W.Short	A.J.Larrick	R.E.Soummers
J.T.Connelly	W.O.Sines	A.F.Pugh	W.R.King
C.L.Gainer	T.J.Stevenson	H.A.Harris	B.J.Mangan
F.M.Galloway	E.Stimson,Jr.	F.H.Becherer,Jr.	G.O.Prosser

         To provide additional Caboose Cars that can be used in heavy pusher
service; arrange, when class I-5 Caboose Cars are on shop tracks for repairs,
to increase the truck centers from 15'-0" to 19'-0", apply ballast to increase
weight and reclassify to I-5d, as covered by the following prints,   copies
attached:-

     V-52757-C - Relocation of Body Bolster.
     T-66946-A - Details of Platform Step.
     V-82116-A - Underframe Arrangement for 19'-0" Truck Centers and Ballast.
     T-82124-A - Ballast Pans.
     Y-75555-B - "AB" Brake Arrangement, showing Modification to Brake
                 Appliances when applying Ballast.
     S-28446-U - Double Elliptic Springs Stock No. 902 -
                 To be applied due to increase in weight when ballast is
                 applied.

         On a number of class I-5 Caboose Cars the truck centers were increased
from 15'-0" to 19'-0", and reclassified I-5c.   Ballast was not applied to these
cars.   When the class I-5c Cars are on shop tracks for repairs, arrange to
apply ballast per print V-82116-A and reclassify to I-5d.

         Application of ballast and the relocation of body bolsters to be
reported on Form 2404-A to Mechanical Engineering Department and others concerned.

Copy - Messrs.   R.W.Eves
  A.B.Lawson   G.F.Wiles   G.R.Palmer   H.P.McQuilkin
  A.H.Keys   Melvin Ennis (6)   W.F.Peck   V.N.Dawson
  J.Hewes, Jr.   C.W.Esch   C.B.Chattin   L.G.Kohler
  C.E.Morley   G.F.Patten   H.T.Murphy   G.H.Flagg
  H.J.Burkley   B.A.Kidwell   C.S.Shelleman
  F.B.Rykoskey   D.M.Lohr   D.A.Wagner

The report on the previous page indicated that a program should be set up to modify cabooses to class I-5D for heavy duty pusher service. Five months later the Mechanical Department had completed the steps necessary for mass modification of the cars and this neo-style letter was issued to the field with instructions. In addition to relocating the trucks from 15 to 19 foot centers, steps also had to be reduced in width to clear the new truck location and elliptic springs had to be increased in strength due to the additional weight of the cars after application of concrete and scrap metal in the floors.

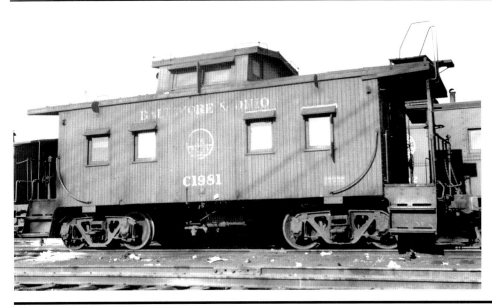

The C-1981 was photographed on the Western Maryland caboose track on January 11, 1949. The car still retains original "K" brakes but has been upgraded with Andrews trucks and long wheelbase. Interesting are the marker light "shields" seen midway between the cupola and marker brackets. They prevent light from the markers bothering trainmen in the cupola, particularly helpful for night backup moves. *Jay Williams collection*

"I referred this to our divisional people, who advised that when this letter was received the repairs to this caboose, including the cupola, were practically completed and, therefore, they did not consider it advisable to remove the cupola and caboose was returned to service September 7th."

Several years later a letter was written by an assistant trainmaster relative to the condition of cabooses at Fairmont, West Virginia. His April 2, 1953, letter ended with this statement:

"Too, it seems that in mine run service all conductors want a full platform caboose, and cock loft removed."

E. Stimson, Jr., Master Mechanic at Grafton responded with his letter of April 17, 1953, in which he stated the following:

"I am not in a position to change all cabooses so they will have a wide platform, neither do I have authority to remove the cupolas."

Of course as previously has been documented the cupolas were removed from a few specific cabooses and it is assumed this was done locally without the knowledge of "the brass".

End Platform Upgrades (1955)

Originally built with wood end platforms and wood-covered steps, many of the I-5 family cars were upgraded over the years with metal end platforms and steps.

Drawing T-85455, dated 12-13-55, documented A-W Super Diamond plate for the end platforms (see vol-

ume 3, page 45).

Drawing U-89399, dated 10-24-61, documented Apex type A plate material for platforms (commonly called grating).

Photos of these various different styles are presented in this chapter.

Marker Light Shields or Wings

Although rare on B&O cabooses, a few photos do show these and there has been questions about what they are and what their purpose was. Applications do not appear to be consistent so we suspect they were random local applications. Sometimes a photo shows them only on one end of the caboose. We suspect this might be for a car assigned to a night run with a backup move of the train shoving the caboose.

Sometimes the "wings" are located close to the cupola, sometimes they are mounted close to the marker light attachment brackets and sometimes they are attached midway between the cupola and marker light bracket.

The purpose of the shields was to prevent a lighted marker light from blinding a crew member riding in the cupola. Some B&O cabooses had a small windshield of sorts located at the center of the cupola window. A lighted marker behind someone riding in the cupola may have created a reflection in the glass of this wind screen. B&O crews were not alone with these applications. C&O wide-vision cabooses came delivered from International Car with the marker light shields as standard equipment. And fans of that road have also wondered what they were!

1961 Rebuilding (I-5Dm)

In order to meet newly-enacted state laws imposed by Pennsylvania, Maryland and New York, relating to sanitary facilities in equipment, B&O officers set up a major caboose upgrading program at the Du Bois shops. This program covered I-10 and I-5 family cupola cabooses. As it relates to the class I-5 family cars the following is provided.

The program began in January 1961 and continued through 1962 upgrading a total of 116 cabooses. See page 78 for a listing of early cars and the gradual implementation of some of the betterments.

External spotting features of cars completed during this upgrading included the following:

- power brake stands on both ends
- all side windows eliminated on stove side
- two side windows eliminated on desk side
- aluminum side cupola windows
- wind screens on cupola side windows
- all cars upgraded to I-5D standards
- oil stoves with side fill pipes
- smoke stack with down draft eliminator
- side grabirons upgraded to "J" type
- new tongue-and-groove side sheathing

More of the upgrades can be seen on our matrix listing on page 78. There were also internal upgrades relating to sanitary facilities.

The side window eliminations were to help prevent freezing of the interior water system.

The changes to these cabooses was so great that we call the upgraded cars I-5Dm, the lower case "m" indicating a heavily modified class I-5D caboose, as well as indicating that it is not an official B&O class. B&O mechanical officers were sometimes slow to show a new class for an upgraded car (look how long it took them to select the I-5C and I-5D classes). Had they waited a few years to select a new class for the I-5Dm cars it would have been in the C&O/B&O era; C&O longago abandoned car classes.

As a side note some may argue that the C&O/B&O diagram sheets show a "class". Some years ago when the author was conducting research in the OH Building at Huntington, West Virginia, we mentioned car class to one of the Chessie System mechanical engineers. He was quick to correct us. "Those classes you see on diagram sheets are intended only to be page identifiers in the diagram book, not car classes", he stated. "We do not use car class terminology".

More Grabiron Changes 1970-1971

During the 1970-1971 rehab program at the Chilli-

Early Radio Tests

Cabooses have been intimately involved in tests of the use of radio in railroad operations over the years.

Tests and applications in the 1950s were documented in volume 3 of this series. Tests in 1944 are documented in this book in the I-16 chapter.

The earliest tests were conducted ca. 1930 involving I-5 caboose C-1979 and class S-1 steam locomotive 6149.

The use of locomotive 6149 perhaps suggests that this was not a local yard test but one that extended between two major terminals such as Brunswick and Baltimore. The poor quality photo of caboose C-1979, above, shows the odd radio antenna (a dipol type) extended across the roof of the caboose, reminiscent of the caboose radios used on the Pennsylvania Railroad. The radio applications were reported as removed from the equipment after a short trial period. *collection of Dwight Jones*

Caboose Helper Ratings

B&O CABOOSE CARS
PUSHER SERVICE

Class	Series	None	Light	Heavy
I-I	C1 to C399		Light	
I-1a	C400 to C499		"	
K-1	C501 to C1399	None		
I-1a	C1401 to C1434		"	
I-2	C1561 to C1570	None		
I	C1599	"		
I-3	C1600 to C1614	"		
I-14a	C1650	"		
I-14	C1660, C1661	"		
I-6	C1676 to C1695	"		
C&C	C1700 to 1711	"		
I-11	C1774, C1775	"		
I-13	C1800 to C1835	"		
I-5	C1900 to C2299		Light	
I-5d	C1901 to C2160			Heavy
I-5c	C1903 to C2260			"
I-16	C2300 to C2374	None		
I-12	C2400 to C2499			Heavy
I-7	C2500		Light	
I-5a	C2501		"	
I-5ba	C2502			Heavy
I-5b	C2503 to C2505		Light	
I-5ba	C2506, C2507			Heavy
I-10	C2600 to C2665		Light	
I-16	C2700 to C2799	None		
I-12	C2800 to C2824			Heavy
I-17	C2850 to C2861			Heavy

cothe shops (when cabooses were painted C&O yellow), some cars received plywood side covering. To make this application easier many cars with the full radius side handholds were unbolted at the bottom attachment point and loosened at the top foot and the handhold then was rotated slightly downward and the bottom foot was welded to the side plate of the truck bolster.

Chessie Repaints

Only a small quantity of I-5 family cabooses were painted into some form of a Chessie System paint scheme.

C-2222. After being retired and sold to a private owner this car was refurbished at the Huntington

THE BALTIMORE AND OHIO RAILROAD COMPANY

30x38—49s   Form 300 Ruled.

I-5   C-1900-C-2299 ——— C-1900-C-2299
I-5c   C-1903-C-2260 ——— C-C-2900-C-3299
I-5D   C-1901-C-2160 ——— C-C-3300-C-3699 .... 19........

OLD NUMBERS			NEW NUMBERS (ASSUMED)	
I-5 [263]	I-5c [94]	I-5D [11]	I-5c	I-5D
C-1900			—	C-3300
		C-1901	—	C-3301
C-1902			—	C-3302
	C-1903		C-2903	C-3303
	C-1904		C-2904	C-3304
C-1905			—	C-3305
		C-1906	—	C-3306
	C-1907		C-2907	C-3307
C-1908			—	C-3308
	C-1909		C-2909	C-3309
	C-1910		C-2910	C-3310
C-1911			—	C-3311
	C-1912		C-2912	C-3312
		C-1913	—	C-3313
C-1914			—	C-3314
C-1915			—	C-3315
C-1916			—	C-3316
	C-1917		C-2917	C-3317
		C-1918	—	C-3318
C-1919			—	C-3319
		C-1920	—	C-3320

This Mechanical Department document from February 1953 shows an early concept of identifying cabooses that had been modified to classes I-5C and I-5D by assigning those modified cabooses a new road number in the C-2900 or C-3300-series. Although this renumbering was not adopted it does make us wonder how this relates to the fact that future caboose numbers C-2910 to C-2924 were skipped by the railroad.

MEMORANDUM ON USE OF CABOOSE CARS IN PUSHER SERVICE.

In the late 1920's experiments were made hauling heavy trains over 17 mile grade and Sand Patch grade with caboose car between rear of train and pusher locomotive. The power was steam, and the caboose cars were our class I-5, which were built in years 1924-1929.

Old files indicate that prior to tests the caboose cars were placed back of pusher locomotive with time lost to replace caboose when pusher locomotive was no longer needed.

It was noted that under heavy pusher service the rear end of caboose car would at times raise, and occasionally the rear truck would derail. This would only happen on a curve or crossover.

When rounding a curve couplers of both the locomotive and caboose would swing about their ends to outside of curve, which would augment the side component of pusher force. Limiting blocks were applied to both the locomotive and caboose couplers, which reduced the coupler swing from about 8 degrees each side of center line to 4 degrees. This feature of limiting blocks welded in each side of coupler housing is now used on all pusher equipment. Recently acquired diesel pusher locomotives have coupler centering devices built in, to prevent misalignment of coupler while pushing.

Tests also indicated that if the I-5 caboose wheelbase was lengthened from 15 feet to 19 feet the overhang between truck center and face of coupler would be reduced by 2 feet, which materially reduced the side component of pusher force tending to lift rear caboose truck from rail. All caboose cars now in pusher service have 19-foot truck centers.

Although application of limiting blocks and the spreading of truck centers produced a satisfactory caboose for pusher service, it was further felt that applying ballast, additional weight in floor would improve the resistance of the caboose from lifting from rail. This ballast, amounting to about 20,000 pounds, has so far been applied to 288 cars of our class I-5d. There are 22 cars remaining in class I-5c in heavy pusher service yet to be ballasted and reclassified I-5d.

In addition to the I-5c and I-5d class of caboose we have the class I-12 (114 cars) and I-17, I-17a (84 cars). These cars are all-steel with 19-foot truck centers and equipped with coupler limiting blocks.

The class I-12 is not ballasted. The class I-17a is ballasted.

There has never been any question concerning the strength of center sills to withstand the force exerted by pusher locomotives. Records show that no caboose sills have been crushed in pusher service.

It has been generally accepted that light pusher service is the force exerted by a 3000 horsepower diesel locomotive of two units, and that heavy pusher service is a force exerted by 6000 horsepower, or four units. Up to the present time three to four units of 1500 horsepower and 62,000 pounds tractive effort each at starting have been used.

car shops and was painted into a Chessie scheme. See the photos in our book on B&O Railroad Museum cabooses for the story. Although this car received its Chessie scheme after it was retired we are including it in this tabulation because it spent considerable time on the railroad after it was painted including moving from Huntington to Baltimore by rail, storage at Baltimore at the old Mt. Clare car shops and storage at Brunswick, Maryland, in the retirement line. It then was rescued by museum officers and accepted into the museum collection where it now resides in B&O red.

C-1987 and C-2175. These two cars were assigned to local service in the Toledo area and were repainted at the C&O Walbridge shops with several C&O wood and first generation steel cabooses into a simplified Chessie scheme which became known as the "Wal-bridge Scheme". Photos are included in this chapter. We recorded that C-1987 was repainted in March 1976 and the C-2175 was likely painted around the same time frame.

Another characteristic of cars painted into the Walbridge scheme was removal of the running boards (roof walks) and cutting the end ladders down to the height of the horizontal end railing.

Wrecks and Mishaps

Wrecks and mishaps were an important part of B&O caboose history. We cover that information in the extensive rosters that are published in this book. Select photos also appear later in this chapter showing some of the more interesting I-5 family mishapsm wrecks and derailments.

I-5 Family Cabooses on Roster by Class

1945

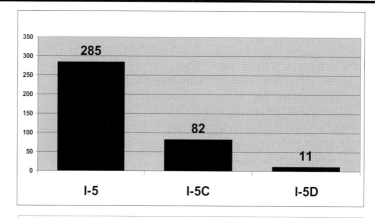

1955

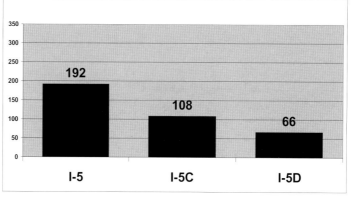

1965

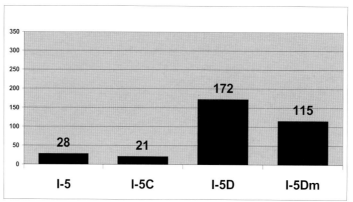

Individual numbers of Class I-5 Cabooses which have had truck centers changed to 19' 0", and steps changed; showing date and station where this work was done.

Caboose No.	Station Changing	Date	Caboose No.	Station Changing	Date
C-1987	Keyser	11-40	C-2090	Keyser	5-41
C-2104	"	12-40	C-1934	"	4-41
C-1998	"	8-40	C-2223	"	3-41
C-2133	Cumberland	12-40	C-2260	"	12-40
C-1937	"	4-42	C-2168	"	11-40
C-1936	"	7-40	C-1938	"	9-40
C-1909	"	4-42	C-2118	"	8-40
C-2135	"	12-40	C-2194	"	6-40
C-2100	"	12-40	C-1917	"	2-42
C-2506	"	12-40	C-2075	"	2-42
C-2507	"	12-40	C-2203	"	1-42
C-2228	"	12-40	C-1993	"	1-42
C-1904	"	12-40	C-2073	"	12-41
C-2185	"	12-40	C-1990	"	12-41
C-1930	"	12-40	C-2099	"	11-41
C-1912	"	8-40	C-1910	"	11-41
C-2160	"	7-35	C-2081	"	10-41
C-2502	"	12-40	C-2079	"	10-41
C-1996	"	12-40	C-2113	"	10-41
C-2230	Glenwood	12-40	C-2112	"	9-41
C-2154	"	12-40	C-2164	"	9-41
C-2237	"	1-41	C-1903	"	9-41
C-2195	Keyser	8-40	C-2080	"	8-41
C-1927	"	12-40	C-2092	"	8-41
C-2155	Glenwood	1-41	C-2097	"	8-41
C-2247	"	1-41	C-1907	"	6-42
C-1961	"	12-40	C-2193	"	6-42
C-2056	"	1-41	C-2000	"	3-42
C-2157	"	4-41	C-2082	"	3-42
C-1972	"	5-41	C-2231	"	3-42
C-2119	Mt. Clare	9-30	C-2101	"	3-42
C-1979	Keyser	2-42	C-1935	"	2-42
C-2093	"	7-41	C-2102	"	3-42
C-2094	"	8-41	C-1994	DuBois	1-41
C-2200	"	7-41	C-2249	"	2-41
C-1985	"	6-41	C-1945	"	1-41
C-1932	"	6-41	C-1970	"	3-41
C-2202	"	6-41	C-2111	"	3-41

The B&O Mechanical Department document on this page and the next, documents early cabooses that were modified to class I-5C and I-5D as well as cabs C-2506 and C-2507 which must have been built with the longer wheelbase at Cumberland. Caboose C-2502 also is listed as modified at Cumberland in December 1940 although this car was displayed at the New York World's Fair in 1939 with the long wheelbase which we suspect was converted at Mt. Clare.

Caboose No.	Station Changing	Date	Caboose No.	Station Changing	Date
C-2138	DuBois	4-41	C-2241	DuBois	11-52
C-2067	"	4-41	C-2052	"	11-52
C-2246	"	2-41	C-2150	"	10-52
C-2060	"	3-41	C-2066	"	11-52
C-2137	"	4-41	C-2158	"	11-52
C-2149	"	4-41			
C-2238	"	5-41			
C-2242	"	5-41			
C-2062	"	5-41			
C-1966	"	12-40			
C-1962	"	1-41			
C-1958	"	1-41			
C-2106	"	10-52			
C-1948	"	10-52			
C-1983	"	10-52			
C-2233	"	10-52			
C-1971	"	10-52			
C-2003	"	10-52			
C-2105	"	10-52			

Individual numbers of Class I-5 Cabooses which have had truck centers changed to 19' 0", steps changed, and ballast applied; showing date and station where this work was done.

Caboose No.	Station Changing	Date	
C-1929	Cumberland	10-41	
C-1901	"	12-40	
C-1931	"	12-40	
C-2160	"	7-35	for trains 117 / 118
C-1920	Keyser	3-32	for W. End Cumb Div
C-1918	"	5-35	
C-1913	Cumberland	7-34	
C-1981	"	4-31	for W. End Cumb Div
C-2084	"	7-35	for trains 117 / 118

The nine cars listed above on the bottom of the memo were the early conversions to what eventually would be class I-5D. Cars C-2160 and C-2084 were assigned to trains 117 / 118 discussed earlier in this section. Cars C-2119, C-1981 and C-1920 were the three test cars converted for service on the West End of the Cumberland Division although C-2119 is listed in the first section of the report as a car not yet ballasted. Note that some of the dates in this report vary by one month from the dates that appear in our roster listings. Many times such dates recorded in the Accounting Department are one month later than the same date recorded in Mechanical Department records.

Part of a typical B&O crew poses on the end platform of caboose C-1946 in the early 1940s at a switchback in Pennsylvania. The I-5 caboose wears a pair of the old bell bottom markers with external "cage" brackets. Even more interesting, the caboose has been equipped with a Westinghouse Clarion whistle which shows above the running boards and is attached to the end of the cupola. Those whistles typically were found only on I-10 class cabooses and required the cab to be equipped with an auxiliary air reservoir. *collection of Dwight Jones*

Variations are always interesting. The Brunswick shops last painted the C-1934, which is shown at Washington, DC, in 1941. Although the car still wears Archbar trucks and has three-point attachment side grabirons the cupola has been modified by sealing one of the side windows as well as the end windows, perhaps an indication this car is assigned to yard/terminal service. *collection of Paul Dunn*

The "AB" Brake

The "AB" brake was made standard for cars built new after September 1, 1933, and for cars that were rebuilt after August 1, 1937. It was required for all cars that were to be used in interchange service after January 1, 1945, by the Board of Directors of the Association of American Railroads upon recommendation of the General Committee of the Mechanical Division. It replaced the type "K" brake.

The desirable characteristics of the new "AB" brake included preliminary quick service, effective throughout the entire length of long trains in level service, accelerated service application, effective protection against leakage and dirt, emergency at any time, higher brake cylinder pressure in emergency situations, and a whole list of other benefits. Essential parts of this new brake were the AB valve and a brake cylinder which had distinctive improvements. See roster listings for dates when specific B&O cabooses were upgraded to have "AB" brakes.

A Westinghouse Clarion whistle shows on the end of the cupola roof on C-1946 at Galeton, Pennsylvania, May 25, 1941. It has recently been painted, and exhibits the newly-adopted Kuhler open-ampersand B&O emblem. The car still wears arch-bar trucks, has type "K" brakes and has had the tool box removed. But there are no ladder-to-roof grabi-rons. *Paul Dunn collection / collection of Dwight Jones*

Last painted at Mt. Clare in June of 1952, C-1925 is shown at Brunswick, Maryland, on May 30, 1953. The car is wearing the 1945 lettering scheme featuring the 36-inch diameter Capitol Dome emblem. *Paul Dunn Collection / collection of Dwight Jones*

A pair of I-5s rest in the yard at Holloway, Ohio, on June 21, 1953. Both cars last were painted at the shops at Lorain, Ohio. The shop is still spelling out their name on the paint stencil rather than using their two-letter station symbol (LO). The C-2057 was painted December 1952 using the then-current 1945 lettering style. *Bob's Photo*

Speedliner Crashes into Work Train
Several Passengers Injured in Blizzard Crash at Sand Patch

On February 19, 1960, a two-unit Speedliner RDC train from Pittsburgh to Baltimore (B&O train #22) crashed into the rear of a standing work train near Sand Patch tower at 6 AM in the morning (also reported as happening at 2:47 PM). Twelve people were seriously injured in the incident, but fortunately there were no fatalities. Other reports indicated there were 20 injured passengers.

Blizzard conditions were occurring in the area at the time of the crash, and it was reported that the engineer could not see the restricted signal and assumed the track ahead was clear. The work train with caboose C-2007 was being used to repair downed lines in the area caused by a two-foot snowfall that week. The Daylight Speedliner was reported as a new model which had been in service only a short time. Lead unit 1961 received front end damage. It was repaired and later returned to service.

The injured were taken to Meyersdale Community Hospital, after being carried a quarter mile through knee-deep snow. A total of 150 passengers were on the train.

A two-unit diesel train with two coaches quickly was assembled at Cumberland and was dispatched to the scene for the passengers while the B&O wreck (relief) train was being readied to depart Cumberland to clean up the wreck.

This wreck spelled the end for the C-2007. The damaged caboose was taken to the Somerset, Pennsylvania, shops where it was written up for dismantle on March 23, 1960. *photos collection of Dwight Jones*

Baltimore, March 16, 1960.

Mr. E. Stimson, Jr.

Please refer to your letter dated March 4th, 1960, file 304-P, concerning condition of B&O X-1672, B&O XM-2844 and caboose car C-2007, which were involved in accident Train 22, Diesel 1961, at Sand Patch, Pa., February 19th, 1960.

I agree with your recommendation that these three units have been damaged beyond economical repairs in this particular accident and that they should be written out of service as being destroyed. This letter will be your authority to report the three units specified above out of service to all concerned by issue of Form 2404-Rev. You will kindly see that when this Form 2404-Rev. is prepared same carries notation indicating that B&O X-1672, B&O XM-2844 and caboose car C-2007 were destroyed in this accident at Sand Patch, February 19th, 1960.

F. B. Rykoskey.

Copy to Mr. C. H. Brown
        Mr. R. P. Bartlett
        Mr. W. C. Reister
        Mr. F. R. Geiselman

The above memo from F. B. Rykoskey (General Superintendent, Motive Power and Equipment) to E. Stimson (Superintendent Motive Power) authorizes the three cars destroyed in the Sand Patch mishap to be written out of service. The next step in the process is to generate a 2404 form (see volume 3 for a sample of this form) which is the formal communication to retire the cars which is distributed to various departments who then can adjust their records accordingly. Not generating a 2404 form is how some cars get scrapped with no record made of their disposition, frustrating future equipment researchers. Others on the distribution list for this memo include C. H. Brown in the Auditing (Property Accounting) department, R. P. Bartlett, Superintendent Car Service, W. C. Reister, Regional Master Car Builder (remember him from page 44 of volume 2—he was not happy about the conversion of M-26 boxcars into cabooses!), and F. R. Geiselman, Mechanical Engineer.

It is interesting to note that the C-2007 was taken to the Somerset shops for disposition. This could mean that it was the Somerset wreck train that was dispatched to the site or that both the Cumberland and Somerset wreck trains were sent due to this being a busy mainline with the need to clear the incident quickly. Both locations were about equidistant from the Sand Patch site.

An odd adaptation of the 1945 lettering showing the addition of the horizontal line above the Baltimore & Ohio lettering. The car was last painted at the Somerset, Pennsylvania, shops in July 1946. The car was stencilled as an I-5 but clearly has the longer wheelbase. The cupola end windows have been sealed. Two chains on the end platform, one to pull the coupler pin and the other to uncouple the air hose, implies use in helper service. *Paul Dunn collection / collection of Dwight Jones*

The C-2033 exhibits a most unusual smoke stack top in this September 1964 view. The car also exhibits the flat stock-style ladder-to-roof handholds on the left side and the round-stock version on the right side indicating a replacement at some point in its career.

C-1926 is shown circa 1962 wearing the 1955 scheme last applied at the Washington, Indiana, shops in December 1958. The car is stencilled as a class I-5D. *Paul Dunn collection / collection of Dwight Jones*

1961 Caboose Upgrading Program

The 1961 caboose upgrade program began in January at the Du Bois car shops. Certain of the specifications were not ironed out until later in February and March, too late to include all of them in the early cabooses outshopped. B&O officials prepared a matrix (retyped below) to indicate the implementation date for the various betterments in this program. It was anticipated that early cars would be returned to the shops to receive those betterments that were missing. Photos of first car C-2165 indicate it never did receive the power hand brakes, aluminum cupola windows or the aluminum cupola window windbreakers.

Caboose Number	Draft Gears	Steel Yokes	Wooden Lockers	Air Gauge Condr. Valve	Power Hand Brake	Aluminum Cup. Windows	Aluminum Windbreakers
C-2165	No	No	No	No	No	No	No
C-2659	No	No	No	No	No	No	No
C-2618	No	No	No	No	No	No	No
C-2158	No	No	No	No	No	No	No
C-2014	No	No	No	No	No	No	No
C-2008	No	No	No	No	No	No	No
	2-3-61						
C-2253	OK	No	No	No	No	No	No
		2-6-61					
C-2010	OK	OK	No	No	No	No	No
			2-8-61				
C-2001	OK	OK	OK	No	No	No	No
				2-10-61			
C-2062	OK	OK	OK	OK	No	No	No
C-2638					No	No	No
					2-15-61		
C-2041	OK	OK	OK	OK	OK	No	No
C-2266	OK	OK	OK	OK	OK	No	No
C-2069	OK	OK	OK	OK	OK	No	No
C-2105	OK	OK	OK	OK	OK	No	No
C-2137	OK	OK	OK	OK	OK	No	No
						2-27-61	
C-2624					OK	OK	No
C-2804	OK	OK	OK	OK	OK	OK	No
C-2657					OK	OK	No
C-2134	OK	OK	OK	OK	OK	OK	No
C-2246	OK	OK	OK	OK	OK	OK	No
C-2635					OK	OK	No
C-1960	OK	OK	OK	OK	OK	OK	No
C-1958	OK	OK	OK	OK	OK	OK	No
C-2150	OK	OK	OK	OK	OK	OK	No
C-2601					OK	OK	No
C-2646					OK	OK	No
							3-31-61
C-2247	OK	OK	OK	OK	OK	OK	OK

More cars were processed through the Du Bois shops than are indicated on this chart. See the extensive roster listings for the I-5 family cars in this chapter for a list of all of the cars. These are the cars that we refer to as class I-5Dm as they exhibit consistent and major differences as compared to normal class I-5D cars.

Julian Barnard photographed C-2001 near Callery, Pennsylvania, on February 13, 1965. This was the ninth car from the Du Bois shops' 1961 program and did not receive all of the program updates (see the table in this chapter). It did get an oil stove and "J" grabirons but not the typical window blankings, power brake stand, aluminum side windows, or wind screens.

The Willard shops applied plywood sides to the C-2001, blanking some of the windows in the process, and painted the car in December 1965. It is shown at Willard on December 24, 1965. It was not unusual for some shops to use non-standard stencils such as these small Capitol Dome emblems (and upside down "B")!

Julian Barnard photographed the C-2272 undergoing repairs at the Willard shops on October 1, 1967. Plywood coverings are being added and windows are being blanked in effect creating a copycat I-5Dm car to the Du Bois version. Of course this car did not receive the sanitary facility upgrades, power brake stand, "J" side grabirons and the other enhancements that were applied at Du Bois. Barney's photos of the car before this work indicated it did have all four side windows on each side. This creates yet more confusion for the discerning modeler who "wants to get it right".

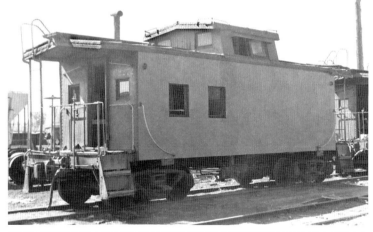

The Willard shops had C-1974 under repair on January 2, 1965. The car must have had a hard coupling on this end as the end platform is bent down, coupler is missing, and the car apparently had to be retrucked with a freight car truck to get it back to the shop. While at the shop it appears that the cupola side window also needed some attention. Note that the car has been strategically placed next to the supply of couplers.

Four photos this page: Julian W. Barnard, Jr.

The C-1976 is undergoing repairs at the Chillicothe shops on December 31, 1970. This car previously had also been repaired and repainted red at Chillicothe. This time the car will receive C&O yellow. A carman is working on the steps and end platform railings. This car is interesting because the two intact windows are by the stove/ice box area instead of at the conductor's desk. *Dwight Jones*

Paul Winters visited the Chillicothe shops in 1962 and recorded C-2206 getting routine repairs on April 28. The wreck (relief) train was still assembled at Chillicothe at this date as can be see in the background left of the caboose. No plywood in use at this early date—tongue-and-groove wood is being used to repair bad sections in the side of the cupola. The repairs here would help this car give B&O another 12 years of active caboose service.

Not to be outdone by the I-5Dm cabooses outshopped from Du Bois in the early 1960s, the shops at Willard released some copycat versions of not only I-5 family cars but also some older wood cupola cabooses. C-1976, painted 8-64 with plywood sides added, is incorrectly stenciled as an I-5. The only similarity between the Willard cars and the Du Bois versions was the window eliminations. *Paul Dunn collection / collection of Dwight Jones*

B&O cabooses often served as positive public relations for the railroad such as class I-5D C-1942 refurbished at the Washington, Indiana, shops and shown here on display at Connersville, Indiana, at a key B&O customer's plant open house in the summer of 1960. Even the wheel rims were highlighted!
collection of Dwight Jones

I-5 Family Retirements by Year

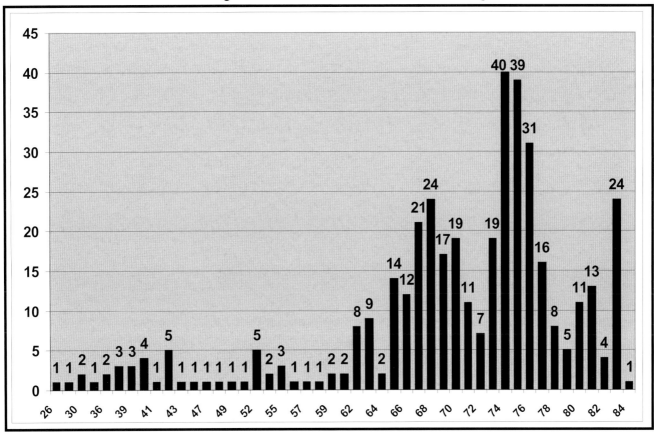

The above graph shows the quantity of I-5 family cabooses that were retired each year beginning with the first retirement in 1926 and ending with the last car to be retired in 1984. Since these cars were among the best on the railroad for their first 35 or so years they were only retired if there was a catastrophic condition. Otherwise B&O's heavy shops kept them repaired and in service. On the right side of the graph one can see two different bell curves. Statisticians refer to this as a bi-modal distribution, an indication that there are two different and distinct factors at work on the population. We can speculate about some of these factors. Caboose pooling, implemented in 1965, reduced the need for cabooses and resulted in retirement of older cars. This was further affected by new steel bay-window cabooses purchased from International Car. The 1970/71 Chillicothe repair program reduced the retirements as I-5 family cars were repaired and returned to service. In the mid-1970s more new cars were received from ICC and FGE, and the Chillicothe-repaired cabooses had reached the end of their three-year expected rehab life.

The Glenwood shops has recently painted the C-1966 (May 1955), stencilling the car as an I-5C. This car has no cupola and the original roof has been replaced with a metal sectional roof, likely reclaimed from a freight car. This suggests that the car had been on fire. Even the siding looks new. *Paul Dunn collection / collection of Dwight Jones*

It is hard to believe that a cupola would be restored to this car and the roof changed back to original style. Perhaps a shop switched numbers on two cars? The Mt. Clare shops last painted C-1966, equipping it with midget electric markers. It also has a firecracker radio antenna on the cupola roof suggesting service in Maryland. Photographed at the Chillicothe shops on October 26, 1971. *Dwight Jones*

A large stencil on the left of this caboose indicates the last painting was completed at the Glenwood, Pennsylvania, shops in May 1937. This car also has a new metal panel roof. It is interesting that both of these cars carry Glenwood shop stencils. Coincidence? Otherwise this car still exhibits many original characteristics: arch-bar trucks, three point side grabs and "K" brakes. *Sid Davies*

Baltimore, Md., August 3, 1961

102 – Caboose Cars – Class I-5b, I-5ba, I-5c and I-5d – Pusher
Service –   (SUPERSEDING LETTER OF February 10, 1961)

Messrs.

G. F. Wiles   (126) L
E. Stimson, Jr. (44) L
W. F. Dadd   (42) L
J. J. Ekin, Jr. (3) L

        This letter embodies previous instructions, revised by
covering additional caboose cars for Heavy Duty Service.

        The Class I-12, I-17 and I-17a caboose cars were built for
Heavy Duty Pusher Service.   Instructions are in effect to change
Class I-5 Caboose Cars for Heavy Duty Pusher Service by increasing
truck centers from 15'-0" to 19'0", reducing overhang two feet on
each end of car, and for identification, Class I-5c has been assigned.

        When Class I-5 and I-5c cars are ballasted, in addition to
relocating truck centers, the class is changed to I-5d.

        Following Caboose Cars have been reported as meeting above
requirements and, in addition to several Class I-5b, I-5ba cars,
will be satisfactory for Heavy Duty Pusher Service:-

                        CLASS I-5C – 41 Cars
                (Wheel Base Changed But Not Ballasted)

C-1910   C-1976   C-2060   C-2102   C-2173   C-2238
C-1915   C-1977   C-2068   C-2106   C-2185   C-2272
C-1945   C-1978   C-2079   C-2110   C-2187   C-2275
C-1948   C-2000   C-2090   C-2138   C-2230   C-2276
C-1949   C-2038   C-2093   C-2150   C-2237   C-2278
C-1953   C-2039   C-2098   C-2155   C-2281
C-1961   C-2040   C-2100   C-2169
          C-2056   C-2170

                        CLASS I-5B – 1 Car
                          (Ballasted)

                            C-2505

                        CLASS I-5BA – 4 Cars
                (Wheel Base Changed and Ballasted)

            C-2502   C-2503   C-2506   C-2507

102 - Caboose Cars - Class I-5b, I-5ba, I-5c and I-5d - Pusher
Service - (SUPERSEDING LETTER OF February 10, 1961)

CLASS I-5D - 235 Cars

(Wheel Base Changed and Ballasted)

C-1900	C-1958	C-2023	C-2097	C-2168	C-2229
C-1901	C-1959	C-2028	C-2099	C-2172	C-2231
C-1902	C-1960	C-2030	C-2101	C-2174	C-2232
C-1903	C-1962	C-2031	C-2103	C-2175	C-2233
C-1904	C-1963	C-2032	C-2104	C-2177	C-2235
C-1906	C-1966	C-2033	C-2105	C-2178	C-2236
C-1907	C-1967	C-2041	C-2112	C-2179	C-2239
C-1908	C-1970	C-2042	C-2113	C-2180	C-2240
C-1909	C-1971	C-2045	C-2114	C-2181	C-2241
C-1912	C-1973	C-2046	C-2115	C-2182	C-2242
C-1913	C-1974	C-2047	C-2116	C-2183	C-2243
C-1914	C-1979	C-2048	C-2119	C-2186	C-2246
C-1917	C-1980	C-2049	C-2120	C-2188	C-2247
C-1918	C-1981	C-2051	C-2123	C-2189	C-2248
C-1919	C-1982	C-2052	C-2124	C-2190	C-2249
C-1921	C-1983	C-2054	C-2129	C-2193	C-2250
C-1922	C-1984	C-2055	C-2131	C-2194	C-2251
C-1923	C-1985	C-2059	C-2132	C-2195	C-2253
C-1925	C-1986	C-2061	C-2133	C-2198	C-2254
C-1926	C-1987	C-2062	C-2134	C-2199	C-2255
C-1927	C-1988	C-2063	C-2135	C-2200	C-2257
C-1928	C-1989	C-2066	C-2137	C-2202	C-2258
C-1929	C-1990	C-2070	C-2139	C-2203	C-2260
C-1930	C-1991	C-2073	C-2141	C-2206	C-2261
C-1931	C-1992	C-2074	C-2142	C-2007	C-2262
C-1932	C-1993	C-2075	C-2143	C-2008	C-2266
C-1933	C-1994	C-2076	C-2149	C-2210	C-2269
C-1934	C-1995	C-2077	C-2151	C-2213	C-2270
C-1935	C-1996	C-2080	C-2152	C-2214	C-2276
C-1936	C-1997	C-2081	C-2154	C-2215	C-2277
C-1937	C-1998	C-2082	C-2157	C-2218	C-2283
C-1938	C-1999	C-2083	C-2158	C-2221	C-2284
C-1939	C-2002	C-2084	C-2159	C-2222	C-2286
C-1941	C-2003	C-2086	C-2160	C-2223	C-2287
C-1944	C-2004	C-2089	C-2161	C-2224	C-2288
C-1950	C-2010	C-2092	C-2162	C-2225	C-2290
C-1954	C-2012	C-2094	C-2163	C-2226	C-2294
C-1955	C-2013	C-2095	C-2164	C-2227	C-2295
C-1956	C-2019	C-2096	C-2165	C-2228	C-2296
					C-2298

A few Class I-5c and I-5d cars were found with slightly less
than 19'-0" or standard wheel base, but this will not affect operation in Heavy Duty Service.

102 – Caboose Cars – Class I-5b, I-5ba, I-5c and I-5d – Pusher
Service (SUPERSEDING LETTER OF 2-10-1961)

Class I-5 Caboose Cars, also in Series C-1900 to C-2299, not
changed as above, are limited to light pusher service.

Changes in Class I-5 Caboose Cars to Class I-5c and I-5d must
be reported to Mechanical Engineering Department and others concerned on Forms 2404-A and 2404-Rev., to insure numbers are included in next General Letter.

F. B. Rykoskey   F. H. Einwaechter

COPY –

Messrs.

H. M. Davenport	T. E. Johnson	W. A. Mullen
P. K. Partee	O. H. Fletcher	H. Raines
C. R. Riley	H. I. Walton	B. J. Mangan
C. T. Williams	R. C. Diamond	G. O. Prosser
A. W. Conley	A. S. Waller	H. A. Lockhart
C. K. Strader	J. F. Robbert	L. G. Kohler
J. R. Frease	E. L. Reeves	J. R. Dietrich
J. F. Stevens	F. R. Geiselman	E. C. Whipp
W. M. Murphey	R. W. Seniff	C. H. Brown
R. J. Cannon	R. B. Fisher	R. P. Bartlett
C. W. Shaw, Jr.	A. W. Gibson	

Once the B&O began modifying I-5 and I-5B cabooses for pusher service it became necessary to communicate to field personnel the numbers of those modified cabooses so there
would be no mistake on what cabooses were qualified for pusher service. Beginning
with a neo-style letter on November 24, 1952, mechanical department personnel began
circulating a memo with an updated list of modified cabooses. As additional cars were
modified the list was updated and a new neo-style letter was issued. A total of 17 letters
were issued over the years including the last one which is reproduced here, and on the
previous two pages, under date of August 3, 1961.

The letters were not 100% accurate and company officers were constantly asking field
personnel to double check specific caboose numbers. Errors were found and the incor-
rect numbers were corrected in the next edition of the neo-style letter.

This car, photographed at Rossford Yard in Toledo on October 19, 1963, exhibits the original window elimination authorized by mechanical officers—eliminating the window by the ice box. Oil for the stove has discolored the side under the fill pipe—good information for modelers' weathering efforts. *Kirk Hise*

Another car with the ice box window eliminated. The oil heater in this car and the car above indicates the cars have been equipped with updated sanitary equipment. The C-2238 was photographed at Rossford Yard, Toledo, on February 6, 1965. *Eileen J. Wolford*

The Chillicothe shops have changed the window configuration of the C-2238 shown here in the yellow scheme and above in the red scheme. This view was taken at Newark, Ohio, in July 1971. The car now has a coal stove replacing the oil unit shown in the photo above. *Paul B. Dunn / collection of Dwight Jones*

In February 1971 the C-2137 is shown behind the B&O Transportation Museum where the caboose assigned to the Mt. Clare switcher often could be found. As a Maryland caboose it has been equipped with Pyle-National-style midget electric markers. The Stemsonite reflectors have been relocated to the brake stand and an additional reflector has been mounted to the end of each step. A recharging receptacle is adjacent to the battery vent above the right truck. More noteworthy is the plywood sides and early yellow paint scheme applied in 1969 at the Mt. Clare shops in Baltimore.

The lettering job was terrible—the "B" is upside down and the stencil tabs ("bridges" in B&O lingo) never were filled in.

The yellow C&O scheme was adopted in earnest at the Chillicothe shops beginning less than three months after this car was painted leading to our speculation that this was a test case for officers at Baltimore. Mr. Borgman was a Car Superintendent at Baltimore.

Few images have surfaced of this unusual scheme due to its retirement in early 1973. See another view in this book's color section.

The paint stencil on this car is difficult to read but looks to us like it reads Somerset, Pennsylvania, in 1967. Perhaps the painters, who did the poor stencilling, had no idea what this stencil was so just restencilled what already was on the caboose.

```
                    Mount Clare Repair Track
                     Baltimore, Maryland
                      October 14, 1969



102 - Caboose C-2137 - I-5-D




Mr. B. J. Borgman


        Referring to Caboose C-2137, this will inform you
that this caboose was outshopped from Mount Clare on October 8,
1969 painted per your instructions as follows:

        Painted diesel yellow ball with B&O blue
          letters.
        Hand grabs and outside trim painted with
          B&O blue with a 2" line of red-orange
          fluorescent paint and 3" line on the end
          sills A&B of the red-orange fluorescent
          paint.

        This for your information.



                                      R. L. Weathers
                                      General Car Foreman
```

Before the yellow paint program started at Chillicothe in January 1970, the shops kept cabooses repaired and painted in the red scheme. In April 1968 the C-1902 was painted and lettered in this transitional lettering scheme—old "B&O" initials and dome emblem but with C&O-style Futura Demibold numbers. Class confusion continues. The car is stencilled as an I-5 short wheelbase car.

Paul Dunn / collection of Dwight Jones

The Du Bois shops worked a number of older cabooses during 1969, painting them in this simplified scheme which featured a Capitol Dome emblem with C&O-style Futura Demibold "B&O" initials in the dome but retaining old B&O-style font for numbers. "Watch Your Step" lettering appears on steps. This car was painted at Du Bois in April 1969 and is shown at Zanesville, Ohio, shortly thereafter.

Paul Dunn / collection of Dwight Jones

What is an I-5Dm?

A total of 116 cars were outshopped from the Du Bois shops during 1961-1962 in this I-5Dm configuration based on shop data and photo analysis.

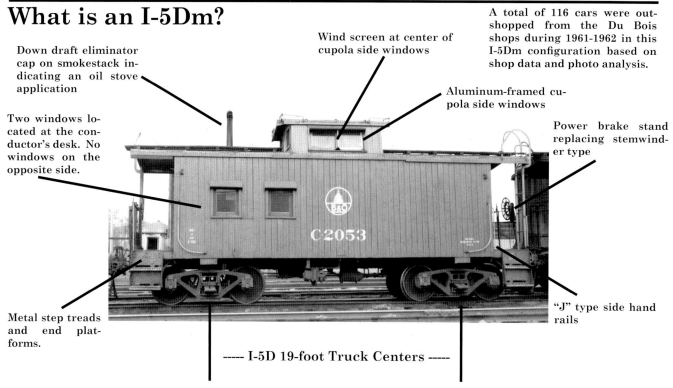

Down draft eliminator cap on smokestack indicating an oil stove application

Wind screen at center of cupola side windows

Aluminum-framed cupola side windows

Two windows located at the conductor's desk. No windows on the opposite side.

Power brake stand replacing stemwinder type

Metal step treads and end platforms.

"J" type side hand rails

----- I-5D 19-foot Truck Centers -----

These two photos show that the painters at the Chillicothe shops were making the transition from the old B&O font to the C&O Futura Demibold font. The C-2135 was painted during March 1968 with old "B&O" and Capitol dome emblem but with new C&O numbers.

The Chillicothe shops refurbished C-2031 in January 1969 painting the caboose the standard B&O red. But C&O influence is taking hold with Futura Demibold "B&O" and numerals. Beginning next year, in January 1970, the Chillicothe shops would start outshopping cabooses in the standard C&O yellow scheme, used on the C&O since 1956. The car was photographed at Columbus, Ohio, in September 1969. *both, Paul Dunn / collection of Dwight Jones*

The first of six cabooses painted red at the Brunswick shops during the 1969-1970 period was I-5Dm C-2089 shown on the Brunswick, Maryland, caboose track on July 31, 1974. The scheme featured a modernized white 38" diameter Capitol Dome emblem with old B&O font numbers. The car is in need of some repair with a roof trim board coming loose and a deteriorated smoke stack top. Note the horn on the end.
Dwight Jones

SOLD

CHANGES

From			To			Date	Place	Original Cost	Betterments
Initial	Number	Class	Initial	Number	Class				
B&O	C-2159	I-5	B&O	C-2159	I-5-D	3-30-53	Gassaway		
B&O	C-2124	I-5	B&O	C-2124	I-5-D	4- 3-53	"		
B&O	C-2081	I-5	B&O	C-2081	I-5-D	4-24-53			
B&O	C-1986	I-5-C	B&O	C-1986	I-5-D	4-28-53			
B&O	C-2257	I-5-C	B&O	C-2257	I-5-D	5- 4-53			

H. S. Arrasmith
_____ Foreman

This B&O 2404 form shows how the shops reported car changes to various offices in Baltimore. The sample above shows a stamp indicating receipt in the office of the Superintendent Car Service. Gassaway shop foreman Arrasmith has completed five I-5 family cars into the latest I-5D configuration. Interesting is the fact that he notes his authority to perform the work as a blueprint letter dated November 24, 1952. From the information provided, we would conclude that his production rate was one caboose per week. Although Gassaway was a rather large shop, caboose work was consolidated at Washington, Indiana; Du Bois, Pennsylvania; and Keyser, West Virginia in 1955. Although it is difficult to pinpoint when some shops were closed, an educated guess would be that Gassaway was closed in July of 1957.

This closeup view under an I-5Dm caboose shows how the railroad created a system to generate power for the electrical system and charge internal batteries. The belt drive, driven off the large cylinder attached to an axle, drives a generator located under a bunk in the car's interior. If this had been an I-5 or I-5C, one would see the underside of the floor boards instead of the ballast pans on this weighted car. *Dwight Jones*

November 25, 1969

Messrs: J. B. Dalton   J. J. Yankovich
         J. F. Grimes   M. W. Phebus
         F. A. deChurch   E. L. Cook
         L. P. Myers   A. J. DiLeonardi
         W. D. Johnson   R. L. Weathers
         W. N. Judy

Gentlemen:

    Attached are copies of Inspection Report covering
B&O Red (or Wooden) Cabooses.

    Arrange to have inspection made of all wooden
cabooses on the B&O. This report must be in this office no later than December 3, 1969.

    Behind Item E of Interior, write in either coal
or oil to denote type of stove.

    If you do not have any Red or Wooden Cabooses,
please advise in writing so that the reports will not
be held up.

                                    B. J. Borgman

cc: Mr. J. L. Cage
     Mr. H. E. Hammer

The last caboose painted into the Brunswick red scheme was the C-2268, shown in the retirement line at Brunswick on July 31, 1975. The car is an I-5Dm but has been stencilled as an I-5C by the Brunswick shops. This car last was painted August 1970 as the yellow paint program was well underway at Chillicothe. *Dwight Jones*

B&O RED CABOOSE

NUMBER _C-1945_ DATE _Dec. 1, 1969_ STATION _Mt. Clare Repair Trk._

1. Interior

    A. Floor   Good _____   Fair _____   Poor _✓_

    B. Windows   Good _____   Fair _____   Poor _✓_

    C. Doors   Good _____   Fair _____   Poor _✓_

    D. Walls - Ceiling   Good _____   Fair _____   Poor _✓_

    E. Stove   Good _____   Fair _____   Poor _✓_

    F. Sink Piping, Etc.   Good _____   Fair _____   Poor _✓_

    G. Seats - Bunks   Good _____   Fair _____   Poor _✓_

2. Exterior

    A. Roof and Sides   Wood _✓_ Metal _____ Good _____ Fair _____ Poor _✓_

    B. Sills and Ends   Good _____   Fair _✓_   Poor _____

    C. Cupalo-Frame   Good _____   Fair _____   Poor _✓_

3. Running Gear   Good _____   Fair _✓_   Poor _____

    Trucks, Etc.   Good _____   Fair _✓_   Poor _____

SUMMARY - 1. Cab needs minor repairs.

            2. Cab needs major repairs. ✓

            3. Cab is not fit for heavy repairs.

R. Lud. uthus
General Car Foreman

The documents on this page and the previous page show how the railroad starts many of the major repair programs—by surveying cars in the fleet to determine how much repair on average may be required for each car (dollars) and then determining how many cars in the fleet will require project repairs which then will lead to a determination of the total cost of the project. With that information an AFE (Authority for Expenditure) can be completed and circulated through various departments for approval signatures. The document on this page is a sample evaluation for caboose C-1945 completed at Mt. Clare. These preliminary inspections led to the yellow caboose program assigned to the Chillicothe shops which began the following month in January 1970.

Believed to be the last B&O wood caboose to be painted red is the C-2056, painted at the Cumberland, Maryland, shops in June 1971. The car had been in service at Morgantown (see the color section) until an accident at a grade crossing damaged the steps and end platform on the right, returning the car to Cumberland and storage in the bad-order line, photographed 8-3-73. The I-5Dm car is stencilled ID-5! *Dwight Jones*

Only one side window is on this class I-5 car, shown at Cumberland on July 31, 1975. The opposite side of this car has no side windows. This single window would have supplied external light for the conductor's desk located at that point. We typically think of cabs assigned to Chicago with this type of reduced window exposures. The car was painted yellow at Chillicothe in February 1971. *Dwight Jones*

R.R. Wallen captured this interesting scene at Springfield, Illinois, on December 25, 1973. The GM&O car is one of five class I-5 cabooses transfered/sold to the Alton Railroad during B&O ownership of that line. More on the GM&O cars in a future volume in this series. *collection of Ed Kirstatter*

Baltimore, Md., August 2, 1960.

Mr. F. H. Einwaechter:

While at Washington, Ind. last week I
observed the installation of sanitary facilities to the
Class I-5 caboose cars.

The second window from the end on the side
of the caboose is not closed off in accordance with the print.
However, the freezer unit sets in front of this window and
blocks it off to the extent the window cannot be cleaned or
raised.

It would seem to me that when this installation
is made the window in question should be closed off.

Will you kindly look into this and let me have
your views.

R. B. Fisher

Baltimore, Md., September 6, 1960.

102 - Caboose Cars - Classes I-5c and I-5d - Sanitary Facilities -
Blanking Off Window at Water Cooler -

Messrs.
E. F. Gross
L. M. Schalk:-

When applying sanitary facilities to Caboose Cars, Classes I-5c
and I-5d, Numbers C-1901 to C-2298, you will please arrange to blank off side
window back of ice box and water cooler.

Attach two copies of print Y-88278-C, which has been revised to
show this change.

Copy -
Messrs.
F. B. Rykoskey
R. B. Fisher   : Refers to your letter of August 2 to Mr. F. H. Einwaechter.
H. J. Burkley
E. Stimson, Jr.
R. A. Garrigus : Copy of above print attached.
W. C. Reister   :

F. H. Einwaechter

CWH-Ers
Enc.

Window Eliminations Chart (not counting I-5Dm cars)

In the table below, a window icon is represented by **W** (indicates the presence of a window), **X** indicates the window has been eliminated, and **P** = Plywood inset.

Caboose Number	Windows Configuration and Side of Caboose					Comments and Opposite Side Windows	Caboose Color	Wheelbase
C-1906	W	W	W	X	stove side	4 windows on desk side	Yellow	long
C-1930	W	W	W	X	stove side		Yellow	long
C-1934	W	W	W	X	stove side		Yellow	long
C-1939	W	W	W	X	stove side	4 windows on desk side	Yellow	long
C-1951	X	W	X	X	desk side	no windows on stove side	Yellow	I-5
C-1957	X	X	X	X	both sides	B&OCT service	Yellow	I-5
C-1970	W	W	W	X	stove side		Yellow	long
C-1976	X	X	W	W	stove side	opp side: 2 wind @ desk	Red & Yel	long
C-1981	W	W	W	X	stove side		Yellow	long
C-1987	W	W	W	X	stove side		Yellow	long
C-1993	W	W	W	X	stove side	4 windows on desk side	Yellow	long
C-1995	W	W	W	X	stove side		Yellow	long
C-1999	W	W	W	X	stove side	4 windows on desk side	Yellow	long
C-2001	W	W	W	X	stove side		Red-DU	long
C-2002	X	W	X	X	stove side	4 windows on desk side	Red	long
C-2008	W	W	X	W	stove side	4 windows on desk side	Red-DU	long
C-2014	W	W	X	W	stove side		Red-DU	long
C-2026	W	W	W	X	stove side	4 windows on desk side	Yellow	long
C-2040	W	W	X	W	stove side	4 windows on desk side	Yellow	long
C-2046	W	W	W	X	stove side	4 windows on desk side	Yellow	long
C-2048	W	W	W	X	stove side	4 windows on desk side	Yellow	long
C-2094	W	X	X	W	desk side	SIRT service	Red	long
C-2098	X	X	W	X	stove side	2 windows offset opp side	Red	long
C-2101	W	W	P	P	stove side	P = Plywood inset	Yellow	long
C-2124	W	W	W	X	stove side		Yellow	long
C-2139	W	W	W	X	stove side	4 windows on desk side	Yellow	long
C-2158	W	W	X	W	stove side	5 windows on desk side	Red-MC	long
C-2165	W	W	X	W	stove side	4 windows on desk side	Yellow	long
C-2175	W	W	W	X	stove side		Yellow	long
C-2200	W	W	W	X	stove side		Yellow	long
C-2203	W	W	W	X	stove side		Yellow	long
C-2204	W	W	W	X	stove side	4 windows on desk side	Yellow	I-5
C-2207	W	W	W	X	stove side		Yellow	long
C-2210	W	W	P	X	stove side	P = Plywood inset	Yellow	long
C-2224	W	W	W	X	stove side	4 windows on desk side	Yellow	long
C-2227	W	W	W	X	stove side		Yellow	long
C-2236	W	W	X	W	stove side		Yellow	long
C-2238	W	W	X	W	stove side	4 windows on desk side	Red	long
C-2238	W	X	X	X	stove side	4 windows on desk side	Yellow	long
C-2245	W	W	W	X	stove side		Red-CE	I-5
C-2248	W	W	W	X	stove side	4 windows on desk side	Yellow	long
C-2250	W	W	W	X	stove side	4 windows on desk side	Yellow	long
C-2258	W	W	W	X	stove side		Yellow	long
C-2261	W	W	W	X	stove side		Yellow	long
C-2272	W	W	X	X	desk side		Red-WR	long
C-2283	W	W	W	X	stove side	4 windows on desk side	Yellow	long
C-2290	W	W	W	X	stove side	4 windows on desk side	Yellow	long
C-2292	W	W	X	W	stove side	4 windows on desk side	Red & Yel	long
C-2293	W	W	W	X	stove side	4 windows on desk side	Yellow	I-5

To assist modelers who desire to number models correctly this chart has been prepared from photos to document a large sampling of cars with window eliminations. In the above chart a window icon indicates the presence of a window, when viewing the side of the caboose; an "X" indicates the window has been eliminated. Also listed is the window configuration on the opposite side if known as well as the color of the caboose (which helps to date the photo) and its class. Unfortunately we do not have photos of the opposite side of all cabooses.

C-2292 is shown undergoing repairs at the Chillicothe shops on February 2, 1975. The car was returned to the Chillicothe shops from its assignment at Dayton, Ohio, where it was involved in a system accident. The Dayton car shops applied some plywood and yellow paint but they apparently had no stencils! An ice box on the end platform indicates interior refurbishment is in process. *Dwight Jones*

This is how the C-2292 looked when outshopped from the Chillicothe shops in September 1970. The car is shown at Rossford Yard, Toledo, on November 1, 1973. It previously had been upgraded with power brake stands and an oil heater, likely at the Washington, Indiana, shops when it was there in

the 1960s where it also received plywood sides. See more about this car in our "PUCO CASE" section in this book. *Kirk Hise photo, collection of Dwight Jones*

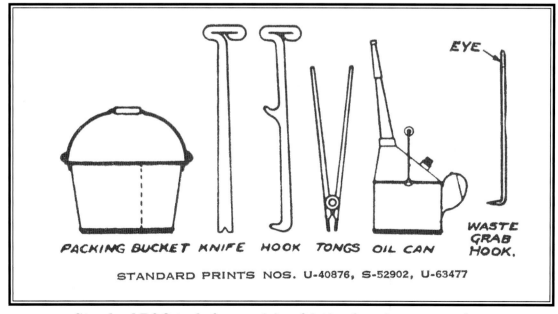

PACKING BUCKET   KNIFE   HOOK   TONGS   OIL CAN   WASTE GRAB HOOK.

STANDARD PRINTS NOS. U-40876, S-52902, U-63477

Standard B&O tools for servicing friction bearings on trucks

Only five I-5 family cabooses were painted into some type of Chessie System paint scheme. No lettering drawings were issued for this class so local shops had to wing it, such as here on the C-1975. Appropriately it was painted July 1, 1975, at Haselton, Ohio. It was in service at New Castle in August 1976 and at Lordstown in June 1977. Silver trucks mimic early Chessie GP40-2s. *Paul Dunn collection / collection of Dwight Jones*

The Grafton, West Virginia, shops painted the C-2165, and misidentified it as the "2165", in April 1975 in this odd Chessie System scheme reminiscent of a similar scheme applied to many C&O and two B&O cabooses at the C&O Walbridge, Ohio, shops. This cab also exhibits a window elimination. Company officials authorized the elimination of the window in front of the ice box. The "R" indicates the car is in Restricted service, in this case due to Age, Yoke and Coupler.

Paul Dunn collection / collection of Dwight Jones

Photographed at the Walbridge shops of the C&O the C-1987 models the "Walbridge Scheme" on May 21, 1977. Note the interesting two-tone step painting. *Dwight Jones*

Timeline of I-5 History Elements

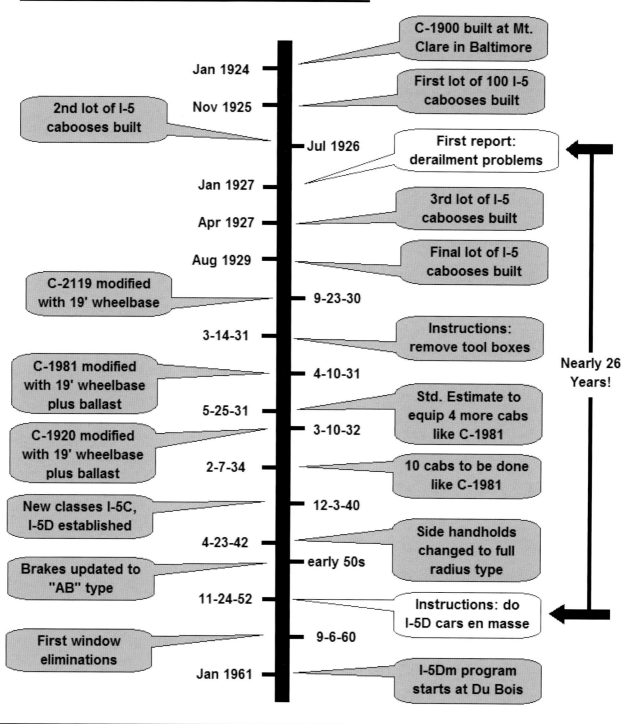

So much happened with the I-5 family of cabooses that this one page summary will help to clarify and give a quick snapshot of the key changes made to those cars from the time they were built to the early 1960s. After the early-to-mid 1960s the cars were primarily in secondary service, which was orchestrated by the introduction of pool service in 1965.

One key takeaway from the above, emphasized by the arrows on the right, is that troubles with the I-5 cars in helper service first were reported in early 1927 with time to make changes before more I-5 cars were built. But it took nearly 26 years before officers determined that I-5 and I-5C cars should be converted to I-5D in large quantities.

Caboose C-1967 was involved in this wreck, probably near Philadelphia, circa 1950. The top photo shows the caboose lying on its side, suffering from both a derailment and a subsequent fire.

B&O wrecker X-43 from Philadelphia is working the right side of the scene while borrowed Reading wrecker 90900 is working from the left, a delicate job since it is working partially inside of a tunnel. B&O diesel yard engine 415 was powering the B&O's wreck (relief) train.

Steam locomotive 4620 was also involved in this wreck and is lying on its side near the tunnels.

The B&O caboose last was painted at the Mt. Clare shops in Baltimore in 1946 where the car was stencilled as an I-5 class although it shows as having the longer 19-foot wheelbase. *Three photos collection of Dwight Jones*

On November 24, 1943, three trains collided near Newton Falls, Ohio, killing two or three (newspapers reported three; ICC report stated two) employees, and injuring as many as 78. The wreck is documented in ICC Accident Report #2745. The caboose is believed to be the C-2237 which was retired in B&O accounts the following month. It appears the car was heavily burned and still was on fire at

the time of the photo. An eastbound B&O freight, stopped in a siding, was rear ended by a PRR freight, which operated over this line. The wreckage then was hit by B&O eastbound passenger train #20 operating on the main at 55 MPH. *collection of Dwight Jones*

This wreck on the Monongah Division (Short Line Subdivision) destroyed I-5C caboose C-2191 which last had been painted at the Keyser shops in July 1953. The July 21, 1955, wreck also involved diesel model AS-16 904 which shows on the left side of this photo. Engine 904 was shoving the caboose eastbound near Lumberport and encountered a head-on collision with engine 4433 westbound. One crew member on the end platform and one inside the caboose jumped to safety. The conductor, riding inside the caboose, was killed. See photo next page. *collection of Dwight Jones*

The "kiss coupling" was just a little too strong for the C-2151, damaged at Newark, Ohio, on July 23, 1975. The car had just received repairs and a repainting at the Chillicothe shops in May of 1975, two months earlier. The only good thing about this view is that it clearly shows that the end platform and steps had been upgraded to the steel grating type. *Bud Abbott*

Caboose C-2182 was removed from service at Fairmont, West Virginia, (we assume the coal hoppers as well) and the string was dispatched to the Chillicothe shops for disposition. Photographed at Chillicothe on May 3, 1975, there was no need to unload anything—the string was sold to scrap dealer Friedman Metals and the cars continued on their journey. The trucks from the caboose were retained at Fairmont. *Dwight Jones*

Odd Wreck Costs Life

This period newspaper photo documented the end for caboose C-2191 in this wreck which occurred on July 21, 1955, near Lumberport, West Virginia. Engines 4433 and diesel 904 crashed head-on, destroying the caboose which was being shoved ahead of one of the engines. Six employees were injured in the wreck, with one trainman being killed. (see photo on previous page)

The Chillicothe shops was busy in the 1970s. Cab C-2122 has just arrived at the shops on July 20, 1973, loaded on a C&O flat car. The car had been damaged at Flora, Illinois, apparently from a rather hard coupling. No repair for this car; it was sold to a Portsmouth, Ohio, scrapper. *Dwight Jones*

The PUCO Case (also known as "The B&O Caboose Case")

Case Synopsis

On April 12, 1960, unions in Ohio filed a complaint with the Public Utilities Commission of Ohio (PUCO) regarding unsafe and unsanitary condition of cabooses operating in the state, primarily out of Toledo. The cars in question were I-1, I-1A and I-5 family cabooses. In this case the PUCO ruled that B&O must equip cabooses with oil stoves and cushion underframes (along with other minor sanitary equipment) any time a caboose is sent for rehabilitation to a "caboose repair shop".

Noting that freshly painted cabooses were being outshopped from Chillicothe in 1970-1971 without cushion underframes or oil stoves, the Unions filed a

The Players

In the second 1971 complaint there were two cabooses that were mentioned, the C-2292 and the C-2022. At the time these two cabooses were shown in the complaint as operating out of Lima, Ohio. Based on dates these two cabooses would just have been assigned to Lima after being released from the shops at Chillicothe where they were painted in the C&O yellow scheme as well as receiving any other repair action deemed necessary.

Caboose C-2292 was painted at Chillicothe in September 1970 while the C-2022 was painted in June of 1970. Cab C-2238, shown below, was painted at Chillicothe in March 1971.

Reading between the lines the complaint apparently alleged that these cabooses had gone through a "caboose repair shop" but had not been upgraded per the 1961 PUCO case settlement. We assume that meant full sanitary equipment, oil heaters, power brake stands and cushion underframes.

We are not exactly sure how the C-2238 got into this case. It was not referenced in the material we have describing the actual 1971 legal proceedings but it was mentioned in a C&O/B&O letter dated August 1, 1972, in regard to this case indicating that C-2238 and C-2292 were operating out of Lima. It is shown here at Benwood on **June 2, 1973.** *Paul B. Dunn*

second complaint with the PUCO in 1971 indicating that B&O was not living up to the 1961 PUCO order. B&O officers countered by indicating that they only had to equip cabooses with said equipment when a caboose was sent to a "caboose repair shop" and that only Du Bois, Pennsylvania, was the B&O "caboose repair shop". Chillicothe was not considered a "caboose repair shop" as only minor work and painting was done there.

This 1971 case was heard by an Attorney Examiner for the PUCO which sided with the B&O. The Unions filed an appeal which then was heard by a three-member panel for the PUCO which threw out the Attorney Examiner's decision and severely chastised the B&O for not complying with the 1961 order.

In the meantime a new union-management agreement had been reached in Baltimore concerning future caboose plans on the B&O (see volume 2 in this caboose series, page 65, for a copy) and it was felt that the Unions would not further push this matter due to the new agreement which documented a specific time line for acquisition of new cabooses. B&O officers had indicated that they would not equip these old, veteran cabooses with cushion underframes due to cost but rather would simply retire the cars from service.

The three cabooses shown on the previous page were the key players of the 1971 complaint. The original 1961 filing contained this listing of cabooses:

C-2047 Toledo to Cincinnati
C-1950 Toledo to Cincinnati
C-2049 Toledo to Cincinnati
C-404   Toledo Territory
C-264   Toledo Territory
C-1413 Toledo Territory
C-418   Toledo Territory
C-360   Toledo Territory
C-2022 Toledo to Cincinnati
C-2213 Toledo to Cincinnati
C-2210 Toledo to Cincinnati
C-495   Toledo Territory

Some of the interesting testimony in this case was provided by S. M. Ehrman (General Superintendent, Car Department, C&O/B&O). Selected dialogue is reproduced following:

> **Photos on the previous page show the C-2292 undergoing repairs at the Chillicothe shops on February 8, 1975, and the C-2022 in service on the caboose track at the C&O's Parsons Yard, Columbus, on April 1, 1973.** *both photos by Dwight Jones*

Q. "Do you have any kind of facility at Chillicothe?"

A. "Yes, we do."

Q. "Tell us about what kind of repair facility that is there so far as cabooses are concerned?"

A. "As far as cabooses, we are merely doing what is classified as minor repair work, refurbishing. In other words, we take the caboose in and any work that is required--could be a coat of paint in order to keep it in the serviceable condition."

Q. "Would you also do some window weather proofing if it was needed?"

A. "Weather stripping as needed."

Q. "And painting?"

A. "And painting, inside and out."

Q. "If a caboose were to receive a cushion draft gear or underframe job, where would you send that caboose?"

A. "That caboose would have to go to Du Bois, Pennsylvania."

Q. "Would it be done at Chillicothe?"

A. "No, sir."

Q. "And if in addition to a cushion underframe draft gear you also were going to put in an oil stove and a chemical or flush-type toilet and/or other things mentioned in the 1961 Commission order, where would those items be installed?"

A. "Du Bois, Pennsylvania."

Q. "Would they be done at Chillicothe?"

A. "No, sir."

Q. "Now, what was the situation, Mr. Ehrman, in 1961 when this order that I speak of, that is, the 1961 order, was issued? Was Chillicothe a major repair point for cabooses then?"

A. "No, sir, it was not. They were not even doing as much as is now being done there with cabooses."

Q. "Where would a caboose have been dispatched for cushion underframe or other items in the 1961 order?"

A. "Du Bois, Pennsylvania."

Q. "So the situation hasn't changed for the last ten years?

A. "Not one bit.

Q. "Now, from your familiarity with the 1961 order that we speak of here, are you aware that it uses the word 'rehabilitate' in one or two instances?

A. "Yes, sir.

Q. "What do you understand, Mr. Ehrman, to be required or involved when you rehabilitate a caboose?

A. "To rehabilitate is the type of repair we're doing at Du Bois at the present time in which we renew and modernize the caboose by putting in all the facilities that are required according to that 1961 order."

From the above it is obvious that railroad officials were making the point that cabooses outshopped from Chillicothe would not be modernized to the 1961 requirements, only cars outshopped from Du Bois would be.

Had the union representatives done their homework they would have questioned the wood cabooses outshopped from Du Bois, particularly those cars in the 1968-1969 program which also did not get the 1961 upgrades either.

A company letter dated April 22, 1971, from T. P. Hackney (C&O/B&O Assistant Vice President, Mechanical), stated the following:

"We interpret the order in this case to mean caboose cars given heavy repairs in our heavy shops where cabs can be made to comply with the Ohio requirements as a part of that heavy repair. This type of work is only performed at Du Bois Shops on the B&O. This was also the case in 1961. At the time the case was decided in 1961, only light running repairs were accomplished at Chillicothe, the same as was done at Cincinnati, Willard and Toledo.

"The light repairs at Chillicothe presently underway are intended to make these very old wood cabooses serviceable for another two or three years until more new cabs can be added to the fleet. Due to age and construction, it is not feasible to make these cars fully meet the Ohio requirements."

A Company letter dated August 1, 1972, indicated that B&O had won the case and "...were able to convince the Attorney Examiner that B&O had not violated the old 1961 case caboose order and further that the complainants had failed to make a case as to unsafe conditions."

Following the Attorney Examiner's report, the attorney for the Brotherhoods filed exceptions which were replied to by the railroad on November 22, 1971. The case then was reviewed by three Commissioners.

The Commissioners apparently were not convinced of the B&O's arguments and the merit of the Attorney Examiner's report and disregarded his report, issuing a "somewhat caustic and critical" report in which they concluded that B&O "dragged its feet" in failing to comply with the 1961 caboose order and further that B&O had "purposely failed" to comply with the 1961 order.

As this case was still under review by Company officers it was noted that it might be just as easy to remove the two cabooses from their northeast Ohio assignment. It was also noted that a new caboose agreement had been signed at Baltimore with the United Transportation Union on October 21, 1971, and it was felt the UTU would therefore not have much interest in pursuing this Ohio complaint since the 1971 agreement called for hundreds of new steel cabooses and also indicated that there would be no wood cabooses used in road service after 1975. See a copy of this agreement on page 65 of volume 2 in this caboose book series.

We finish this section with more testimony from C&O/B&O's Ehrman:

Q. "First of all, what is a cushion-type draft underframe.

A. "This is what they call a sliding sill, s-i-l-l, underframe, which takes care of the shock you get when they have slack action.

Q. "Now, bearing these words in mind that I just gave you, cushion-type draft underframe, as used by Mr. Alexander [the PUCO Attorney Examiner], I will ask you then if that terminology would be the same as cushion-type draft gear or underframe?

A. "As I stated a little earlier, I think that needs a little clarification.

Q. "Would you do so?

A. "A draft gear cushioning in that operation is what we call a replaced center sill. Now, a cushion underframe is the sliding type that I just mentioned that takes care of the shock itself. You do not have a draft gear in that car.

Q. "Now, let me see if I understand you correctly. You say a cushion draft gear --

A. "A draft gear is a cushioning device.

Q. "A draft gear then could be used in conjunction with a stationary underframe?

A. "That is correct.

Q. "And would that have some of the affect of cushioning impact of switching and slack action?

A. "Very little in a caboose car. It is too light.

Q. "Now, what is the difference between that type of an installation, a cushion gear and a stationary underframe, and a cushion-type draft gear or underframe?

A. "In your draft gear your center sill is secure to the body of the car and your draft gear is applied to each end behind and between your coupler in order to take some of the shock. However, those draft gears are of a high capacity nature which renders them practically nothing in the way of cushioning devices.

"Now, a cushion underframe -- you have an arrangement of springs which take up the shock. These are mounted inside of a sliding sill which slides underneath the body of the caboose car.

Q. "Now, you are speaking of this sliding body type that's known as a cushion underframe? That is what your understanding was that was specified in the order in 1961?

A. "Yes, sir.

Q. "All right. Now, one step further, presently does caboose 2292 or 2238 have this sliding type cushion draft underframe installed in it?

A. "No, sir, they do not.

Q. "And assuming that in 1963 giving credit to Mr. Alexander's report, assuming that there was a sliding draft cushion underframe in caboose 2238, would your mechanical department take out such a draft gear and put the old style back in?

A. "No, sir.

Q. "Would that be almost unheard of?

Q. "Due to the age of that car, if that sliding or cushion frame had become damaged to the extent it would have to be removed, we would have scrapped the caboose. We would not have changed that part of it.

Q. "If circumstances, which I hope never come about, if this Commission would order the B&O Railroad to install a cushion-type draft gear or underframe under caboose No. 2292 and also caboose 2238, what action would you take relative to such an order?

A. "I am afraid the cabs would be scrapped.

Q. "Mr. Ehrman, did I understand from your prior testimony that the so-called blue cabooses are your newer type cabooses?

A. "Yes, sir.

Q. "And is it a fact that such newer and more modern cabooses [have the] cushion draft underframe, the sliding type which you have just described, put in?

A. "Yes, sir. They do, keeping in mind that the purpose of such cushion draft type sliding underframes are to cushion the jolts from slack action either when the train is running, starting or stopping."

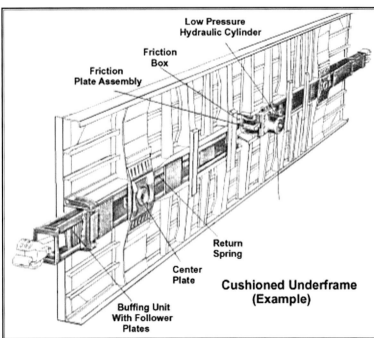

Low Pressure
Hydraulic Cylinder

Friction
Box

Friction
Plate Assembly

Return
Spring

Center
Plate

Buffing Unit
With Follower
Plates

**Cushioned Underframe
(Example)**

At left a representative drawing of a cushioned underframe.
courtesy Wabtec Corporation; copyright © 2003 Wabtec Corporation

For an example of a cushion draft gear see page 125.

Roster Copyright © 2016 by Dwight Jones   **DO NOT COPY**

Number	Pic ?	Built	Early "CF"	"AB" Brakes	I-5C	I-5D	I-5Dm	ACI Plate	1970-71 Paint	Misc. Paint	Retired	Disposition	Comments
C1900	Yes	1-24		7-53		GS 4-16-54					6-63	Sold from Parkersburg to Dr. Edward Shupala	(see Vol III); now burned up in Ohio
C1901	Yes	11-25	8-34	7-53		CU 12-40	DU 10-61	CE 4-3-70	CE 4-70	CE 3-75	9-79	Sold: Chillicothe Fire Department 8-16-79, for fire chief	(see Vol V); now private owner
C1902	Yes	11-25		3-53		WA 12-11-57		11-16-69	CE 9-71		4-74	Donated to White Water Valley RR, Connersville, IN 1-31-74;	sold on AFE 55613; (see Vol II)
C1903	Yes	11-25		10-52	KY 9-41	KY 10-13-55					4-70	Dismantled at B&O shops, Du Bois, PA, 4-30-70	scrapped
C1904	Yes	11-25		10-50	CU 12-40	KY 12-28-55	DU 6-62	CE 10-9-70	CE 10-70		11-75	Sold to Jim Dunnett, Athens, GA 9-30-75 for $1000	ACI again: Lima 3-27-75 (see Vol I & II)
C1905		11-25									2-45	Destroyed: Fire: Laurel, MD 2-8-45	scrapped
C1906	Yes	11-25	7-34	6-53				CE 5-28-71	CE 5-71		6-24-83	Donated to Parks & Recreation, Petersburg, WV; AFE 59286	now used on Durbin & Greenbrier tourist train out of Durbin, West Virginia (see Vol I)
C1907	Yes	11-25		7-53	KY 6-42	GS 5-29-53					7-62	Used as a cabin at Tygart Lake, Grafton, WV; sold 6-13-62	(see Vol IV); now scrapped
C1908	Yes	11-25		6-50		WA 3-30-56					2-65	System Accident: O'Bannon, OH; dismantled: WA	scrapped
C1909	Yes	11-25		11-51	CU 4-42	KY 5-25-56	DU 3-62	Yes	CE 10-71		8-79	Sold at MTC to Brett Properties, Baltimore 5-21-79	(see Vol III)
C1910	Yes	11-25		7-53	KY 11-41	Yes-DJ verified					6-62	Sold 6-5-62 from Hamilton, OH, to Jim Newton, Hamilton, OH	(see Vol I); resold to new owner (see Vol V)
C1911		11-25									10-30	Accident: Altamont, MD 3-20-30; 2404 Report: MTC: 1-5-31	wreck also reported as 3-2-30 2404 copy is in this publication
C1912	Yes	11-25		5-52	CU 8-40	KY 1-23-57					8-75	Sold to Granville Tennis Club, Heath, OH, 5-13-75 for $800	(see Vol I)
C1913	Yes	11-25	8-34	7-53				CE 6-18-71	CE 6-71		10-77	Sold: John Parkin, Hag, MD 9-23-77; at McD's-Winchestr., VA	(see Vol I & III)
C1914	Yes	11-25				GS 10-29-54					7-62	Used as a cabin at Tygart Lake, Grafton, WV; sold 6-13-62	(see Vol IV); now scrapped
C1915	Yes	11-25		DU 10-23-53	10-53			CE 2-12-71	CE 2-71		12-76	Donated to City of Willard, OH 8-2-76; AFE 56696	(see Vol I); displayed in city park
C1916	Yes	11-25		8-52	Yes-DJ verified						5-71	Donated to City of Garrett, IN, 9-30-66; park display	AFE 54434; (see Vol I)
C1917	Yes	11-25		12-51	KY 2-42	KY 3-8-57					4-72	Sold from CU to A.H. Slocum, Martinsburg, WV 2-28-72 $824	private display near Romney, WV (see Vol V)
C1918	Yes	11-25	8-35	5-52							7-62	Used as a cabin at Tygart Lake, Grafton, WV; sold 6-13-62	cement floor at CU 5-21-35 (see Vol IV); now scrapped
C1919	Yes	11-25		5-52		KY 1-3-56		CE 9-28-70	CE 9-70		7-74	Sold to Art Davis, Wooster, OH, 6-13-74 for $250	
C1920	Yes	11-25	4-32								10-59	Wrecked KY 9-2-59 while being handled by yard engine	3-32 record shows steel underframe
C1921	Yes	12-25		7-49		MTC 8-18-54		CE 9-28-70	CE 9-70		9-75	Sold: T.J. O'Brien, IA, 6-20-75; At Mid-Continent Ry. Mus. $800	
C1922	Yes	12-25		9-50		MTC 10-6-54					5-75	Sold: Majestic Mining, Widen, WV (body only) 10-23-74	subsequently scrapped; no cupola later years
C1923	Yes	12-25		MTC 8-31-51		MTC 11-10-54					2-66	Dismantled: B&O Shops, Somerset, PA 1-5-66	scrapped
C1924		12-25									8-57	Wrecked 7-20-57 at N. Vernon, IN, train #3.	scrapped
C1925	Yes	12-25		2-51		MTC 12-6-54	DU 9-61				5-72	Sold: A.H. Slocum, Martinsburg, WV 5-10-72 $832	sold along with C1917 (see Vol V)
C1926	Yes	12-25		5-51		WA 12-10-56					9-6-83	Donated: Hampshire County Parks, Romney, WV, 9-6-83	Destroyed: fire: Keyser, WV, 10-31-34 sold on AFE 59605; (see Vol III);
C1927	Yes	12-25		1-51	KY 12-40	See Note >		CE 8-17-70	CE 8-70		7-74	Sold: Art Davis, Wooster, OH; 6-13-74 $250	Inspected: D. Jones 9-25-93: car was I-5C; (see Vol II); KY reported I-5D 3-20-56
C1928	Yes	12-25		GS 1-29-54		GS 1-29-54					3-74	Sold: La Rosa Fuel; Fairmont, WV 11-30-73 $800	See Note 1
C1929	Yes	12-25	12-34	12-52				CE 6-4-70	CE 6-70		6-76	Donated to New Carlisle, OH, Rotary Club 4-19-77 AFE 56916	ACI also reported: GW 1-6-70; car burned by vandals before delivery and scrapped
C1930	Yes	12-25	8-34	5-50		CU 12-40		CE 3-18-71	CE 3-71		2-80	Sold: Fay Fleming, Clarksburg, WV, 1-17-80; (see Vol V)	scrapped March 2012; trucks to Byesville, OH caboose
C1931	Yes	12-25	8-34	GS 8-14-53		DU 8-25-61	DU 8-61				6-71	Donated: 5-19-71 to city of Tipp City, OH; AFE 54522	telcon with city June 1993; they indicated cab had been gone from city park for several years
C1932	Yes	12-25		7-50	KY 6-41	KY 2-26-54		CE 7-10-70	CE 7-70		7-77	Sold: private owner, Somerset, PA	sold 8-5-77 (see Vol V)
C1933	Yes	12-25		10-49		WA 11-28-56					3-68	Sold: 2-15-68; on OH Div '61; sold with 2 others	sale order 5555 suggests sales to a scrap dealer
C1934	Yes	12-25		2-51	KY 4-41			No	CE 1-71		9-15-83	Sold: Mansbach Metal from Russell, KY, 9-15-83	Fire: Mt. Clare, MD, 3-3-53 $1600 damage
C1935	Yes	12-25		MC 10-23-53	KY 2-42						9-67	Sold: Harry Smuck, Baltimore, MD, 9-19-67 $450	(see Vol I)
C1936	Yes	12-25		8-53	CU 7-40	GS 8-7-53					9-75	Sold: private owner, Chillicothe, OH, 6-17-75 $400	Painted KY 6-57; (see Vol V)
C1937	Yes	12-25		8-50	CU 4-42	MTC 8-17-55	DU 3-62				4-68	Dism: 3-18-68 Brunswick, MD due to wreck at Kensington, MD	wrecked 2-16-68; wreck photo: Trains Magazine
C1938	Yes	12-25		10-51	KY 9-40	WA 12-30-58					12-74	Sold: Art Davis, Wooster, OH 11-7-74	(see Vol II)
C1939	Yes	12-25		5-52				CE 12-11-70	CE 12-70		3-80	Donated: city of Washington C.H., OH, 2-26-80 AFE 57977	(see Vol II)
C1940	Yes	12-25		7-53				CE 4-27-70	CE 4-70		9-75	Sold: Mike Staley, Apple Creek, OH; 6-9-75; $800	Telcon: Mike said it has a concrete floor (see Vol II)
C1941	Yes	12-25		5-50	Yes	MTC 7-29-54					11-68	Destroyed: Dola, WV 2-20-67	Insp: MTC--stenciled I-5 but is "I-5C" 4-20-54
C1942	Yes	12-25		10-52	long wheelbase			CE 8-31-70	CE 8-70		12-78	Sold: 8-7-78 Ron Jedlicka, Columbus; $391.04 body scrap'd	system accident: Dayton, Ohio 12-27-75
C1943	Yes	12-25		5-52							4-63	Dismantled: B&O shops, Washington, IN	scrapped

Roster Copyright © 2016 by Dwight Jones **DO NOT COPY**

Number	Pic ?	Built	Early "CF"	"AB" Brakes	I-5C	I-5D	I-5Dm	ACI Plate	1970-71 Paint	Misc. Paint	Retired	Disposition	Comments
C1944	Yes	12-25		4-51		MTC 12-24-54					7-74	Don: Brunswick, MD, Potomac River Festival 4-18-74;	Minor fire damage: Baltimore, MD, 11-7-51 (see Vol I); AFE 55667; later to high school
C1945	Yes	12-25		8-50	DU 1-41		DU 9-61				11-74	Sold: Art Davis 11-7-74 Wooster, OH	(see Vol II)
C1946	Yes	12-25				DU 5-61		CE 10-30-71	CE 10-71	CU RUS 5-75	7-20-83	Sold: Mansbach Metal from Brunswick, MD 7-20-83	scrapped
C1947		12-25									9-47	Destroyed: Finney, OH, 8-6-47 2404 form: Storrs, OH, 9-22-47	rear end collision with work train
C1948	Yes	12-25		5-52	DU 10-6-52	DU 5-29-61	DU 5-61				9-70	Sold: Wilkoff Co., Youngstown, OH for scrap 7-16-70	scrapped
C1949	Yes	12-25		6-50	DU 8-31-53						5-70	Dismantled: B&O shops, Du Bois, PA, 4-30-70	scrapped
C1950		12-25		4-51		WA 3-23-56					11-68	Dismantled: B&O shops, Chillicothe, OH 11-12-68	scrapped
C1951	Yes	12-25		3-52				CE 2-23-71	CE 2-71		4-77	Donated: community of Mt. Savage, MD 12-7-76;	AFE 56884 (see Vol I)
C1952	Yes	12-25		DU 8-14-51				CE 3-5-71	CE 2-71		6-80	Sold: Columbus Hardware Supply 6-18-80	Damaged: fire: Connellsville, PA, 10-5-29 (see Vol IV)
C1953	Yes	12-25		12-52	DU 12-9-52	DU 8-8-61	DU 8-61				1-81	Removed from ownership--car could not be found on the system	Last record: photos show in service at Chicago 11-13-66
C1954	Yes	12-25		11-50		MTC 3-14-55	DU 3-62	CE 9-9-70	CE 9-70		1-71	Dest: Fire: Mt. Clare shops 1-10-71,	cut up at Du Bois, 3-10-71
C1955	Yes	12-25		PV 6-25-54		PV 6-21-54	DU 9-61				11-67	Destroyed: Fire: Willard, OH, 11-8-67	scrapped
C1956	Yes	12-25		6-53	DU 6-3-53	DU 12-12-56	DU 12-61				9-73	Sold: Mrs. Robert Masters, Bowerstown, OH 9-26-73 $800	(see Vol I)
C1957	Yes	12-25		4-53				CE 2-19-70	CE 2-70	CE 12-74 RUS	8-17-83	Sold: Mansbach Metal from Brunswick, MD 8-17-83	scrapped
C1958	Yes	12-25		1-49	DU 1-41	DU 2-21-56	Partial 3-61				3-67	Dismantled: Pittsburgh, PA, B&O shops 3-31-67	scrapped
C1959	Yes	12-25		4-52		KY 6-17-57	DU 9-61				4-70	Dismantled: B&O shops, Du Bois, PA 4-30-70	scrapped
C1960	Yes	12-25		3-52		DU 4-4-56	Partial 3-61				2-67	Dismantled: B&O shops, Willard, OH 2-3-67	scrapped
C1961	Yes	1-26		PV 11-27-53	GW 12-12-40	DU 9-22-61	DU 9-61				4-70	Destroyed: Willard, OH, on B&O 4-6-70.	Damaged: fire: New Castle, PA, 12-14-44
C1962	Yes	1-26		5-50	DU 1-41	DU 11-23-56					7-68	Sold: Indiana Metals, Inc. as scrap 7-10-68	scrapped
C1963	Yes	1-26		12-48		DU 6-22-56	DU 6-61	CE 7-24-70	CE 7-70		5-73	Donated: Phillip Barbour High School, Phillippi, WV 5-17-73	AFE 55380 Scrapped circa 1988
C1964		1-26									3-42	Sold: Alton Railroad	one of six I-5 cars sold to Alton
C1965	Yes	1-26									12-52	Destroyed: Fire: Wellsboro, IN 2-25-52; 2404: DU 12-26-52	Damaged: fire: Tracy, IN, 2-25-52
C1966	Yes	1-26		3-53	DU 12-40	DU 1-31-57	DU 9-61				10-73	Sold: C.F. Dozer, Chillicothe, OH 10-3-73 $800	Destroyed: fire: Demmler, PA, 11-21-36 (reblt after fire with cupola ?) (see Vol V)
C1967	Yes	1-26		11-51		KY 3-26-56		CE 6-22-71	CE 6-71		8-73	Sold: Alan Norris, Westerville, OH 8-24-73 $800	(see Vol III)
C1968		1-26									3-42	Sold: Alton Railroad	one of six I-5 cars sold to Alton
C1969	Yes	1-26		1-51							2-68	Sold: 2-15-68; OH / NE Div, '61 Pic shows still I-5 in '61	sales order 5555 suggests sale to a scrap dealer
C1970	Yes	1-26		10-50	DU 3-41	KY 11-1-55		CE 6-11-71	CE 6-71		9-75	Donated: city of Parkersburg, WV, 9-16-75; AFE 56409	burned by city and scrapped circa 1985
C1971	Yes	1-26		GW 8-13-51	DU 10-16-52	DU 4-24-56	DU 9-61				1-74	Donated: village of Ottawa, OH, 1-31-74; AFE 55669	(see Vol I); displayed in city park
C1972		1-26			GW 5-8-41						10-52	Wrecked: DU 10-16-52 Damaged: Fire 8-31-48	Condemned 10-16-52
C1973	Yes	1-26		12-52		DU 11-13-56	DU 9-61				6-71	Body only donated to Boy Scouts, New Haven, OH 6-3-71;	trucks cut up at BW 6-1-71; (see Vol V) AFE 54523
C1974	Yes	1-26		11-52	DU 11-24-52	DU 1-23-57	DU 9-61				1-71	Sold: Cravat Coal Co, 1-6-71; Dest: 8-19-70 Stillwater, OH	(see Vol I)
C1975	Yes	1-26		4-53			DU 9-61	CE 11-21-70	CE 11-70	HA 7-75	5-78	Renumbered X150 at Haselton, OH, 5-24-78 (wreck service);	later to 911505; sold private owner 8-86; later scrapped; (see Vol V); AFE 57496
C1976	Yes	1-26		1-53	1-53			CE 1-15-71	CE 1-71		2-74	Sold: Little River Railroad, 2-27-74, Coldwater, Michigan	(see Vol II)
C1977	Yes	1-26		DU 12-7-53	12-53						7-70	Sold: S.C. Johnson 7-30-70 See Note 2	dam. fire: Sodom, PA, 6-13-33 sold with C2298 (Grand View, WI)
C1978	Yes	1-26		10-50	DU 6-19-53		DU 7-61				5-74	Donated: Mar-Lu-Ridge, Jefferson, MD, 5-22-74	AFE 55714; (see Vol II)
C1979	Yes	1-26		MTC 8-31-52	KY 2-42	KY 6-11-57	DU 4-62	CE 9-17-70	CE 9-70		8-81	Sold: Portsmouth Iron & Metal as scrap 8-30-81 from CE	system accident at Dayton, OH, 2-3-77
C1980	Yes	1-26		6-53		WA 2-10-60		CE 7-2-70	CE 7-70		12-80	Fire dam: 10-13-79 Cin. and Dism: Cincinnati, OH 12-2-80	trucks retained at Cincinnati, sold: Portsmouth Iron & Metal as scrap
C1981	Yes	1-26	9-31	3-52				CE 7-9-71	CE 7-71		9-15-83	Sold: Mansbach Metal from Russell, KY, 9-15-83	scrapped
C1982	Yes	1-26		DU 8-10-51		DU 1-16-59		Yes	CE 10-71	CE 4-77	12-76	Cut up as scrap at Indianapolis ca. Early 1987	scrapped
C1983	Yes	1-26		2-55	DU 10-13-52	DU 1-8-57	DU 4-61	CE 10-9-70	CE 10-70		7-75	Donated: American Legion, Brunswick, MD, AFE 56043	Damaged: fire: Smithfield, PA, 12-2-46 (see Vol II)
C1984	Yes	1-26		7-50		DU 2-28-56	DU 6-61	CE 7-16-70	CE 7-70		5-78	Sold: Midwest Steel from Mt. Clare, MD, 5-16-78	ACI also reported at Curtis Bay 7-29-69; Fire damaged at Locust Point 5-14-75
C1985		1-26		3-50		KY 6-41					6-66	Dismantled: B&O, Wilsmere, DE, 8-10-65	
C1986		1-26		3-52		GS 4-28-53					11-75	Sold: Stan Grueninger, Cincinnati, OH, 11-6-75; $1000	(see Vol I); now in Cincinnati park
C1987	Yes	1-26		3-51	KY 11-40	KY 11-14-55		CE 12-6-70	CE 12-70	WAL 3-76	3-31-82	Donated: 40&8 Voiture, local 553, Grand Rapids, MI, 3-31-82	AFE 58630

Roster Copyright © 2016 by Dwight Jones **DO NOT COPY**

Number	Pic ?	Built	Early "CF"	"AB" Brakes	I-5C	I-5D	I-5Dm	ACI Plate	1970-71 Paint	Misc. Paint	Retired	Disposition	Comments
C1988	Yes	1-26		1-51		WA 12-8-55					10-70	Dest: Fire: B&OCT, Barr Yard, 10-19-70; cut up at CE 5-5-71	scrapped
C1989	Yes	1-26		11-49		MTC 9-15-54					11-75	Donated: Lions Club, Eureka, WV, 11-24-75; AFE 56468	(see Vol II)
C1990		1-26			KY 12-41	KY 10-3-55					7-65	Dismantled, B&O shops, Washington, IN	scrapped
C1991	Yes	1-26		6-53		GS 4-16-54					10-68	Sold: private owner, 10-23-68; AFE 53190	(see Vol V)
C1992	Yes	1-26		9-52		KY 9-17-57					1-81	Removed from ownership--car could not be found 1-15-81	(see Vol V)
C1993	Yes	1-26		8-52	KY 1-42	KY 10-21-55		CE 10-1-70	CE 9-70	CE 12-74	6-76	Sold: Donald Shriner from WR, Ohio, 6-21-76; $800	Fire damaged at CE 1-1-75 (see Vol II); car has new brake wheel
C1994	Yes	2-26		6-53	DU 1-41	DU 11-30-56					11-74	Sold: Art Davis, Wooster, Ohio, 11-7-74	(see Vol II)
C1995	Yes	2-26		MTC 2-1-52				CE 9-1-71	CE 8-71		11-76	Sold: George Silcott, Worthington, Ohio, 11-29-76; $1000	Silcott was an Ohio dealer; final dispo. unknown Destroyed: fire: Mt. Clare, MD, 8-26-53
C1996	Yes	2-26		3-52	CU 12-40	KY 4-12-57	DU 3-62	CE 11-28-70	CE 11-70		2-80	Sold: Sandusky Contractors, Inc., 2-25-80 from Brunswick	on display; (see Vol V)
C1997	Yes	2-26		8-50		WA 7-1-57		CE 11-20-70	CE 10-70		8-75	Sold: Friedman Metals, 8-6-75, from Chillicothe	Fire damaged at CE 1-1-75
C1998	Yes	2-26		GS 7-21-54	KY 8-40	GS 7-21-54					12-63	Dismantled: B&O shops, Benwood, WV	scrapped
C1999	Yes	2-26		12-52		WA 6-26-59		No	CE 1-71		10-75	Sold: Ronnie Drake Construction, Walkerton, IN, 10-7-75	(see Vol II &IV); this company purchased three I-5 family cabooses
C2000	Yes	2-26		4-52	KY 3-42			CE 2-25-70	CE 2-70	CU 4-75 / RUS	8-17-83	Sold: Mansbach Metal, Ashland, KY, 8-12-83	sold from Clarksburg, WV
C2001	Yes	7-26		11-52		DU 2-61	Partial 2-61				5-66	Fire at Chicago 1-66 and dism at Chicago 5-66	scrapped
C2002	Yes	7-26		1-51		DU 12-27-56	DU 9-61				3-67	Sold: Darby Wood Products, Hagerstown, MD, 3-21-67	sold from SO; AFE 52349 (see Vol V)
C2003	Yes	7-26		10-52	DU 10-13-52	DU 4-11-56	DU 9-61	CE 6-26-70	CE 6-70		8-77	Sold: private owner, Roseville, MI, 8-29-77 $1000	on display; (see Vol V)
C2004		7-26		7-51		DU 1-25-56	DU 2-61				6-63	Dest: Fire: on P&LE at Lucas, PA; cut up at SO	scrapped
C2005	Yes	7-26		LO 2-5-54							9-65	Dismantled, B&O shops, Du Bois, PA	scrapped
C2006	Yes	7-26		PV 10-21-55			DU 4-61				1-71	Fire damaged at Barr yd 1-12-71; cut up at Chillicothe, 5-5-71	Damaged: fire: New Castle, PA, 1-16-34
C2007	Yes	7-26		DU 11-23-55		DU 11-23-55					3-60	Wrecked Sand Patch 2-19-60; 2404 form made SO 3-23-60	scrapped due to wreck; see this book for wreck photos and story
C2008	Yes	7-26		11-52			Partial 1-61				5-65	Destroyed: Fire: Willard; dismantled at Willard	scrapped
C2009	Yes	7-26		See Note >							4-70	Dismantled at B&O shops, Du Bois, PA, 4-30-70	photo: car has long wheelbase, no cupola
C2010	Yes	7-26		2-55		DU 1-30-57	Partial 2-61				11-67	Sold: Indiana Metals, Inc. as scrap, E. Chicago, IN, 11-1-67	scrapped
C2011	Yes	7-26		10-50		DU 8-23-61	DU 8-61				9-73	Sold: R.D. Williams, Indiana, PA, 9-11-73; $800	(see Vol II)
C2012	Yes	7-26				DU 11-18-57	DU 7-61			BY 1966	2-75	Sold: priv. owner, Dayton, OH, 2-24-75. Yellow ends: B&OCT	Damaged: fire: New Castle, PA, 10-26-29 sold: moved by rail to Yellow Springs, OH
C2013	Yes	7-26		11-51		PV 8-2-55	DU 3-62				1-67	Sold: W.A. Lakel, Wilsmere, DE, 1-25-67, with C-2042	Wilmington & Western RR; Lakel was the B&O area Trainmaster; (see Vol I)
C2014	Yes	7-26		5-52			Partial 1-61				12-69	Sold: Eugene Nasbaum, St. Anne, IL, 12-5-69.	telcon with owner: car has concrete floor (see Vol I)
C2015	Yes	7-26		3-51		DU 8-24-61	DU 8-61				4-69	Dismantled, B&O shops, Holloway, OH, 4-15-69	scrapped
C2016		7-26									2-53	Old date--no doubt scrapped by B&O	scrapped
C2017		7-26									3-41	Destroyed: Fire: Walkerton, IN 3-2-41;	2404 form: Garrett 3-13-41
C2018	Yes	7-26		2-55		DU 8-22-61	DU 8-61	CE 4-9-71	CE 4-71		7-77	Dismantled, B&O shops, Garrett, IN, 7-20-77;	trucks sent to Willard
C2019	Yes	7-26		3-52		KY 7-1-57		CE 1-15-71	CE 1-71		9-80	Donated: City of Wheeling, West Virginia; AFE 58971	(see Vol I)
C2020		7-26									12-53	Old date--no doubt scrapped by B&O	scrapped
C2021	Yes	7-26		5-51		DU 8-11-61	DU 8-61	CE 1-22-71	CE 1-71		11-75	Sold: Eastman Kodak Co., Rochester, NY, 11-3-75 $1000	Damaged: fire: Dayton, OH, 3-26-40 (see Vol I)
C2022	Yes	7-26		9-50				CE 6-18-70	CE 6-70		11-74	Sold: Art Davis, Wooster, Ohio 11-7-74	(see Vol II)
C2023	Yes	7-26		12-50		WA 3-1-56		CE 7-24-70	CE 7-70		4-76	Sold: James K. Vinton, Mooresville, IN, 4-6-76 $1000	(see Vol II & IV)
C2024	Yes	7-26		4-50				CE 7-10-70	CE 7-70		3-76	Sold: Harvey Cohn, Owings Mills, MD, 3-31-76	(see Vol IV)
C2025	Yes	7-26		12-50							12-66	Sold: H. Wolfe Metal Co., New Castle, PA, 12-29-66 from WA	scrapped
C2026	Yes	7-26		10-50				CE 10-30-70	CE 10-70		12-75	Sold: Mansbach Metal, Ashland, KY, 12-11-75 from CE	car has new brake wheel fire damaged at Lima 10-1-75
C2027	Yes	7-26		3-51		WA 8-3-61					4-68	Dismantled, B&O shops, Willard, OH, 4-26-68	scrapped
C2028	Yes	7-26		3-53		WA 2-20-59		CE 11-20-70	CE 10-70		11-74	Sold: Whitewater Valley RR, Connersville, IN, 11-5-74 $300	(see Vol II)
C2029		8-26									5-39	Sold: Alton RR 5-31-39	one of six I-5 cars sold to Alton
C2030	Yes	8-26		6-51		WA 12-28-55		CE 2-25-70	CE 2-70		10-83	Donated: city of Spencer, WV, 10-25-83; Cab at BW 7-15-81	sold on AFE 59606; (see Vol II)
C2031	Yes	8-26		2-51		WA 4-29-59		CE 7-9-71	CE 6-71		8-75	Donated: CofC Valley City, Ohio, 8-15-75; AFE 56375	(see Vol I)

Number	Pic ?	Built	Early "CF"	"AB" Brakes	I-5C	I-5D	I-5Dm	ACI Plate	1970-71 Paint	Misc. Paint	Retired	Disposition	Comments
C2032	Yes	8-26		1-52		WA 5-21-57		Yes	CE 9-71		4-76	Donated: Lavalette little league, Lavalette, WV, 4-26-76	AFE 56337; telcon 10-26-93 car was concession stand at ball field; scrapped ca. 1984
C2033	Yes	8-26		7-50		WA 3-30-59					3-68	Dismantled: B&O shops, Brunswick, MD, 3-18-68	scrapped
C2034	Yes	8-26		1-53							11-68	Sold: International Car Co., Kenton, OH, 11-8-68	disposition unknown;
C2035	Yes	8-26		6-52		DU 8-9-61	DU 8-61	CE 4-9-71	CE 4-71		9-75	Sold: Jim Dunnett, Athens, GA, 9-30-75; $1000	(see Vol IV) at lake along interstate E of Athens
C2036	Yes	8-26		11-51							5-80	Dism: Indianapolis; Body sold: Portsm. Iron & Metal, 5-9-80	Minor fire damage: Wapakoneta, OH, 12-3-46 wreck damage on one end at Indianapolis
C2037	Yes	8-26		5-52							12-63	Dismantled, B&O shops, Garrett, IN	scrapped
C2038	Yes	8-26		6-53	DU 7-17-53						2-66	Dismantled, B&O shops, Willard, OH, 1-25-66	scrapped
C2039	Yes	8-26		5-53	DU 5-5-53						10-67	Donated: Camp Tomahawk, 10-67; AFE 52508	See Note 3
C2040	Yes	8-26		DU 9-18-53	9-53	WA 5-21-62	Note > 6-62	CE 12-6-70	CE 12-70		8-81	Sold: Portsmouth Iron & Metal from CE 8-21-81	Also reported: "I-5C" to "I-5D" at DU 9-18-53 Externally cab has power brake wheel only
C2041	Yes	8-26		PV 2-27-52	PV 8-2-55		Partial 2-61	CE 11-13-70	CE 11-70		7-75	Sold: George Silcott ($800), Worthington, Ohio, 7-24-75	also reported to "I-5D" 7-61; Silcott was a dealer; disposition unknown
C2042	Yes	8-26		3-52	KY 9-6-57	DU 12-61					4-67	Sold: Wilmington & Western RR, DE, 4-13-67, with C-2013	sold on AFE 52351 (see Vol I & II)
C2043	Yes	8-26		2-55	DU 8-18-61	DU 8-61					11-74	Sold: Springboro Clinic, Carlisle, OH, Dr. T.C. Garland; 11-5-74	sold from CE ($800); (see Vol II); now scrapped
C2044	Yes	8-26		12-49				CE 5-28-71	CE 5-71		12-75	Sold: All Aboard shop, to Brookville, IN, 12-19-75; $1000	burned by locals and scrapped ca. 1982 (see Vol V)
C2045	Yes	8-26		8-53		WA 8-6-53		CE 10-8-70	CE 10-70		9-75	Sold: Ronnie Drake Construction, Walkerton, IN, 9-3-75	(see Vol II); this company purchased three I-5 family cabooses
C2046	Yes	8-26		12-51		WA 10-24-55		CE 8-4-70	CE 7-70		8-81	Sold: Portsmouth Iron & Metal from Chillicothe 8-21-81	Destroyed: fire: Dayton, OH, 9-26-75
C2047	Yes	8-26		7-51		WA 6-22-56					6-69	Sold: Falls Motel--excursion use in Kentucky, 6-9-69	car scrapped when tourist train went out of business; (see Vol IV)
C2048	Yes	8-26		4-50		WA 5-15-53		Yes	CE 10-71		11-74	Sold: Art Davis, Wooster, Ohio, 11-7-74	(see Vol II)
C2049	Yes	8-26		9-51		WA 5-13-57					6-69	Dismantled: B&O shops, Brunswick, MD, 6-5-69	scrapped
C2050	Yes	8-26		1-50	?						8-73	Sold: E.H. Castle, Rowlesburg, WV, 8-8-73; $800	was at Cool Springs Park; (see Vol II); now displayed: Rowlesburg, WV
C2051	Yes	8-26		WA 10-9-53							5-69	Dismantled: B&O shops, Chillicothe, OH, 5-13-69	scrapped
C2052	Yes	8-26		11-52	DU 11-7-52	DU 6-15-56	DU 4-61	CE 2-10-70	CE 2-70		8-5-83	Sold from Ridgeley to Mansbach Metal, Ashland, KY, 8-5-83	scrapped
C2053	Yes	8-26		3-52		DU 8-10-61	DU 8-61	CE 4-27-71	CE 4-71	CE 3-75	RUS 8-17-83	Sold: Mansbach Metal, Ashland, KY from BW, 8-17-83	Accident: 9-12-74: Cumberland, OH System Acc: 11-11-76, Parkersburg, WV
C2054	Yes	8-26		4-51	DU 7-30-53	DU 2-9-59					7-70	Sold: Fate-Root-Heath Co., Plymouth, OH, 7-10-70	(see Vol II)
C2055	Yes	8-26		7-53	KY 6-3-57						4-76	Sold: Mary Andrews McVey, Lexington, KY, 4-26-76; $1050	(see Vol IV)
C2056	Yes	8-26		6-51	GW 1-28-41	DU 8-17-61	DU 8-61	CU 11-14-69		CU 6-71	1-76	Donated: private organization, Cumberland, MD, 1-21-76	AFE 56524 (see Vol V)
C2057	Yes	8-26		12-52				No	CE 5-70		10-74	Donated: St. Paul Lutheran Church, Sandusky, OH, 10-4-74	AFE 55836; (see Vol I)
C2058	Yes	8-26		1-53							7-63	Destroyed: Fire, Toledo, OH 2-63	scrapped
C2059	Yes	8-26		8-52	MTC 2-23-54						11-74	Sold: Art Davis, Wooster, Ohio, 11-7-74	(see Vol II)
C2060	Yes	8-26		5-50	DU 3-41		DU 3-62				1-74	Donated: town of Barton, Maryland, 1-11-74	AFE 55605 (see Vol III)
C2061	Yes	8-26		4-53	DU 4-15-53	WA 8-1-60					12-71	Sold from Baltimore to Peter Fedak, Bethesda, MD, 12-13-71	sold for $800; (see Vol II)
C2062	Yes	8-26		10-52	DU 5-41	DU 5-29-56	Partial 2-61	GW 11-11-69	CE	Yes	4-74	Sold: Lawrence J. Kuhn, Strongsville, OH, 4-29-74; $800	(see Vol II)
C2063	Yes	8-26		2-51							9-15-83	Sold: Mansbach Metal from Russell, KY, 9-15-83	scrapped
C2064	Yes	8-26		12-52						CE 6-77	3-82	Sold: United Iron & Metal from Mt. Clare, 3-24-82	system accident: Riverside: 4-16-80
C2065	Yes	8-26		PV 8-31-55			DU 7-61	CE 6-11-70	CE 6-70		10-75	Sold: DABO Inc., Wooster, OH, 10-28-75; sold from CE	DABO is Art Davis (see Vol II)
C2066	Yes	8-26		11-52	DU 11-14-52	DU 2-13-59	DU 9-61				3-73	Sold: Midwest Steel & Alloy Corp., Cleveland, OH, 3-30-73	scrapped
C2067		8-26		1-51	DU 4-41	DU 10-8-54					4-55	Fire Damaged: Destroyed: Allegheny, PA 2-17-55	Damaged: fire: Allegheny, PA, 2-17-55 condemned: Cumberland 4-29-55
C2068	Yes	8-26		2-53	DU 2-27-53	DU 6-21-61	DU 6-61	CE 2-12-71	CE 2-71		2-76	Dest: Fire: LO 2-7-76; Dism: Lorain, Ohio, 11-16-76	
C2069	Yes	8-26		6-53			Partial 2-61	GW 10-8-69	CE 3-70		6-74	Sold: Carl Nourse, Columbus, OH, 6-18-74; $800	(see Vol IV)
C2070	Yes	8-26		7-52		WA 3-20-59					4-75	Sold: private owner, Muskegon, MI, 4-15-75	(see Vol V)
C2071		8-26									3-42	Sold to Alton Railroad	one of six I-5 cars sold to Alton
C2072		8-26		6-52							9-65	Dismantled: B&O shops, Du Bois, PA	scrapped
C2073	Yes	8-26		5-51	KY 12-41	KY 10-11-55					10-67	Sold: Red Clay Valley Rwy Equip. Co. from MTC, 10-17-67	AFE 52585; (see Vol V)
C2074	Yes	8-26		5-50	MTC 7-15-54						9-15-83	Sold: Mansbach Metal from Russell, KY, 9-15-83	inspected at MTC 4-20-54, lettered I-5C but found to be I-5
C2075	Yes	8-26		11-52	KY 2-42	KY 9-20-57					1-81	Sold at Ridgeley to Brock Scrap and Salvage, 1-8-83	painted BW 12-63

Number	Pic ?	Built	Early "CF"	"AB" Brakes	I-5C	I-5D	I-5Dm	ACI Plate	1970-71 Paint	Misc. Paint	Retired	Disposition	Comments
C2076	Yes	8-26		2-49		DU 3-28-56	DU 4-61				6-71	Donated: WV School for the Deaf, Romney, WV, 6-10-71	AFE 54579 (see Vol III)
C2077	Yes	8-26		5-51		DU 12-31-56					12-67	Sold: Indiana Metals, Inc. as scrap, E. Chicago, IN, 12-6-67	scrapped
C2078	Yes	8-26		3-53	was a "C"?	DU 12-1-61	DU 12-61	CE 4-3-70	CE 4-70		3-76	Sold: Harvey Cohn, Owings Mills, MD, 3-31-76; $1000	2404 form shows "I-5C" to "I-5D"; (see Vol IV)
C2079	Yes	8-26			KY 10-41		DU 3-62				3-76	Sold: Harvey Cohn, Owings Mills, MD, 3-31-76; $1000	(see Vol IV)
C2080	Yes	8-26		7-49	KY 8-41	WA 4-20-60		CE 1-20-70	CE 7-70		3-73	Sold: Robert Fracci, Mentor, OH, 3-27-73; $800	(see Vol II)
C2081	Yes	8-26		7-53	KY 10-41	GS 4-24-53	DU 5-61				9-77	Don: WV Army National Guard., Huntington, WV, 9-19-77;	AFE 56971; shipped from CE (see Vol I) body only (no longer there)
C2082	Yes	8-26		6-50	KY 3-42	KY 4-23-56		CE 5-6-71	CE 5-71		5-79	Don: Bluegrass RR Museum, Lexington, KY, 5-17-79;	AFE 57600 (see Vol I & III); scrapped spring 2014
C2083	Yes	8-26		5-53	DU 5-21-53	DU 12-20-56					4-74	Destroyed and Dismantled: Keyser, WV, 4-22-74	(see Vol III); number changed to C2225
C2084	Yes	8-26	8-35	5-52				CE 8-11-70	CE 8-70		11-76	Sold: Tom Jones, Stow, Ohio, 11-11-76 for $1000	cement floor at CU 7-10-35; (see Vol III)
C2085	Yes	8-26									8-38	Acc: Landsdowne, MD, 10-17-37; Destroyed: Fire	2404 form: MTC 8-6-38
C2086	Yes	8-26		11-50		MTC 9-23-55	DU 4-62			BW 6-69	5-78	Sold: Midwest Steel, from MTC, 5-16-78	fire damaged: Locust Point 5-4-75
C2087	Yes	8-26									12-39	Rebuilt to C2503 at Cumberland, MD, 12-7-39	
C2088		8-26									2-50	Old date--no doubt scrapped by B&O	scrapped
C2089	Yes	8-26		5-49		KY 11-23-55	DU 4-62	BW 11-11-70		BW 5-69	5-78	Sold: Midwest Steel, from Mt. Clare, 5-16-78	scrapped
C2090	Yes	8-26		3-53	KY 5-41						11-65	Dismantled: B&O shops, Garett, IN	I-5 to I-5C at Lorain, OH, 3-6-53
C2091		9-26									3-40	Rebuilt and renumbered to caboose C2504, CU, 1-3-40	
C2092	Yes	9-26		3-51	KY 8-41	MTC 10-4-55	DU 4-62				3-67	Dismantled: B&O shops, Brunswick, MD, 3-16-67	scrapped
C2093	Yes	9-26		11-51	KY 7-41						9-65	Dismantled: B&O shops, Du Bois, PA	scrapped
C2094 (1st)		9-26									10-26	destroyed Swan Creek, WV, 10-4-26 with 2 other cabs	scrapped
C2094 (2nd)	Yes	9-26		4-52	KY 8-41	KY 10-26-55					1-70	Dismantled: Arlington, NY, 1-15-70; on SIRT	Renumbered from C2100 (1st) Damaged: fire: Berkeley Springs, WV, $1200
C2095	Yes	9-26		3-52		KY 11-21-56		Yes	CE 9-71		9-78	Sold: Jack Amatucci, Brunswick, MD, 9-28-78; $1200	(see Vol III); now displayed Mt. Airy, MD (see Vol V)
C2096	Yes	9-26		1-52	DU 4-22-55		DU 12-61				1-81	Removed from ownership, car could not be found (1-15-81)	newspaper clip. @ Balt. Early 60s in serv., photo: destroyed: fire: Baltimore, 2-20-66
C2097	Yes	9-26		1-51	KY 8-41	MTC 9-12-55	DU 3-62				6-76	Sold: Portsmouth Iron & Metal from Chillicothe, 11-27-79	Reported as destroyed Halethorpe Calvert Dist., Locust Point, MD, 1-16-74
C2098	Yes	9-26		6-53	DU 6-12-53						11-66	Sold: from SO, Black Diamond RR, Flemington, NJ, 11-66	Also reported sold: Merritt, Inc., Flemington, NJ (see Vol V)
C2099	Yes	9-26		2-53	KY 11-41	KY 7-9-57					8-67	On display: Severn, MD, at garden center	(see Vol II)
C2100 (1st)		9-26									1-27	Renumbered to become C2094 (2nd) at Riverside, MD	
C2100 (2nd)	Yes	4-27		5-52	CU 12-40						12-68	Dismantled: B&O shops, Du Bois, PA, 12-11-68	scrapped
C2101	Yes	4-27		7-52	KY 3-42	KY 12-12-56		CE 1-20-70	CE 1-70		6-76	Sold: George W. Barnette, JR., 6-24-76	See Note 4
C2102	Yes	4-27		7-52	KY 3-42						4-70	Dismantled: B&O shops, Du Bois, PA, 4-30-70	scrapped
C2103	Yes	4-27		1-52		KY 12-7-55		CE 2-23-71	CE 2-71		6-74	Sold: Interlake, Inc., Newport, KY, 6-13-74; $800	scrapped on Interlake's property, Newport, KY
C2104	Yes	4-27		5-52	KY 12-40	GS 6-11-54		CE 4-27-71	CE 4-71		RUS 8-17-83	Sold: Mansbach Metal, Ashland, KY, 10-12-83;	sold from Russell, KY
C2105		4-27		12-50	DU 10-23-52	DU 3-8-56	Partial 2-61				8-65	Dismantled: B&O shops, Du Bois, PA	scrapped
C2106	Yes	4-27		10-52	DU 10-6-52	DU 8-14-61	DU 8-61				6-68	Dismantled: B&O shops, Brunswick, MD, 6-27-68	scrapped
C2107		4-27									12-48	Old date--no doubt scrapped by B&O	scrapped
C2108		4-27									3-42	Sold to Alton Railroad	One of six I-5 cars sold to Alton
C2109	Yes	4-27		DU 12-1-53							3-68	Destroyed: Newark, NJ, on CNJ 3-23-68	scrapped
C2110	Yes	4-27		8-50	1-53	DU 8-7-61	DU 8-61	CE 1-27-70	CE 1-70		11-77	Sold: Winters RR Service, Inc., N. Collins, NY, 11-28-77; $900	Damaged: fire: Du Bois, PA, 4-29-48; (see Vol V)
C2111		4-27			DU 3-41						4-52	Destroyed: Fire	scrapped
C2112	Yes	4-27		11-49	KY 9-41	GS 4-9-54					7-62	Grafton, WV, used as cabin at Tygart Lake, sold 6-13-62	(see Vol IV); now scrapped
C2113	Yes	4-27		2-51	KY 10-41	WA 11-13-56					6-72	Sold: Dr. Byron Bernard, Cincinnati, OH, 6-2-72; $800	(see Vol V); resold and moved down south
C2114	Yes	4-27		11-52		KY 9-3-57		CE 4-23-71	CE 4-71		RUS 8-17-83	Sold: Mansbach Metal, Ashland, KY, 10-12-83;	scrapped
C2115	Yes	4-27		5-52		DU 12-5-56	DU 4-61	CE 1-29-70	CE 1-70		11-72	Donated: American Legion, Chillicothe, Ohio, 11-5-72;	AFE 55117; (see Vol I), displayed in city park
C2116	Yes	4-27		6-50		DU 2-1-56	DU 6-61	CE 4-10-70	CE 4-70		8-73	Donated: Roweton Boys Ranch, Chillicothe, OH, 8-7-73;	AFE 55432; (see Vol II)
C2117		4-27									3-40	Rebuilt to caboose C2505 at Cumberland, 1-25-40	

Number	Pic ?	Built	Early "CF"	"AB" Brakes	I-5c	I-5D	I-5Dm	ACI Plate	1970-71 Paint	Misc. Paint	Retired	Disposition	Comments
C2118		4-27		6-52	KY 8-40						9-52	Rear end collision: Chestnut Hill WV, 8-3-52	2404 form: Benwod 9-2-52
C2119		4-27		7-50	MTC 9-30	KY 11-18-55					3-69	Dismantled: B&O shops, Cowen, WV, 3-20-69; AFE 53302	then donated: John Douglas, Otter, WV / See Note 5
C2120	Yes	4-27		GS 9-25-53	GS 9-26-53	DU 12-61					3-73	Sold: Midwest Steel and Alloy, Cleveland, Ohio, 3-30-73	scrapped
C2121		4-27									4-30	Accident: 1-18-30, near E. Side, Philadelphia, PA	also reported: BW, MD
C2122	Yes	4-27		LO 10-23-53		DU 8-15-61	DU 8-61	CE 5-18-70	CE 5-70		8-72	Sys. Acc: Flora, IL, 8-17-72; Sold: scrapper, Portsmouth, OH	Sold: M.D. Friedman, Portsmouth, OH (see Vol I) as C-2122 (2nd)
C2123	Yes	4-27		6-50		KY 12-15-55		CE 7-16-70	CE 7-70		RUS 8-17-83	Sold: Mansbach Metal, Ashland, KY, 8-12-83	scrapped
C2124	Yes	4-27		7-53	GS 4-3-53			CE 12-18-70	CE 12-70		12-75	Sold: George Silcott, Worthington, OH,12-19-75 $1000	at an oil company at PV then to depot (see Vol IV); burned and rebuilt at PV depot
C2125	Yes	4-27		7-52			Yes		CE 9-71		11-74	Sold: Whitewater Valley RR, Connersville, IN, 11-5-74; $800	(see Vol III)
C2126		4-27									10-40	Rebuilt to caboose C2506 at Cumberland 9-10-40	
C2127	Yes	4-27		11-50		DU 8-28-61	DU 9-61			CU 7-74	11-77	Donated: city of Columbus Grove, Ohio, 11-3-77; AFE 57098	later to Westminster, Ohio, on Dave Lee farm; (see Vol II)
C2128	Yes	4-27						CE 5-28-70	CE 5-70		6-76	Sold: George W. Barnette, Jr., 6-24-76	See Note 4
C2129	Yes	4-27		11-49		KY 4-16-57		No	CE 5-70		11-74	Sold: Whitewater Valley RR, Connersville, IN, 11-5-74; $800	(see Vol III)
C2130	Yes	4-27		1-55							1-82	Sold: Midwest Steel, from Haselton, Ohio, 1-29-82	scrapped
C2131	Yes	4-27		6-51		MTC 1-4-55					2-66	Dismantled: B&O shops, Somerset, PA, 1-6-66	scrapped
C2132	Yes	4-27		6-52	GS 2-10-54			CE 8-11-70	CE 8-70		6-77	Donated: Chi Rho House, Inc., Newark, OH, 6-28-77	AFE 56972; (see Vol II)
C2133	Yes	4-27		10-52	CU 12-40	KY 6-29-56	DU 3-61				1-70	Dismantled: B&O, Arlington, NY, 1-15-70 on SIRT	scrapped
C2134	Yes	4-27		6-53		DU 8-29-55	Partial 3-61				11-66	Sold: R. E. Summers, from Chillicothe, 10-31-67	(see Vol II); displayed at Washington, PA home; later scrapped
C2135	Yes	4-27		12-52	CU 12-40	KY 1-30-56		CE 3-12-71	CE 3-71		7-72	Sold: Daniel Fandrey, Newark, OH, 7-3-72 for $522.50	(see Vol III)
C2136	Yes	4-27									7-55	Cond: DU, certificate #5, 7-13-55; Dism: Du Bois shops	scrapped
C2137	Yes	4-27		11-52	DU 4-41	DU 11-30-55	Partial 2-61			MTC 10-69	3-73	Sold: Midwest Steel & Alloy Corp., Cleveland, OH, 3-30-73	special yellow paint scheme at Baltimore in 1969; painted at Mount Clare
C2138	Yes	4-27		see note 1-22-54	DU 4-41			No	CE 8-71		10-83	Sold: Luria Brothers, Cleveland, OH, 10-13-83	also reported: Brier Hill Scrap Co., Haselton PV and GRF reported AB brakes 1-22-54
C2139	Yes	5-27		LI 2-15-52		WA 1-30-57		Yes	CE 8-70	CE 10-77	7-77	Sold scrap: D.J.Joseph, Wilder, KY; burned & scrapped	burned and scrapped at scrap dealer 10-87 per telcon with scrapper
C2140	Yes	5-27		11-51							8-69	Dismantled: B&O shops, Du Bois, PA, 8-7-69	scrapped
C2141	Yes	5-27		6-53	WA 4-28-53	DU 12-61		BW 10-24-69		BW 10-69	6-73	Sold: Thomas Ward, Baltimore, MD, 6-25-73 on s.o. # 4723 $800	(see Vol III)
C2142		5-27		KY 2-18-52		KY 11-3-55					5-66	Dismantled: B&O shops, Brunswick, MD	scrapped
C2143	Yes	5-27		1-53		KY 7-26-57	DU 10-61				10-83	Retired at Youngstown and sold to Luria Brothers (scrapper)	sold 10-13-83
C2144	Yes	5-27		3-52							6-64	Sold: private owner, Somerset, PA	(see Vol V)
C2145		5-27		5-52							8-63	no data; assigned to Benwood 1961	reproduction displayed in Holloway, OH, park
C2146		5-27									9-36	Acc: 2-13-36, Bridgeport, West Virginia; scrapped	scrapped
C2147	Yes	5-27		5-52							7-62	Grafton, WV, used as cabin at Tygart Lake, sold 6-13-62	(see Vol IV); now scrapped
C2148		5-27			GW 12-26-40						8-49	Old date--no doubt scrapped by B&O	scrapped
C2149	Yes	5-27			DU 4-41	DU 5-2-56	DU 9-61	CE 4-10-70	CE 7-71		6-76	Donated: Historic Ellicott City, MD, 6-14-76; AFE 56883	(see Vol I)
C2150	Yes	5-27		12-48	DU 10-28-52		Partial 3-61	CE 3-30-70	CE 3-70		6-74	Sold: Art Davis, Wooster, Ohio, 6-13-74; $250	fire damaged: Oak Hill, OH, 2-12-74; (see Vol II)
C2151	Yes	5-27		12-51	WA 5-21-53			CE 12-31-70	CE 12-70	CE 5-75	8-75	Sold: Ralph Smith, Newark, OH, 8-13-75.	system acc: Newark, 7-23-75; (see Vol I)
C2152	Yes	5-27		3-51		WA 12-18-55					12-75	Donated: City of Loogootee, IN, 12-23-75; later to French Lick, IN	AFE 56525; (see Vol IV); at French Lick museum/tourist line
C2153	Yes	5-27		1-52		WA 12-10-57					9-60	Fire Damaged: Renick, Ohio, 8-31-60; scrapped	scrapped
C2154	Yes	5-27		9-52	GW 12-28-40	DU 5-17-56	DU 8-61				3-68	Sold: private owner, Pittsburgh, PA, 3-21-68	(see Vol V)
C2155	Yes	5-27		9-52	GW 1-15-41	DU 8-29-61	DU 9-61				7-77	Sold: Mansbach Metal, Ashland, KY, 7-21-77, trucks kept at PR	destroyed: fire: Baden, WV 1-5-76
C2156		5-27									3-42	Sold: Alton Railroad	One of six I-5 cars sold to Alton
C2157	Yes	5-27		7-51	GW 4-25-41	DU 10-10-55	DU 5-61				9-77	Sold: H. Phillip Schobeloch, Chillicothe, 9-28-77; $1000	(see Vol I & IV)
C2158	Yes	5-27		6-51	DU 11-13-52	DU 6-28-56	Partial 1-61				8-73	Sold: E. H. Castle, Rowlesburg, WV, 8-8-73, $800	(see Vol II & IV); at Cool Springs Park
C2159	Yes	5-27		7-49	GS 3-30-53			CE 9-1-71	CE 9-71		RUS 8-17-84	Sold: Mansbach Metal, 8-17-84, Ashland, KY	System Accident: Parkersburg, WV 11-11-76
C2160	Yes	5-27	8-35	MTC 8-31-51							11-67	Sold: Indianapolis Union Railway, 11-17-67; AFE 52641	cement floor at CU 7-18-35; one of three I-5 cars sold to IURY
C2161	Yes	5-27		7-53		DU 11-8-55	DU 6-61				8-73	Sold: E. H. Castle, Rowlesburg, WV, 8-8-73; $800	(see Vol II & IV); at Cool Springs Park

Number	Pic?	Built	Early "CF"	"AB" Brakes	I-5C	I-5D	I-5Dm	ACI Plate	1970-71 Paint	Misc. Paint	Retired	Disposition	Comments
C2162	Yes	5-27		4-53		DU 1-19-56	DU 6-61	GW 1-29-70	CE 5-70		6-74	Sold: Art Davis, Wooster, Ohio, 6-13-74; $800	(see Vol II)
C2163	Yes	5-27		7-51	12-53	DU 6-24-55					4-70	Dismantled: B&O shops, Du Bois, PA, 4-30-70	scrapped
C2164	Yes	5-27		3-51	KY 9-41	MTC 12-17-54		CE 3-31-71	CE 3-71		11-75	Sold: Bud Brady, Elyria, OH, 11-3-75; $1000	(see Vol II)
C2165	Yes	5-27		10-49		DU 12-24-58	Partial 1-61	CE 3-5-71	CE 3-71	GRF 4-75	RUS 8-17-83	Sold: Mansbach Metal, Ashland, KY, 8-17-83	car at Benwood 8-5-80
C2166		5-27		12-49							4-71	Destroyed: Fire: Barr Yd; Sold: Industrial Salvage, 4-19-71	Destroyed: Fire: Chicago on B&OCT 3-7-71
C2167		5-27									7-58	Cond: WA, certificate #3, 6-25-58; also Cond: WA 7-28-58	scrapped
C2168	Yes	5-27		5-53	KY 11-40	DU 1-24-57				DU 8-68	10-75	Sold: DABO, Inc., Wooster, OH, 10-28-75, (DABO is Art Davis)	also reported to "I-5C" at DU 5-14-53 painted DU 8-68 w/yellow ends for B&OCT svc.
C2169	Yes	5-27		GA 4-1-54	GA 4-1-54			CE 3-12-71	CE 3-71		10-74	Sold: Charles H. Prinz, Dayton, Ohio, 10-29-74; $800	(see Vol II)
C2170	Yes	5-27		6-53	DU 6-16-53			CE 4-20-70	CE 4-70		3-73	Sold: B.L. Rhodes Co., Chardon, Ohio, 3-27-73; $800	(see Vol I)
C2171	Yes	5-27		9-52	?						10-69	Sold: private owner, 10-16-69	Damaged: fire: Hancock, WV, 10-25-48 with C-2324; (see Vol V)
C2172	Yes	5-27		10-51		GS 6-28-54	DU 12-61				10-73	Sold: Warther Museum, Inc., Dover, OH, 10-16-73; $800	renumbered to C2122 at museum; (see Vol I)
C2173	Yes	5-27		10-51	CE 12-2-55			CE 5-21-70	CE 5-70		11-74	Sold: Art Davis, Wooster, Ohio, 11-7-75	Last I-5C conversion--at Chillicothe !; System Accident: Brooklyn Jct., WV, 3-16-73
C2174	Yes	6-27		LI 8-24-51	WA 2-19-57						8-68	no data in Huntington files assigned to Tol Div 1961	
C2175	Yes	6-27		4-50	WA 9-13-60			CE 3-26-71	Probably	WAL 6-76	4-81	Sold: Kenneth Gill--Grand Rapids, MI, 4-1-81 on sales order 4692	(see Vol III)
C2176	Yes	6-27		12-52							3-68	Sold: Joe Kear, Chillicothe, Ohio, 3-6-68; AFE 52739	(see Vol IV)
C2177	Yes	6-27		1-55		KY 2-1-56	DU 3-62			BW 12-69	5-78	Sold: Midwest Steel, Mt. Clare, MD, 5-16-78	scrapped
C2178	Yes	6-27		7-52		KY 10-25-57					10-63	Sold from Du Bois to private owner from DU	(see Vol V); used as cabin; no trucks
C2179	Yes	6-27		5-51		KY 12-2-55					9-63	Sold: Norris Boucher from Du Bois, PA, shops	(see Vol V); located near Luthersburg, PA now scrapped
C2180	Yes	6-27		7-53		KY 5-8-57					8-67	Donated: city of Vienna, West Virginia; AFE 52401	Damaged: fire: Brunswick, MD, 1-18-40 (see Vol III)
C2181	Yes	6-27		1-55		MTC 9-27-54	DU 4-61			MTC 1-64	6-76	Sold: Betty Porter, Pataskala, OH 6-9-76; $1000	MTC inspected 5-54: cab is I-5 but stenciled I-5C; (see Vol II), resold, moved along I 70
C2182	Yes	6-27		GS 10-8-54		GS 10-8-54					5-75	Sold: Friedman Metals, from Chillicothe, OH, 5-7-75	trucks retained at FR when sold
C2183	Yes	6-27		10-52		KY 6-5-57		CE 6-18-70	CE 6-70		11-74	Sold: Art Davis, Wooster, Ohio, 11-7-74; (see Vol II)	fire damaged: Lockland, OH, 5-7-74
C2184		6-27			Yes						5-56	Destroyed: Wreck: Cumbo yard, 5-24-56; taken to Keyser shop	also reported wrecked on 5-1-56 at Cumbo
C2185	Yes	6-27		1-55	CU 12-40	DU 4-10-62	DU 6-62				8-68	Dismantled: B&O shops, Brunswick, MD, 8-2-68	scrapped
C2186	Yes	6-27		10-50		MTC 5-2-55					2-68	Sold: M. Jane Rettenstein Hospital, Chillicothe, 2-16-68; $350	(see Vol I)
C2187	Yes	6-27		3-53	DU 3-23-53	DU 5-10-61	DU 5-61	Yes	CE 10-71		8-79	Don: Bangor, MI, Downtown Devel. Authority, 8-17-79;	AFE 57825 sold from Chillicothe; (see Vol II)
C2188	Yes	6-27		6-53		GS 6-19-53					7-62	Condemned: MTC 6-19-62 2404 form: MTC 6-29-62	I-5D class; assigned Balt Term. 1961 Damaged: fire: Parkersburg, WV, 6-12-43
C2189	Yes	6-27		5-51		KY 6-22-56					RUS 8-17-83	Sold: Mansbach Metal, Ashland, KY, 8-17-83	car located at Fairmont, WV, 8-5-80
C2190	Yes	6-27		5-50		KY 5-7-56					1-74	Sold: Bridgeville, PA, Public Library, 1-2-74; $800	(see Vol I)
C2191	Yes	6-27									10-55	Wrecked 7-55 in collision on Monongah Division	wrecked 7-21-55 on Short Line Subdivision with engine 4433 and diesel 904
C2192	Yes	6-27									6-64	Sold: William M. Bill, Frederick, MD	later to a restaurant at Thurmont, MD (see Vol II); still later scheduled for auction
C2193	Yes	6-27		12-51	KY 6-42	WA 3-2-60					7-68	Destroyed: on B&O at Flora, IL, 7-9-68	scrapped
C2194	Yes	6-27		5-50	KY 6-40	WA 2-23-60					9-68	Dismantled: B&O shops, Washington, IN, 9-28-68	Destroyed: Shoals, IN, 9-28-68
C2195	Yes	6-27		7-51	KY 8-40	KY 12-28-56					1-75	Sold: George Fee, 1-8-75 $800 AFE 55923	See Note 6
C2196	Yes	6-27		3-51							6-76	Given to former Cincinnati Police Chief "off the books"	(see Vol V)
C2197		6-27									6-52	Destroyed: Fire 10-45	scrapped
C2198	Yes	6-27		1-55		KY 3-16-56		CE 3-10-70	3-70	7-71	10-80	Sold: Cravat Coal, Holloway, Ohio, 10-23-80	(see Vol IV)
C2199	Yes	6-27			8-54 see note >	KY 11-3-55					6-69	Sold: W.D. Ferguson, Steamburg, NY, 6-9-69	* also reported MTC 4-20-54 (see Vol II)
C2200	Yes	8-29		1-55	KY 7-41	KY 9-30-55		CE 9-17-70	CE 9-70		8-73	Sold: private owner, Wheeling, WV, 8-8-73	(see Vol V)
C2201		8-29									5-39	Acc: Point of Rocks, MD, 5-3-39; MTC issued report	scrapped
C2202	Yes	8-29		MTC 8-14-51	KY 6-41						11-75	Donated: Grove City, Ohio, Jaycee's, 11-7-75; AFE 56488	later to Green's Farm, Orient, OH; (see Vol I)
C2203	Yes	8-29		5-51	KY 1-42	MTC 7-20-55		CE 10-1-70	CE 9-70		4-77	Sold: Becky Eller, Proctor, West Virginia, 4-19-77	(see Vol I & III)
C2204	Yes	8-29		4-50				CE 11-21-70	CE 11-70		3-76	Sold: Harvey Cohn, Owings Mills, MD, 3-31-76; $1000	(see Vol IV)
C2205	Yes	8-29		11-52							5-69	Dismantled: B&O shops, Chillicothe, OH, 5-13-69	scrapped

Number	Pic ?	Built	Early "CF"	"AB" Brakes	I-5C	I-5D	I-5Dm	ACI Plate	1970-71 Paint	Misc. Paint	Retired	Disposition	Comments
C2206	Yes	8-29		4-53		WA 5-31-57					9-74	Sold: private owner-- PA, 9-11-74	sold for $800; (see Vol V)
C2207	Yes	8-29		12-50		WA 2-4-59		CE 12-14-70	CE 12-70		1-76	Sold: H.W. Martell, Kent, Ohio, 1-13-76; $1000	Mr. Martell is associated with Thomas Asphalt Paving Co.; (see Vol II)
C2208	Yes	8-29		2-53		WA 2-13-59		Yes	CE 10-70		3-75	Sold: Warehouse Services, Columbus, OH	(see Vol II & IV)
C2209		8-29									7-36	Acc: Middletown, OH, 6-2-36; Ivorydale report 7-30-36	scrapped
C2210	Yes	8-29		11-49		WA 5-29-56		CE 4-30-70	CE 5-70	CU 5-74	4-77	Sold: Don Plotkin, Monticello, IL, 4-14-77 from CE	kept at the Monticello (IL) Railway Museum (see Vol III)
C2211		8-29									4-38	Fire: 3-21-38; 2404 form made out at Ivorydale, OH	Damaged: fire: Miamisburg, OH, 3-21-38
C2212	Yes	8-29		11-49				CE 8-4-70	CE 7-70		12-75	Sold: Replicap Products, Greenville, Ohio, 12-4-75	sold for $1000; (see Vol III)
C2213	Yes	8-29		11-50		DU 3-29-60		CE 12-31-70	CE 12-70		8-81	Sold: Portsmouth Iron & Met'l. as scrap, 8-21-81	fire damaged at Barr Yard 12-1-76
C2214	Yes	8-29		GRF 1-14-54		KY 1-5-56					7-67	Dismantled: B&O shops, Fairmont, WV, 7-11-67	AFE 52172
C2215	Yes	8-29		3-51	8-54	KY 4-19-57	DU 3-62				11-67	Sold: Ron Sherry, Coopersburg, PA, 11-10-67	AFE 52620; (see Vol I)
C2216	Yes	8-29		7-50							11-67	Sold: Indianapolis Union Railway, 11-17-67	AFE 52641; one of three I-5 family cars sold to IURY
C2217	Yes	8-29		6-50		GS 12-22-53					4-59	Wrecked 3-3-59, Brooklyn Jct, WV, diesel 9243	scrapped
C2218	Yes	8-29		5-53		MTC 1-21-54		CE 4-23-71	CE 4-71		7-76	Sold: private owner, Sugarcreek, Ohio, 7-15-76	(see Vol V)
C2219		8-29									10-40	Rebuilt to B&O caboose C2507 at Cumberland 10-4-40	had been reported as accident 8-24-33 at Locust Point
C2220		8-29									1-32	Accident: Locust Point, Baltimore, 1-24-32	also reported: wrecked, Della, MD 1-24-32 MTC made out 2404 form: 1-26-34
C2221	Yes	8-29		4-50			DU 3-62	BW 10-24-69		BW 10-69	3-76	Sold: Harvey Cohn, Owings Mills, MD, 3-31-67; $1000	(see Vol IV)
C2222	Yes	8-29		MTC 8-14-51		KY 2-8-57		CE 6-11-70	CE 6-70	HTG 1975	1-75	Sold: Virginia Tanner, Baltimore, 1-13-75	AFE 55923; later to B&O RR Museum see book *B&O RR Museum Cabooses*
C2223	Yes	8-29		4-50	KY 3-41	DU 12-19-55	9-61	CE 4-9-71	CE 6-70		10-76	Sold: Ruth Nash, Harpers Ferry, WV, 10-28-76	(see Vol II)
C2224	Yes	8-29						CE 2-26-71	CE 2-71		12-76	Sold: Commercial Logistics Corp, 12-16-76 $1000	Jeffersonville, IN, at elementary school (see Vol II)
C2225 (1st)	Yes	8-29		8-52		KY 10-17-55	Yes				7-75	Donated: Historical Society of Mineral Co., WV, AFE 55612	(see Vol III); C-2225 (2nd) renumbered from C-2083 at Keyser; car located Burtonsville, MD
C2226	Yes	8-29		GS 11-27-53				CE 3-6-70	CE 3-70		5-72	Donated: Davies County CofC-- Washington, IN, 5-9-72;	AFE 54971; (see Vol V)
C2227	Yes	9-29		7-52		KY 2-29-56		CE 3-18-71	CE 3-71		9-15-83	Sold: Mansbach Metal, Ashland, KY, from Russell, 9-15-83	car at Grafton, WV, July 1981
C2228	Yes	9-29		3-50	CU 12-40	KY 11-16-55					6-66	Dismantled: B&O shops, Chillicothe, OH	scrapped
C2229	Yes	9-29		10-51				CE 6-26-70	CE 6-70		12-81	Donated: Bridgeport, WV, Booster Club, 4-3-82; AFE 58702	car at Grafton, WV, July 1981; (see Vol I)
C2230	Yes	9-29		PV 9-1-53	GW 12-14-40	DU 8-7-61	DU 8-61				12-80	Re#'d XM915 @HA 12-11-80; Dism: Youngstown 5-11-83	Sold: Luria Brothers 9-10-83 (scrapper)
C2231	Yes	9-29		11-50	KY 3-42	KY 5-28-57					9-66	Sold: Bill C. Armagost, Coal & RR Co., from Somerset, PA	refurbished at Ill. Rwy. Museum; (see Vol IV)
C2232	Yes	9-29				GS 11-19-54		CE 5-18-70	CE 5-70		11-74	Sold: Whitewater Valley RR, Connersville, IN, 11-5-74	Sold for $800; (see Vol I)
C2233	Yes	9-29		6-53	DU 10-13-52	DU 2-2-56	DU 5-61	CE 12-31-70	CE 12-70	RUS	8-17-83	Sold: Mansbach Metal, Ashland, KY, 7-23-83	car at Clarksburg, WV, 8-5-80
C2234	Yes	9-29		6-52							1-67	Sold: D.B. Frampton, Columbus, Ohio, from Somerset, PA	(see Vol I)
C2235	Yes	9-29		DU 10-25-55		DU 10-25-55	9-61	GW 10-2-69	CE 3-70		4-77	Donated: Boy Scouts, Evans City, PA, 4-19-77	AFE 56888; now displayed in downtown Mars, PA (see Vol II)
C2236	Yes	9-29		6-51		DU 10-28-55		CE 4-9-71	CE 4-71		1-76	Sold: R.G. Robertson, Ft. Wayne, IN, 1-14-76; $1000	Damaged: fire: Butler Jct., PA, 12-9-54; (see Vol I)
C2237	Yes	9-29		9-52	GW 1-41	DU 6-14-61	DU 6-61	GW 9-18-69	CE 3-70		6-74	Sold: Art Davis, Wooster, Ohio, 6-13-74; $800	(see Vol III)
C2238	Yes	9-29		11-48	DU 5-41	DU 9-15-61		CE 3-26-71	CE 3-71		7-82	Don: Western MD College, Westminster, MD, 10-82	changed to WM 1895 for display purposes AFE 59010; (see Vol I)
C2239	Yes	9-29		9-50		WA 1-15-54		CE 2-10-70	CE 2-70		10-79	Sold: Ronnie Drake Constr. Co., Walkerton, IN, 10-7-75	sold for $1000; this company purchased three I-5 family cabs; see Note 7
C2240	Yes	9-29		6-53		WA 6-22-53		CE 5-28-70	CE 5-70		8-73	Sold: T. Smith, Brecksville, OH 8-2-73; $800	(see Vol II)
C2241	Yes	9-29		11-52	DU 11-3-52	DU 2-15-56	DU 6-61				2-65	Dismantled: B&O shops, Benwood, WV, 9-65	Damaged: fire: New Castle, PA, 11-29-45
C2242	Yes	9-29		1-50	DU 5-41	DU 10-17-55	DU 4-61	GW 11-3-69	CE 5-70	RUS	8-17-83	Sold: Mansbach Metal, Ashland, KY, 8-17-83	car at Brunswick, MD, 8-5-80
C2243	Yes	9-29		7-52		KY 1-23-56	DU 10-61				4-69	Dismantled at Cumberland due to fire, 4-2-69	scrapped
C2244	Yes	9-29		12-48		DU 7-14-61	DU 7-61				3-70	Dism: FR 1-14-71; Dest: Chilton Siding, PA	painted SO 8-59; destroyed Chilton Siding, PA, 3-25-70
C2245	Yes	9-29		1-51							7-74	Sold: C.E. Ruff, Newark, Ohio, 7-25-74; $836	(see Vol II)
C2246	Yes	9-29		DU 9-1-53	DU 2-41	DU 2-20-59	Partial 3-61	GW 10-20-69			3-70	Dest: Rankin, PA; Dism: Chillicothe, OH, 7-17-70	destroyed by fire 3-24-70, Rankin, PA
C2247	Yes	9-29		10-52	GW 1-10-41	DU 6-4-56	DU 3-61				2-65	Dest: Fire: Jacobs Creek, PA; New Castle reported	scrapped
C2248	Yes	9-29		5-52		GS 7-31-53		CE 1-29-71	CE 1-71	CE 4-77	2-84	Sold: Mansbach Metal from Russell, KY, 2-13-84; AFE 58097	scrapped
C2249	Yes	9-29		6-53	DU 2-41	DU 5-9-56	DU 7-61	CE 3-18-70	CE 3-70		5-78	Sold: Midwest Steel, from MTC 5-16-78	fire damaged at MTC 4-11-75

Number	Pic ?	Built	Early "CF"	"AB" Brakes	I-5C	I-5D	I-5Dm	ACI Plate	1970-71 Paint	Misc. Paint	Retired	Disposition	Comments
C2250	Yes	9-29		2-51		KY 1-18-56		CE 9-9-70	CE 9-70		9-80	Donated: Boy Scouts, Ft. Wayne, IN, 9-16-80	AFE 57916; sold from Chillicothe; (see Vol IV)
C2251	Yes	9-29		12-51		KY 5-23-56					4-74	Don: St. Francis & St. Mary Churches, Brunswick, MD	donated 4-18-74; sold on AFE 55666 telcon with church: they know nothing about this
C2252	Yes	9-29		4-51							12-68	Donated: City of Deshler, OH, 12-19-68	scrapped ca. 1990; (see Vol I)
C2253		9-29		4-53	DU 4-27-53	DU 8-30-55	Partial 2-61				4-69	Dismantled: B&O shops, Du Bois, PA, 4-21-69	scrapped
C2254	Yes	9-29		3-53		GS 12-10-53					7-62	Grafton, WV, used as cabin at Tygart Lake; sold 6-13-62	(see Vol III & IV); now scrapped
C2255	Yes	9-29		9-49		WA 6-10-57		CE 1-29-70	CE 1-70		1-73	Dism: Holloway; used as building; sold: private owner	Dism: HO 1-31-73; (see Vol IV)
C2256	Yes	9-29		11-51							11-68	Sold: International Car Corp., Kenton, OH, 11-8-68	disposition from ICC unknown
C2257		10-29		5-53		GS 5-4-53					6-69	Dismantled: B&O shops, Benwood, WV, 6-16-69	scrapped
C2258	Yes	10-29		9-52		GS 7-24-53		Yes	CE 2-71		11-83	Sold: scrap dealer Mansbach Metal, 11-22-83;	scrapped
C2259		10-29									8-38	Acc: Mt. Clare 8-21-38; Acc: Hastings, WV, 7-30-37	2404 form: MTC 8-22-37
C2260	Yes	10-29		2-51	KY 12-40	KY 12-20-55		Yes	CE 8-71	CE 5-75	8-21-80	Sold: Portsmouth Iron & Metal as scrap 8-21-81	Limbo at Chillicothe 11-27-79
C2261	Yes	10-29		2-53		GS 7-30-54		CE 1-29-71	CE 1-71		6-76	Donated: Boy Scouts, Perry, OH, 6-16-76	AFE 56532; (see Vol III)
C2262	Yes	10-29	DU 12-21-53		12-53	DU 3-5-56	DU 5-61	CE 6-18-71	CE 6-71		7-81	Sold: Luntz Corp., from Willard, OH, 7-31-81	Luntz is a scrap company
C2263	Yes	10-29	LO 10-14-53								9-65	Dismantled: B&O shops, Du Bois, PA	Damaged: fire: Painesville, OH, 7-20-44
C2264	Yes	10-29		9-52							4-69	Dismantled: B&O shops, Willard, OH, 4-28-69	scrapped
C2265	Yes	10-29	LO 8-10-53								9-65	Dismantled: B&O shops, Du Bois, PA	scrapped
C2266	Yes	10-29		11-56		DU 11-26-56	Partial 2-61				11-74	Sold: Art Davis, Wooster, OH, 11-7-74	equipped with electric lights; (see Vol II)
C2267	Yes	10-29		5-50		DU 8-4-61	DU 8-61	CE 5-4-71	CE 4-71		6-74	Sold: Art Davis, Wooster, OH, 6-13-74; $250	accident: Cicero, IL, 2-14-73; fire damage
C2268	Yes	10-29				DU 8-16-61	DU 8-61	Yes		BW 8-70	6-76	System Acc: BW 6-15-74 Cab at BW 8-5-86 wreck damage	Damaged: fire: Willard, OH, 2-26-47 scrapped due to wreck damage
C2269	Yes	10-29		10-52		DU 2-15-57	DU 7-61	CE 5-4-71	CE 4-71		11-74	Sold: Art Davis, Wooster, OH, 11-7-74	
C2270	Yes	10-29		12-50		DU 3-20-59	DU 7-61	CE 9-1-71	CE 9-71		7-76	Donated: Kent Historical Society, Kent, OH, 7-6-76	AFE 56688; (see Vol II)
C2271	Yes	10-29		2-55		DU 8-21-61	DU 8-61	CE 1-5-71	Probably		7-75	Dismantled: B&O shops, Du Bois, PA, 7-3-75	scrapped
C2272	Yes	10-29		6-53	3-54 see note >						12-68	Dismantled: Arlington, New York, 12-4-68, on SIRT	* I-5C also reported: GA 10-22-53
C2273		10-29									12-43	Wrecked near Warren, OH per photo in this book	scrapped
C2274	Yes	10-29		4-52							11-74	Sold: Art Davis, Wooster, OH, 11-7-74	damaged by fire
C2275		10-29	See Note 1-21-54		see note > 1-21-54						7-65	Dismantled: B&O shops, Du Bois, PA	*DU and GRF reporting 1-21-54;
C2276	Yes	10-29	DU 9-8-53		DU 9-8-53	DU 4-24-61	DU 4-61				11-77	Sold: Jack Warble, Morristown, IN, 11-10-77	(see Vol II)
C2277	Yes	10-29	LO 2-18-52			DU 5-17-57	DU 5-61				5-75	Sold: Williston Northampton school, Easthampton, Mass	sold: 5-29-75; (see Vol I)
C2278	Yes	10-29		6-53	DU 6-29-53					DU 9-68	6-75	Sold: private owner, Kalamazoo, MI, 6-5-75, s.o. # 4590, $800	later to Coloma, MI, at photo studio; (see Vol III) painted DU 9-68 w/yellow ends for B&OCT svc.
C2279	Yes	10-29									9-71	Destroyed: fire: Barr Yard 1-23-71;	cut up at Chillicothe 9-8-71
C2280	Yes	10-29		4-51							4-66	Damaged: Barr Yard, 12-65; Dismantled: Garrett, IN	Dismantled: Garrett; 3-2-66
C2281	Yes	10-29	DU 10-9-53		10-53						8-71	Sold as scrap: M. D. Friedman, 8-26-71	scrapped
C2282	Yes	10-29		7-52							7-70	Sold: Fate-Root-Heath Co., Plymouth, OH, 7-10-70	(see Vol I)
C2283	Yes	10-29		1-51		WA 1-14-57		CE 1-22-71	CE 1-71	CE 5-75	9-81	Don: W. Agusta Hist. Soc., 9-4-81, Mannington, WV	sold on AFE 58415; (see Vol I)
C2284	Yes	10-29		2-51		WA 6-8-59					3-68	Sold: 2-15-68; pic @ NE '63 assigned NE Div 1961	sales order 5555 suggests sale to a scrapper
C2285	Yes	10-29		1-51							?	Last reported on OH-NE Div 1964	
C2286	Yes	10-29		11-50		WA 6-1-56					5-69	Dismantled: B&O shops, Chillicothe, OH, 5-12-69	scrapped
C2287	Yes	11-29		12-48		WA 2-3-56					11-67	Sold: Indianapolis Union Railway, 11-17-67; AFE 52641	one of three I-5s sold to IURY
C2288		11-29		3-50		WA 4-16-59					7-65	Dismantled: B&O shops, Washington, IN	scrapped
C2289	Yes	11-29		4-51							6-69	Sold: Falls Motel, Cumberland, KY, 6-9-69; used on tourist train	scrapped when tourist operation went out of business; (see Vol I & IV)
C2290	Yes	11-29		7-52		WA 11-30-56		CE 12-11-70	CE 12-70		8-75	Donated: Village of Cowden, IL, 8-15-75; AFE 56338	acquired by private owner and displayed on farm; (see Vol V)
C2291	Yes	11-29		10-51							11-67	Destroyed: Toledo, OH, 11-4-67	scrapped
C2292	Yes	11-29		4-51		WA 12-6-61		CE 9-19-70	CE 9-70	CE 2-75	8-81	Sold: Portsmouth Iron & Metal, 8-21-81 from Chillicothe, OH	car has new brake wheel Limbo at Chillicothe 8-28-80
C2293	Yes	11-29		2-53				CE 11-28-70	CE 11-70		5-75	Donated: Greenfield, Ohio, Hist. Society, 5-21-75; AFE 56501	Damaged: fire: North Vernon, IN, 2-28-47 (see Vol III); vandals burned--scrapped

Number	Pic ?	Built	Early "CF"	"AB" Brakes	I-5c	I-5D	I-5Dm	ACI Plate	1970-71 Paint	Misc. Paint	Retired	Disposition	Comments
C2294	Yes	11-29		12-51		WA 2-12-57					7-70	Destroyed: Arlington, New York, 7-1-70; on SIRT	scrapped
C2295	Yes	11-29		12-50		WA 6-15-56					5-69	Dismantled: B&O shops, Chillicothe, OH, 5-13-69	scrapped
C2296	Yes	11-29		2-53		WA 5-6-60					2-76	Donated: Kiwanis Club, Flora, IL, 2-24-76; AFE 56520	displayed in park; (see Vol V)
C2297	Yes	11-29		4-53							8-70	Sold: Williams Trailer Sales, Frazeyburg, OH, 8-3-70	built with a steel body; displayed: Frazeyburg
C2298	Yes	11-29		6-53		WA 6-22-53					7-70	Sold: S. C. Johnson Co. from Chillicothe, 7-30-70	sold with C1977; displayed: Grand View, WI, town hall; See Note 2; (see Vol V)
C2299	Yes	11-29		5-51							2-74	Destroyed: Fire: Rossford, OH, 2-8-74	Dismantled: Chillicothe, OH, 11-29-74

Notes

A. (see Vol ...) indicates that we have photographed the caboose at its private owner location and more information can be found by examining what is in a specific volume of our *C&O/B&O Cabooses, Private Owner and Display Cabooses* books. (see Volume V) indicates we have photographed the caboose and it will likely appear either in volume V or volume VI in this series, both of which are future planned publications.

B. In most of our rosters we provide a "Photo ?" column to indicate if an image exists for that car. The term "YES" indicates the author has photographed the car while the term "Photo" indicates an image from another source. Because of the large number of I-5 family photos in our collection it was evident that sorting them into those two categories was going to be a Herculean chore. Therefore we show only a "YES" to indicate that an image exists regardless of the photographer.

C. "CF" in column four stands for Concrete Floor. Other columns indicate modification dates and paint dates.

1. C-1928 was sold to the LaRosa Fuel Company in 1974 at Fairmont, West Virginia. This company owned much land in West Virginia and the owner (now deceased) was reported as one of the wealthiest men in the state. Reportedly he was responsible for the large shopping area located at the southeast corner of route 50 and I-79 at Clarksburg. He also built a large golf course nearby which had some railroad themes and tracks laid. In telcons with many members of the family during July and August 2016 the caboose last was known to be at or near Maybie, WV, in the mid-1980s. Maybie is at the end of a B&O coal branch; the tracks have long been removed. The caboose is presumed scrapped.

2. C-1977 and C-2298 were purchased from Chillicothe in 1970 by the S. C. Johnson Company (famous for many household cleaning products). The two cars were moved to the Wisconsin area where the company owns much land. Our photos show the C-2298 was repainted red and lettered for the B&O at the Chillicothe shops before shipment, likely the C-1977 as well. After several years the C-2298 was given to the town of Grand View, Wisconsin, and today sits behind the town hall. Our request made to the S. C. Johnson Company during 2016 for information on the other caboose was not responded to.

3. C-2039 was donated to Camp Tomahawk in 1967. There is more than one camp with this name. We contacted two which were located in B&O territory and our request for information was not responded to.

4. C-2101 and C-2128 were purchased in 1976 by George W. Barnette, Jr. He is believed to be the one located at Wise, Virginia (now deceased). One contact at this company provided conflicting information while another did not return our call for information on these two cabooses.

5. C-2119 was reported as given to John Douglas at Otter, West Virginia, from Cowen in 1969. In a July 2016 telcon with his widow she advised they wanted the caboose but could not find anyone to move the caboose therefore never received it. It likely was scrapped at Cowen.

6. C-2195 was sold to a George Fee in 1975. This person was from the Chicago area and moved the caboose to a farm in Wisconsin; it later was resold and moved to a new location; see Volume V.

7. The Ronnie Drake Construction Company (in Indiana) purchased three cabooses (C-1999, C-2045, C-2239). The C-2239 has never turned up anywhere and our searches for information about the disposition of this caboose were fruitless.

8. Out of 400 I-5 road numbers there is only one car that exists for which we do not know, for sure, what number it was. One of the I-5D cars showed up on the West Virginia Northern Railroad, probably in the mid-1960s, and was repainted in the road's white, black and blue scheme. After closure of that line it went to Durbin, West Virginia, where it operates with sister C-1906 on a tourist train. We have never located any company documentation for the sale of this caboose by the B&O leading to our speculation that it was given to the WVN "off the books". We do have an educated guess on this car—which we'll present in Volume V.

For more help with roster interpretation see page 23 as well as the Notes section at the end of the I-16 roster.

We welcome updates and additions to any of our roster listings which are considered living documents.

Shops That Modified Cars to I-5C Class
and quantity completed at each shop

The two Pareto charts on this page have been tabulated from the raw data listed in our roster. Although we do not have data for every caboose, enough information has been collected to validate the trends shown by these graphs. The I-5C graph above shows that two primary shops were assigned to spread the trucks that resulted in the I-5C class. The data we have collected indicates that the Chillicothe shops completed the very last I-5C caboose and it was the only one they did! The chart below shows that there were three primary shops that participated in the I-5D modification program. It is interesting to note that the Washington, Indiana, shops did many I-5D cabooses but apparently did not do any I-5C changes.

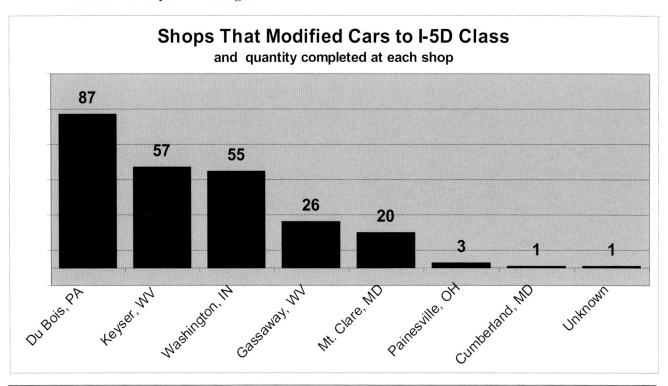

Shops That Modified Cars to I-5D Class
and quantity completed at each shop

I-5 Family Assignments

Cab #	Date	Assignment	Cab #	Date	Assignment	Cab #	Date	Assignment
C-1900	4-5-51	Gassaway, WV, shopped	C-1913	7-22-74	Parkersburg, WV, Viscose turn	C-1928	10-20-61	Wheeling Division
C-1900	10-3-52	Parkersburg, WV, pool	C-1913	3-14-75	Parkersburg, WV	C-1928	12-1-65	MR Pool, Monongah Division
C-1900	8-18-53	Gassaway, WV, shopped	C-1914	4-5-51	Parkersburg to Grafton pool	C-1928	1-1-69	Fairmont, WV, MR Pool
C-1900	1-22-54	Shopped, Gassaway, WV	C-1914	10-3-52	Grafton to Salem, WV, pool	C-1929	4-5-51	Grafton to Cowen service
C-1900	3-1-54	Gassaway, shopped	C-1914	8-18-53	Grafton to Salem pool	C-1929	10-3-52	Grafton, WV, unassigned
C-1900	2-10-58	Parkersburg High yard ind. Turn	C-1914	10-27-53	Clarksburg, WV, assigned	C-1929	8-18-53	CL to Benwood assigned turn
C-1901	4-5-51	Grafton to Cowen service	C-1914	11-2-53	Clarksburg, WV, assigned	C-1929	1-22-54	Trains 99-100, BD to Clarksburg
C-1901	10-3-52	Grafton to Salem, WV, pool	C-1914	1-22-54	Shopped, Gassaway, WV	C-1929	2-10-58	Fairmont to Clarksburg turn
C-1901	8-18-53	Grafton to Salem, WV, pool	C-1914	3-1-54	Grafton, WV, shopped	C-1929	10-20-61	Toledo-Indianapolis Division
C-1901	11-2-53	Clarksburg, WV, assigned	C-1914	2-10-58	Clarksburg, WV, industrial turn	C-1929	1-12-64	Toledo-Indianapolis Division
C-1901	1-22-54	Grafton to Salem, WV pool	C-1915	1-16-59	Garrett, IN, to Robey St, Chicago	C-1930	4-5-51	Grafton to Cowen service
C-1901	3-1-54	Grafton to Salem Pool	C-1915	5-5-61	Garrett, IN, operating into Illinois	C-1930	10-3-52	Grafton to Cowen, WV
C-1901	3-8-54	Grafton to Salem, WV, pool	C-1915	10-20-61	Akron-Chicago Division	C-1930	8-18-53	Trains 91-86 GRF to Cowen, WV
C-1901	5-25-61	Akron-Chicago Division	C-1915	10-15-64	Garrett, IN assigned	C-1930	1-22-54	Trains 91-86, GRF to Cowen, WV
C-1901	9-27-61	Akron Division	C-1915	7-8-69	Zanesville to Parkersburg local	C-1930	2-10-58	CL to Brook. Jct, High Cars train
C-1901	6-1-66	Chillicothe, OH, freight pool	C-1916	1-13-58	shopped, Du Bois, PA	C-1930	12-1-65	CL to Benwood, assigned turn
C-1901	1-1-68	Chillicothe trains 84, 84	C-1916	10-20-61	Akron-Chicago Division	C-1930	1-1-69	Clarksburg-Elenboro district run
C-1901	7-1-69	Chillicothe to McBee turnaround	C-1916	10-15-64	Garrett, IN assigned	C-1930	7-22-74	Clarksburg, WV, yard turn #8
C-1901	3-14-75	Chillicothe, OH	C-1917	8-15-56	Hagerstown, MD, pool	C-1930	3-14-75	Clarksburg, WV
C-1902	7-25-64	Cincinnati to Youngstown, KY	C-1917	6-5-61	Cumberland, MD	C-1931	4-5-51	Grafton to Cowen service
C-1902	10-20-61	St. Louis Division	C-1918	4-5-51	Trains 82-83, Grafton to GS	C-1931	10-3-52	Parkersburg, WV, pool
C-1902	1-12-64	St. Louis Division	C-1918	10-3-52	GRF to GS trains 82-83	C-1931	8-18-53	Train 99 & 2nd 86 GRF to Cowen
C-1902	7-8-69	Rider for Newark to Willard local	C-1918	8-18-53	Trains 82-83, GRF to Gassaway	C-1931	1-22-54	Trains 99-92, GRF to Cowen
C-1903	8-15-56	Hagerstown, MD, pool	C-1918	1-22-54	Trains 82-83, GRF to Gassaway	C-1931	2-10-58	Grafton, WV, extra service
C-1904	7-22-54	shopped Mount Clare	C-1918	3-1-54	Trains 82-83, Mon Div	C-1931	8-25-61	Akron Division
C-1904	12-15-55	at KY shop for Monongah Div	C-1918	2-10-58	Grafton to Gassaway, trns 83-82	C-1931	10-20-61	Akron-Chicago Division
C-1904	9-6-56	Brunswick, MD, work train	C-1919	3-1-54	Gassaway, WV, shopped	C-1932	9-6-56	Baltimore, MD, terminal service
C-1904	9-10-56	Brunswick, MD, work train	C-1919	8-15-56	Brunswick, MD, pool	C-1932	9-10-56	Baltimore, MD, terminal
C-1904	6-21-61	Maryland	C-1919	1-12-64	Toledo-Indianapolis Division	C-1932	2-10-58	#5 Cowen District Run
C-1904	7-17-61	BW to Hagerstown, turnaround	C-1920	4-5-51	Grafton to Salem, WV, pool	C-1932	12-1-65	Parkersburg to Millwood dist run
C-1904	1-12-64	Toledo-Indianapolis Division	C-1920	10-3-52	Grafton to Salem, WV, pool	C-1932	1-1-69	Sent to Du Bois shop
C-1904	3-14-75	Lima, OH	C-1920	8-18-53	Trains 2nd 99-92, GRF to CW	C-1932	7-22-74	Ravenswood, WV, district turn
C-1906	4-5-51	Grafton to Cowen service	C-1920	1-22-54	Shopped, Grafton, WV	C-1932	3-14-75	Ravenswood, WV
C-1906	10-3-52	G&B pool, Monongah Division	C-1920	3-1-54	Grafton, WV, shopped	C-1933	10-20-61	Ohio-Newark Division
C-1906	8-18-53	G&B Pool, Monongah Division	C-1920	2-10-58	Shopped, Keyser, WV	C-1933	5-19-62	Chillicothe, OH, pool
C-1906	1-22-54	G&B Pool, Monongah Division	C-1921	3-12-48	Brunswick, MD	C-1933	4-17-63	Southwest Pool, Newark, OH
C-1906	3-1-54	G&B Pool	C-1921	4-3-50	Millville, WV	C-1933	6-4-63	Newark, OH, pool
C-1906	2-10-58	Grafton to Cowen, trains 91-86	C-1921	5-18-53	Baltimore Div, operating thru DE	C-1933	6-22-63	Newark to Cincinnati pool
C-1906	12-1-65	MR Pool, Monongah Division	C-1921	5-11-54	to MC for I-5D then to Mon. Div	C-1933	1-12-64	Ohio-Newark Division
C-1906	1-1-69	Pennsboro, WV, work train	C-1921	2-10-58	MR Pool, Monongah Division	C-1933	1-15-64	Newark to Cincinnati pool
C-1906	7-22-74	Gassaway, WV, district turn	C-1921	12-1-65	Fairmont, WV, yard	C-1933	1-18-64	NE to Cincinnati pool service
C-1906	3-14-75	Gassaway, WV	C-1921	1-1-69	Fairmont, WV, MR Pool	C-1934	8-19-53	shopped: MC send to Wheel. Div
C-1907	3-1-54	Benwood, WV extra cab	C-1921	7-22-74	Fairmont, WV, tramp caboose	C-1934	11-13-53	sending to Wheeling Division
C-1907	7-26-61	Benwood, WV	C-1921	3-14-75	Fairmont, WV	C-1934	2-10-58	MR Pool, Monongah Division
C-1908	10-20-61	Toledo-Indianapolis Division	C-1922	5-11-54	to MC for I-5D then to Mon. Div	C-1934	12-1-65	FR to Clarksburg assigned turn
C-1908	5-19-62	Blanchester, OH, work train	C-1922	2-10-58	Parkersburg, WV, extra service	C-1934	1-1-69	Clarksburg to FR assigned turn
C-1908	6-4-63	Chillicothe locals 85 and 86	C-1922	12-1-65	Cowen, WV, #4 district turn	C-1934	7-22-74	Fairmont to Clarksburg turn
C-1908	1-12-64	Ohio-Newark Division	C-1922	1-1-69	Trains 50-51, Gassaway to GRF	C-1934	3-14-75	Clarksburg, WV
C-1908	1-15-64	Chillicothe to Stock Yards local	C-1922	7-22-74	Gilmer, WV, unfit; scrap	C-1935	8-19-53	shopped: MC send to Wheel. Div
C-1909	8-19-53	shopped: MC send to Wheel. Div	C-1922	3-14-75	Gassaway, WV	C-1935	9-29-53	shopped: GS for Wheeling Div
C-1909	9-29-53	shopped: GS for Wheeling Div	C-1923	5-18-53	Baltimore Div, operating thru DE	C-1935	11-13-53	sending to Wheeling Division
C-1909	9-6-56	Winchester to Strasburg, VA, turn	C-1923	5-11-54	to MC for I-5D then to Mon. Div	C-1935	2-10-58	SC&M RR assigned
C-1909	9-10-56	Winchester to Strasburg turn	C-1923	2-10-58	Parkersburg to Grafton, WV, pool	C-1935	12-1-65	Somerset, PA, shop 9-13-65
C-1909	10-20-61	Akron-Chicago Division	C-1923	12-1-65	Somerset, PA, shops; to be sold	C-1936	4-5-51	Parkersburg to Grafton pool
C-1909	3-14-75	Mt. Clare, Baltimore, MD	C-1925	7-26-61	Benwood, WV	C-1936	10-3-52	Parkersburg, WV, pool
C-1910	11-13-53	sending to Wheeling Division	C-1925	9-5-61	Pittsburgh Division	C-1936	8-18-53	Parkersburg to Grafton pool
C-1910	3-1-54	Lorain, OH, extra cab	C-1925	4-28-72	Cumberland, MD, for sale	C-1936	1-22-54	Parkersburg to Grafton pool
C-1912	4-5-51	Trains 80-81, Grafton to GS	C-1925	8-19-53	shopped: MC send to Wheel. Div	C-1936	2-10-58	Parkersburg to Salem work train
C-1912	10-3-52	GRF to GS trains 80-81	C-1925	9-29-53	shopped: GS for Wheeling Div	C-1936	12-1-65	Buckhannon, WV, district turn
C-1912	8-18-53	Trains 80-81, GRF to Gassaway	C-1925	5-11-54	to MC for I-5D then to Mon. Div	C-1936	1-1-69	Buckhannon, WV, #2 district run
C-1912	1-22-54	Trains 80-81, GRF to Gassaway	C-1925	8-29-55	Fairmont, WV	C-1936	7-22-74	Buckhannon, WV, district run
C-1912	3-1-54	Trains 80-81 Mon. Div	C-1926	10-20-61	Ohio-Newark Division	C-1937	9-6-56	Brunswick, MD
C-1912	2-10-58	Short Line mine run, Monong. Div	C-1926	4-17-63	Newark, OH, pool	C-1937	9-10-56	Brunswick, MD
C-1912	12-1-65	Grafton to Salem, WV, pool	C-1926	6-22-63	Willard to Benwood pool	C-1937	6-21-61	Maryland
C-1912	1-1-69	Grafton to Salem, WV, pool	C-1926	1-12-64	Ohio-Newark Division	C-1937	7-17-61	Alex. Sub-Div local freight
C-1912	7-22-74	Cowen, WV, extra cab	C-1926	1-18-64	Newark Division, pool service	C-1938	1-12-64	Toledo-Indianapolis Division
C-1912	3-14-75	Cowen, WV	C-1926	1-1-69	Fairmont, WV, MR Pool	C-1938	4-28-72	Chillicothe, OH, fire damaged
C-1913	10-3-52	Grafton, WV, unassigned	C-1926	7-22-74	Fairmont, WV, extra cab	C-1939	4-5-51	Parkersburg to Grafton pool
C-1913	4-5-51	Grafton to Cowen service	C-1926	3-14-75	Fairmont, WV	C-1939	10-3-52	Grafton to Salem, WV, pool
C-1913	8-18-53	CL to Benwood assigned turn	C-1927	7-25-50	Brunswick, MD	C-1939	8-18-53	Shopped, Gassaway, WV
C-1913	1-22-54	Parkersburg to Grafton pool	C-1927	7-26-61	Parkersburg, WV	C-1939	1-22-54	Fairmont to Benwood pool
C-1913	3-1-54	Parkersburg to Grafton pool	C-1927	12-1-65	Ravenswood to Graham dist. run	C-1939	3-1-54	Benwood to Fairmont Pool
C-1913	2-10-58	Grafton to Salem, WV, pool	C-1927	1-1-69	Parkersburg, WV, city ind. turn	C-1939	8-31-54	Benwood to Fairmont pool
C-1913	12-1-65	Gassaway, WV, work train rider	C-1927	7-22-74	Monongah Division assigned	C-1939	2-10-58	Clarksburg, WV, industries
C-1913	1-1-69	Trains 51-50, Grafton to GS	C-1928	7-26-61	Benwood, WV	C-1939	12-1-65	Ravenswood to Pt. Pleasant run

I-5 Family Assignments

Cab #	Date	Assignment
C-1939	1-1-69	Parkersburg, WV, work train
C-1939	7-22-74	Cowen, WV, #5 district turn
C-1939	3-14-75	Cowen, WV
C-1940	4-5-51	Grafton to Salem, WV, pool
C-1940	10-3-52	Parkersburg to CL Local
C-1940	8-18-53	Clarksburg to Parkersburg local
C-1940	1-22-54	Shopped, Gassaway, WV
C-1940	3-1-54	Gassaway, shopped
C-1940	4-11-55	shopped Gassaway, WV
C-1940	2-10-58	Grafton to Salem, WV, pool
C-1940	12-1-65	Trains 41-48, GRF to Cowen turn
C-1940	1-1-69	Cowen, WV, work train service
C-1940	7-22-74	Fairmont, rider on Kilarn Branch
C-1941	5-11-54	to MC for I-5D then to Mon. Div
C-1941	2-10-58	Grafton to Salem, WV, pool
C-1941	12-1-65	Trains 43-42, Grafton to CW turn
C-1942	5-5-61	St. Louis Division
C-1942	1-12-64	St. Louis Division
C-1943	8-16-56	New Castle, PA, extra cab
C-1943	4-13-60	DU shop; from Chicago Division
C-1943	4-14-60	DU shop to WA shop for St.L.Div
C-1943	5-5-61	St. Louis Division
C-1944	5-11-54	to MC for I-5D then to Mon. Div
C-1944	2-10-58	Grafton, WV, extra service
C-1944	12-1-65	Parkersburg, for condemnation
C-1944	1-1-69	Cowen, WV, #9 district run
C-1944	7-22-74	Parkersburg, low yard shop track
C-1945	8-16-56	B&O Pool, AK Div, oper. in PA
C-1945	8-16-56	Akron Division, B&O Pool
C-1945	9-25-61	Akron Division
C-1945	10-20-61	Akron-Chicago Division
C-1946	1951	Elk Run Jct., PA
C-1946	5-2-51	Riker, PA assigned
C-1946	9-6-51	Punxsutawney, PA
C-1946	3-3-54	Buffalo Division assigned
C-1946	4-13-55	Du Bois, PA assigned
C-1946	5-19-55	shopped, Du Bois, PA
C-1946	10-14-55	shopped, Du Bois, PA
C-1946	11-3-55	DU shop; to be sent to Glenwood
C-1946	5-5-61	Pittsburgh Division
C-1948	9-6-51	shopped, Du Bois, PA
C-1948	5-25-61	Pittsburgh Division
C-1948	5-29-61	Pittsburgh Division
C-1949	5-5-61	Garrett, IN, operating into Illinois
C-1949	10-20-61	Akron-Chicago Division
C-1950	10-20-61	Toledo-Indianapolis Division
C-1950	1-12-64	Toledo-Indianapolis Division
C-1951	12-13-51	Chicago Division
C-1951	1-16-59	Garrett, IN, to Robey St, Chicago
C-1951	5-5-61	Garrett, IN, operating into Illinois
C-1951	10-20-61	Akron-Chicago Division
C-1951	10-15-64	Garrett, IN assigned
C-1952	5-5-61	Garrett, IN, not assigned
C-1952	10-20-61	Akron-Chicago Division
C-1952	6-1-66	Ivorydale, OH, pool cab
C-1952	9-1-66	Ivorydale, OH, pool cab
C-1952	7-8-69	Philo, OH, district run
C-1953	8-16-56	B&O Pool, AK Div, oper. in PA
C-1953	5-25-61	Akron-Chicago Division
C-1953	8-8-61	Akron Division
C-1953	10-20-61	Akron-Chicago Division
C-1954	9-29-53	shopped; GS for Wheeling Div
C-1954	5-11-54	to MC for I-5D then to Mon. Div
C-1954	9-6-56	Georgetown Local (Baltimore Div)
C-1954	9-10-56	Georgetown Local (Balt Div)
C-1954	6-21-61	Maryland
C-1954	7-17-61	DC side, Met Sub-div local
C-1955	8-16-56	Akron Div, Lake Pool
C-1955	5-25-61	Akron-Chicago Division
C-1955	9-21-61	Akron Division
C-1955	10-20-61	Akron-Chicago Division
C-1955	8-16-56	Akron Div, Lake Pool
C-1955	5-25-61	Akron-Chicago Division
C-1955	9-21-61	Akron Division
C-1955	10-20-61	Akron-Chicago Division

Cab #	Date	Assignment
C-1956	10-20-61	Akron-Chicago Division
C-1957	1-16-59	Garrett, IN to Barr Yard, Chicago
C-1957	5-5-61	Garrett, IN, operating into Illinois
C-1957	10-20-61	Akron-Chicago Division
C-1957	10-15-64	Garrett, IN assigned
C-1958	3-15-61	Pittsburgh Division
C-1958	10-20-61	Akron-Chicago Division
C-1959	3-1-54	Cleveland, OH, extra cab
C-1959	8-31-61	Akron Division
C-1959	10-20-61	Akron-Chicago Division
C-1960	1951	Butler Jct, PA
C-1960	4-3-53	Butler Jct, PA
C-1960	3-3-54	Buffalo Division assigned
C-1960	10-28-54	assigned between FB and Kane
C-1960	4-13-55	Butler Jct, PA
C-1960	5-19-55	Foxburg Branch, PA
C-1960	6-8-55	Butler Jct, PA
C-1960	8-19-55	Butler Jct, PA
C-1960	10-14-55	Butler Jct, PA
C-1960	1-23-56	Butler Jct, PA, sending to DU
C-1960	4-4-56	shopped, Du Bois, PA
C-1960	1957	Butler Jct, PA
C-1960	4-57	Butler Jct, PA
C-1960	8-1-57	Butler Jct, PA
C-1960	11-13-58	Butler assigned Bruin switcher
C-1960	8-10-59	Northern Sub; Buffalo Division
C-1960	11-3-59	Bruin, PA, switcher
C-1960	6-20-60	Bruin, PA, switcher
C-1960	3-10-61	Buffalo Division
C-1960	6-19-61	Trains 85-86, Butler, PA
C-1960	8-11-61	Trains 87-88, Foxburg, PA side
C-1960	11-14-61	DU shop; billed to Punxsutawney
C-1960	6-21-62	Kane to Mt. Jewett assigned
C-1960	2-27-63	Trains 87-88, Kane, PA side
C-1960	10-15-64	Garrett, IN assigned
C-1961	8-16-56	B&O Pool, AK Div, oper. in PA
C-1961	5-25-61	Akron-Chicago Division
C-1961	9-22-61	Akron Division
C-1961	10-20-61	Akron-Chicago Division
C-1962	2-27-53	PV shop to DU shop for repair
C-1962	5-5-61	Garrett, IN, operating into Illinois
C-1962	10-20-61	Akron-Chicago Division
C-1962	10-15-64	Garrett, IN assigned
C-1963	8-16-56	B&O Pool, AK Div, oper. in PA
C-1963	5-25-61	Akron-Chicago Division
C-1963	6-28-61	Akron Division
C-1963	10-20-61	Akron-Chicago Division
C-1966	5-25-61	Pittsburgh Division
C-1966	9-15-61	Pittsburgh Division
C-1966	1-1-69	Pt. Pleasant, WV, district run
C-1967	3-1-54	Benwood, WV, extra cab
C-1967	7-26-61	Parkersburg, WV
C-1967	12-1-65	Clarksburg, WV, industrial turn
C-1967	1-1-69	Clarksburg, WV, shopped
C-1969	10-20-61	Ohio-Newark Division
C-1969	4-17-63	Southwest Pool, Newark, OH
C-1969	6-22-63	Newark to Cincinnati pool
C-1969	1-12-64	Ohio-Newark Division
C-1969	1-18-64	NE to Cincinnati pool service
C-1969	6-1-66	Ivorydale, OH, pool cab
C-1969	9-1-66	Ivorydale, OH, pool cab
C-1970	9-6-56	Hagerstown, MD, turn
C-1970	9-10-56	Hagerstown, MD, turn
C-1970	6-21-61	Maryland
C-1970	7-17-61	Georgetown turnaround, Balt Div
C-1970	12-1-65	Trains 49-40, Grafton to CW turn
C-1970	1-1-69	Brooklyn Jct., WV, AM dist. run
C-1970	7-22-74	sent to Chillicothe from Mon. Div
C-1970	3-14-75	Newark, OH
C-1971	8-16-56	Painesville, OH, extra cab
C-1971	5-25-61	Akron-Chicago Division
C-1971	9-18-61	Akron Division
C-1971	10-20-61	Akron-Chicago Division
C-1972	10-27-50	shopped, Du Bois, PA
C-1972	1951	shopped, Du Bois, PA

Cab #	Date	Assignment
C-1972	9-6-51	shopped, Du Bois, PA
C-1972	5-26-53	DU shop; condemned 10-16-52
C-1973	5-25-61	Akron-Chicago Division
C-1973	9-13-61	Akron Division
C-1973	10-20-61	Akron-Chicago Division
C-1974	8-16-56	B&O Pool, AK Div, oper. in PA
C-1974	5-25-61	Akron-Chicago Division
C-1974	9-8-61	Akron Division
C-1974	10-20-61	Akron-Chicago Division
C-1975	8-16-56	Akron Div, Lake Pool
C-1975	5-25-61	Akron-Chicago Division
C-1975	9-20-61	Akron Division
C-1975	10-20-61	Akron-Chicago Division
C-1976	3-6-45	Foxburg, PA, assigned
C-1976	5-29-46	Foxburg, PA, assigned
C-1976	8-16-56	B&O Pool, AK Div, oper. in PA
C-1976	10-20-61	Akron-Chicago Division
C-1977	10-20-61	Akron-Chicago Division
C-1977	10-15-64	Garrett, IN, to Lima, OH
C-1978	10-31-45	Riker, PA assigned
C-1978	10-27-50	shopped, Du Bois, PA
C-1978	9-6-51	Du Bois installed A-1 cab valve
C-1978	11-28-51	shopped, Du Bois, PA
C-1978	1-16-52	Du Bois, PA
C-1978	6-17-53	DU shop; billed to Punxsutawney
C-1978	6-24-53	shopped, Du Bois, PA
C-1978	3-3-54	Buffalo Division assigned
C-1978	10-28-54	assigned between Butler and FB
C-1978	4-13-55	Butler Jct, PA
C-1978	5-10-55	Butler Jct, PA
C-1978	7-55	Butler Jct, PA
C-1978	8-17-55	Butler Jct, PA
C-1978	8-19-55	Butler Jct, PA
C-1978	9-15-55	Butler Jct, PA
C-1978	10-14-55	Butler Jct, PA
C-1978	12-10-56	Butler Jct, PA
C-1978	1957	Butler Jct, PA
C-1978	8-1-57	Butler Jct, PA
C-1978	12-17-58	Butler, PA, extra cab
C-1978	8-10-59	Northern Sub; Buffalo Division
C-1978	11-3-59	Kane-Marienville-Mt.Jew. switchr
C-1978	6-20-60	Kane-Marienville-Mt.Jew. switchr
C-1978	5-25-61	Pittsburgh Division
C-1978	7-27-61	Buffalo Division
C-1978	8-11-61	Riker Yard (PX), PA, extra cab
C-1978	10-17-61	Rochester, NY, pool
C-1978	2-27-63	Riker to Glenwood, PA pool
C-1978	10-15-64	Garrett, IN assigned
C-1979	5-18-53	Baltimore Div, operating thru DE
C-1979	9-6-56	Baltimore, MD, terminal service
C-1979	9-10-56	Baltimore, MD, terminal
C-1979	6-21-61	Maryland
C-1979	7-17-61	Frederick, MD, yard job
C-1979	1-12-64	Toledo-Indianapolis Division
C-1979	3-14-75	Dayton, OH
C-1980	8-15-56	S. Brnch. Local-Petersbg. layover
C-1980	7-25-61	Washington, IN to Cincinnati
C-1980	10-20-61	St. Louis Division
C-1980	1-12-64	St. Louis Division
C-1980	7-1-69	Ivorydale (Cincy), OH
C-1980	3-14-75	Cincinnati, OH
C-1981	4-5-51	Grafton to Cowen service
C-1981	10-3-52	Parkersburg, WV, pool
C-1981	8-18-53	Parkersburg to Grafton pool
C-1981	1-22-54	Parkersburg to Grafton pool
C-1981	3-1-54	Parkersburg to Grafton pool
C-1981	2-10-58	Clarksburg to Benwood, WV, turn
C-1981	12-1-65	Belington to Grafton, WV, local
C-1981	1-1-69	Grafton, WV, to Elkins local
C-1981	7-22-74	Rider-Coalton Sub-div. Mon. Div
C-1982	1-13-58	shopped, Du Bois, PA
C-1982	1-17-59	DU shop; being sent to Garrett, IN
C-1982	5-5-61	Garrett, IN, not assigned
C-1982	10-20-61	Akron-Chicago Division
C-1982	10-15-64	Garrett, IN assigned

I-5 Family Assignments

Cab #	Date	Assignment
C-1982	1-1-69	Clarksburg, WV, MR work train
C-1982	7-22-74	Fairmont, WV, extra cab
C-1982	3-14-75	Fairmont, WV
C-1983	10-27-50	shopped, Du Bois, PA
C-1983	1951	shopped, Du Bois, PA
C-1983	9-6-51	shopped, Du Bois, PA
C-1983	4-3-61	Pittsburgh Division
C-1983	3-14-75	Newark, OH
C-1984	5-25-61	Pittsburgh Division
C-1984	6-7-61	Pittsburgh Division
C-1984	3-14-75	Mt. Clare, Baltimore, MD
C-1985	7-22-54	shopped Mount Clare
C-1985	9-6-56	Riverside (Balt) emergency svc.
C-1985	9-10-56	Riverside Yard, (Balt), emergency
C-1985	5-3-57	Baltimore Div operating thru DE
C-1985	6-21-61	Maryland
C-1985	7-17-61	Wilsmere, DE, work train rider
C-1986	4-5-51	G&B Pool, Monongah Division
C-1986	10-3-52	Parkersburg, WV, pool
C-1986	8-18-53	Grafton to Salem pool
C-1986	10-27-53	Clarksburg, WV, assigned
C-1986	11-2-53	Clarksburg, WV, assigned
C-1986	1-22-54	Grafton to Salem pool
C-1986	3-1-54	Grafton to Salem, WV pool
C-1986	2-10-58	Grafton to Gassaway, trns 80-81
C-1986	12-1-65	Cowen, WV, #9 district turn
C-1986	7-22-74	Cowen, WV, extra cab
C-1986	3-14-75	Cowen, WV
C-1987	9-6-56	Baltimore, MD, terminal service
C-1987	9-10-56	Baltimore, MD, terminal
C-1987	6-21-61	Maryland
C-1987	7-17-61	Winchester, VA, district turn
C-1987	7-25-61	Cincinnati to Washington, IN
C-1987	7-1-67	Brighton, OH, outside transfer
C-1987	7-1-69	Brighton (Cincy), OH, transfer
C-1988	10-20-61	St. Louis Division
C-1988	1-12-64	St. Louis Division
C-1988	7-25-61	Washington, IN to N. Vernon, IN
C-1989	5-11-54	to MC for I-5D then to Mon. Div
C-1989	2-10-58	Parkersburg to Grafton, WV, pool
C-1989	10-20-61	St. Louis Division
C-1989	12-1-65	MR Pool, Monongah Division
C-1989	7-22-74	Fairmont, WV, extra cab
C-1989	3-14-75	Fairmont, WV
C-1990	8-15-56	Hagerstown, MD, pool
C-1990	5-5-61	Indianapolis Division
C-1990	1-12-64	Toledo-Indianapolis Division
C-1991	11-13-53	shopped: GS from Balt Division
C-1991	3-1-54	Gassaway, WV, shopped
C-1991	7-26-61	Benwood, WV
C-1991	12-1-65	Benwood, WV, extra cab
C-1992	1-31-57	Piedmont Local (WV)
C-1992	6-5-61	M&K Jct., WV, work train
C-1993	8-15-56	Hagerstown, MD, pool
C-1993	10-20-61	Ohio-Newark Division
C-1993	4-17-63	Newark, OH, pool
C-1993	6-22-63	Willard to Benwood pool
C-1993	1-12-64	Ohio-Newark Division
C-1993	1-18-64	Newark Division, pool service
C-1993	7-8-69	Shopped, Newark, OH
C-1993	3-14-75	Chillicothe, OH
C-1994	1-16-59	Garrett, IN to Willard, OH
C-1994	5-5-61	Garrett, IN, not assigned
C-1994	10-20-61	Akron-Chicago Division
C-1994	10-15-64	Garrett, IN to Lima, OH
C-1994	7-22-74	Benwood, WV, condemned
C-1995	8-19-53	shopped: MC send to Wheel. Div
C-1995	11-13-53	MTC sending to Wheeling Div
C-1995	3-1-54	Parkersburg to Huntington, WV
C-1995	7-22-54	shopped Mount Clare
C-1995	7-26-61	Parkersburg, WV
C-1995	12-1-65	Parkersburg, WV, work train
C-1995	7-22-74	Moundsville, WV, switcher
C-1996	3-1-54	Lorain, OH to New Castle pool
C-1996	10-20-61	Akron-Chicago Division
C-1996	12-1-65	trains 61-62, GS to Charleston
C-1996	7-22-74	Grafton, WV, extra service
C-1996	3-14-75	Grafton, WV
C-1997	10-20-61	Ohio-Newark Division
C-1997	5-19-62	Chillicothe to Portsmouth switcher
C-1997	6-4-63	Chillicothe, Toledo Div distr run
C-1997	1-12-64	Ohio-Newark Division
C-1997	1-15-64	2nd Toledo Div dist run (CE)
C-1997	3-25-65	Chillicothe, OH
C-1997	6-1-66	Wellston district run
C-1997	1-1-68	Wellston, OH district run from CE
C-1997	7-1-69	Chillicothe to Wellston district run
C-1998	3-1-54	Gassaway, WV, shopped
C-1998	7-26-61	Parkersburg, WV
C-1999	7-25-61	Cincinnati to Washington, IN
C-1999	10-20-61	St. Louis Division
C-1999	1-12-64	St. Louis Division
C-1999	3-14-75	Cincinnati, OH
C-2000	8-19-53	sending CU Div to Wheeling Div
C-2000	11-13-53	sending to Wheeling Division
C-2000	3-1-54	Parkersburg to Brk. Jct.
C-2000	7-26-61	Parkersburg, WV
C-2000	12-1-65	Brooklyn Jct., WV, district run
C-2000	7-22-74	Benwood, Natrium Switcher
C-2001	4-8-60	DU shop; sides, floors stripp'd off
C-2001	2-8-61	Akron Division
C-2001	10-20-61	Akron-Chicago Division
C-2002	5-25-61	Akron-Chicago Division
C-2002	9-6-61	Akron Division
C-2002	10-20-61	Akron-Chicago Division
C-2003	5-25-61	Pittsburgh Division
C-2003	8-30-61	Pittsburgh Division
C-2004	2-28-61	Pittsburgh Division
C-2005	3-1-54	Cleveland to Willard, OH, run
C-2005	10-20-61	Akron-Chicago Division
C-2006	8-16-56	B&O Pool, AK Div, oper. in PA
C-2006	4-6-61	Akron Division
C-2006	10-20-61	Akron-Chicago Division
C-2007	5-25-61	Pittsburgh Division
C-2008	8-16-56	B&O Pool, AK Div, oper. in PA
C-2008	1-13-58	shopped, Du Bois, PA
C-2008	4-8-60	DU shop; sides, floors stripp'd off
C-2008	1-30-61	Akron Division
C-2008	10-20-61	Akron-Chicago Division
C-2009	1-16-59	Garrett, IN to Willard, OH
C-2009	5-5-61	Garrett, IN, not assigned
C-2009	10-20-61	Akron-Chicago Division
C-2010	8-16-56	B&O Pool, AK Div, oper. in PA
C-2010	2-6-61	Akron Division
C-2010	10-20-61	Akron-Chicago Division
C-2011	8-16-56	B&O Pool, AK Div, oper. in PA
C-2011	5-25-61	Akron-Chicago Division
C-2011	8-23-61	Akron Division
C-2011	10-20-61	Akron-Chicago Division
C-2012	8-27-56	Glenwood Pool, PA
C-2012	11-30-56	Butler to Glenwood, PA pool
C-2012	12-14-56	Riker to Glenwood pool
C-2012	1957	Punxsutawney, PA
C-2012	1-8-57	Elk Run Jct., PA
C-2012	11-13-58	Riker yard to Glenwood, PA
C-2012	12-11-58	Elk Run Jct., PA
C-2012	8-10-59	Riker Yard to Glenwood, PA, pool
C-2012	10-13-59	Riker to Glenwood pool, PA
C-2012	10-28-59	Elk Run Jct., PA
C-2012	3-4-60	shopped, Du Bois, PA
C-2012	6-20-60	Riker, PA Vintondale Run
C-2012	5-25-61	Buffalo Division
C-2012	7-28-61	Buffalo Division
C-2012	8-11-61	Riker Yard (PX), PA, extra cab
C-2012	10-15-64	Garrett, IN assigned
C-2013	8-16-56	B&O Pool, AK Div, oper. in PA
C-2013	10-20-61	Akron-Chicago Division
C-2014	8-16-56	Painesville, OH, extra cab
C-2014	1-13-58	shopped, Du Bois, PA
C-2014	4-8-60	DU shop; sides, floors stripp'd off
C-2014	1-27-61	Akron Division
C-2014	10-20-61	Akron-Chicago Division
C-2015	8-16-56	B&O Pool, AK Div, oper. in PA
C-2015	8-24-61	Akron Division
C-2015	10-20-61	Akron-Chicago Division
C-2018	8-16-56	B&O Pool, AK Div, oper. in PA
C-2018	1-10-58	Akron Division
C-2018	5-25-61	Akron-Chicago Division
C-2018	8-22-61	Akron Division
C-2018	10-20-61	Akron-Chicago Division
C-2019	10-20-61	Toledo-Indianapolis Division
C-2019	1-12-64	Toledo-Indianapolis Division
C-2019	7-22-74	Brooklyn Jct., WV, district turn
C-2019	3-14-75	Benwood, WV
C-2021	8-11-61	Akron Division
C-2021	10-20-61	Akron-Chicago Division
C-2021	7-8-69	Newark Division pool service
C-2021	3-14-75	Benwood, WV
C-2022	10-20-61	Toledo-Indianapolis Division
C-2022	1-12-64	Toledo-Indianapolis Division
C-2023	10-20-61	Ohio-Newark Division
C-2023	5-19-62	extra cab, Chillicothe, OH
C-2023	6-4-63	Washington, IN, shops
C-2023	1-12-64	Ohio-Newark Division
C-2023	3-14-75	Indianapolis, IN
C-2024	10-20-61	Ohio-Newark Division
C-2024	5-19-62	Chillicothe, OH, pool
C-2024	6-4-63	Chillicothe to Portsmouth local
C-2024	1-12-64	Ohio-Newark Division
C-2024	1-15-64	Portsmouth to Chillicothe local
C-2024	3-25-65	Chillicothe, OH
C-2024	6-1-66	CE to Oak Hill turnaround
C-2024	1-1-68	Chillicothe to Oak Hill turnaround
C-2024	7-1-69	Chillicothe Paint St. district run
C-2024	3-14-75	Chillicothe, OH
C-2025	1-13-58	shopped, Du Bois, PA
C-2025	10-20-61	Ohio-Newark Division
C-2025	5-19-62	Chillicothe, OH, pool
C-2025	6-4-63	CE sent to Benwood 6-27-63
C-2025	1-12-64	Ohio-Newark Division
C-2025	1-15-64	Chillicothe, OH, pool service
C-2025	6-1-66	Chillicothe, OH, freight pool
C-2026	9-18-54	Parkersburg, WV
C-2026	10-20-61	Ohio-Newark Division
C-2026	5-19-62	Chillicothe, OH, pool
C-2026	6-4-63	CE loaned to Cincinnati
C-2026	1-12-64	Toledo-Indianapolis Division
C-2026	7-1-67	Ivorydale, OH, transfer service
C-2026	3-14-75	Lima, OH
C-2027	10-20-61	Ohio-Newark Division
C-2027	5-19-62	Newark, OH, pool
C-2027	4-17-63	Southwest Pool, Newark, OH
C-2027	6-4-63	Newark, OH, pool
C-2027	6-22-63	Newark to Cincinnati pool
C-2027	1-12-64	Ohio-Newark Division
C-2027	1-15-64	Newark to Cincinnati pool
C-2027	1-18-64	NE to Cincinnati pool service
C-2028	7-25-61	Jeffersonville, IN-Youngstown, KY
C-2028	10-20-61	St. Louis Division
C-2028	1-12-64	St. Louis Division
C-2030	10-20-61	Toledo-Indianapolis Division
C-2030	1-12-64	Toledo-Indianapolis Division
C-2031	10-20-61	Toledo-Indianapolis Division
C-2031	4-17-63	Lake Erie local, Newark, OH
C-2031	6-22-63	Lake Erie local, rear cab (NE)
C-2031	1-12-64	Ohio-Newark Division
C-2031	1-18-64	Lake Erie local (Newark, OH)
C-2031	7-1-69	Columbus to Washington CH local
C-2031	7-8-69	Columbus to Washington CH local
C-2031	3-14-75	Newark, OH
C-2032	10-20-61	Ohio-Newark Division
C-2032	5-19-62	Newark, OH, pool
C-2032	6-4-63	Washington, IN, shops
C-2032	6-20-63	Ivorydale, OH, transfer service
C-2032	1-12-64	Ohio-Newark Division

Cab #	Date	Assignment
C-2032	7-8-69	Newark Division pool service
C-2033	7-25-61	Cincinnati to Youngstown, KY
C-2033	10-20-61	St. Louis Division
C-2033	1-12-64	St. Louis Division
C-2034	7-25-61	Storrs (Cin) to Cochran
C-2034	10-20-61	St. Louis Division
C-2034	1-12-64	St. Louis Division
C-2034	12-1-65	St. Joe switcher, Storrs, OH
C-2034	6-1-66	St. Joe switcher, Storrs, OH
C-2034	9-1-66	St. Joe switcher, Storrs, OH
C-2034	7-1-67	Storrs to Sedamsville job
C-2035	8-9-61	Akron Division
C-2035	10-20-61	Akron-Chicago Division
C-2035	6-1-66	Washington CH district run
C-2035	7-8-69	Newark Division pool service
C-2036	10-20-61	Akron-Chicago Division
C-2036	1-12-64	Toledo-Indianapolis Division
C-2036	4-28-72	Indianapolis, IN, for sale
C-2037	1-16-59	Garrett, IN, to Robey St, Chicago
C-2037	5-5-61	Garrett, IN, operating into Illinois
C-2037	10-20-61	Akron-Chicago Division
C-2038	5-5-61	Garrett, IN, operating into Illinois
C-2038	10-20-61	Akron-Chicago Division
C-2038	10-15-64	Garrett, IN assigned
C-2039	5-5-61	Garrett, IN, not assigned
C-2039	10-20-61	Akron-Chicago Division
C-2040	8-16-56	B&O Pool, AK Div, oper. in PA
C-2040	8-1-57	GW repaired and to But Jct, PA
C-2040	11-13-58	Butler assigned Kane switcher
C-2040	8-10-59	Northern Sub; Buffalo Division
C-2040	10-28-59	shopped, Du Bois, PA
C-2040	11-3-59	Billed- Du Bois shop, from Butler
C-2040	4-13-60	DU shop; from Buffalo Division
C-2040	4-14-60	DU shop to WA shop for St.L.Div
C-2040	1-12-64	St. Louis Division
C-2040	3-14-75	Indianapolis, IN
C-2041	8-16-56	Lake Pool, Akron Division
C-2041	2-15-61	Akron Division
C-2041	10-20-61	Akron-Chicago Division
C-2042	12-13-51	Akron Division
C-2042	3-1-54	Lorain, OH, extra cab
C-2042	10-20-61	Akron-Chicago Division
C-2043	8-16-56	B&O Pool, AK Div, oper. in PA
C-2043	8-18-61	Akron Division
C-2044	10-20-61	Ohio-Newark Division
C-2044	5-19-62	Chillicothe, OH, pool
C-2044	6-4-63	Portsmouth to Chillicothe local
C-2044	1-12-64	Ohio-Newark Division
C-2044	1-15-64	Chillicothe, OH, pool service
C-2044	6-1-66	Chillicothe locals 85 and 86
C-2044	1-1-68	Chillicothe, OH, trains 85, 86
C-2044	7-1-69	Chillicothe locals 85 and 86
C-2044	3-14-75	Marietta, OH
C-2045	10-20-61	Ohio-Newark Division
C-2045	5-19-62	Chillicothe, OH, pool
C-2045	6-4-63	Chillicothe, OH, pool
C-2045	1-12-64	Ohio-Newark Division
C-2045	1-15-64	Chillicothe, OH, pool service
C-2045	6-1-66	Chillicothe, OH, freight pool
C-2045	7-8-69	Columbus to Newark local
C-2045	3-14-75	Newark, OH
C-2046	10-20-61	Toledo-Indianapolis Division
C-2046	1-12-64	Toledo-Indianapolis Division
C-2046	3-14-75	Dayton, OH
C-2047	10-20-61	Toledo-Indianapolis Division
C-2047	1-12-64	Toledo-Indianapolis Division
C-2048	10-20-61	Ohio-Newark Division
C-2048	5-19-62	extra cab, Chillicothe, OH
C-2048	4-17-63	Newark, OH, pool
C-2048	6-22-63	Willard to Benwood pool
C-2048	1-12-64	Ohio-Newark Division
C-2048	1-18-64	Newark Division, pool service
C-2048	7-8-69	Shopped, Newark, OH
C-2048	3-14-75	Newark, OH
C-2049	10-20-61	Toledo-Indianapolis Division
C-2049	1-12-64	Toledo-Indianapolis Division
C-2050	10-20-61	Toledo-Indianapolis Division
C-2050	1-12-64	Toledo-Indianapolis Division
C-2050	7-1-69	Ivorydale, OH, L&N transfer
C-2051	10-20-61	Ohio-Newark Division
C-2051	5-19-62	CE loaned to Newark, OH
C-2051	4-17-63	Unassigned, Newark, OH
C-2051	6-22-63	Newark to Cincinnati pool
C-2051	1-12-64	Ohio-Newark Division
C-2051	1-15-64	Chillicothe, OH, pool service
C-2051	6-1-66	Chillicothe, OH, freight pool
C-2052	4-12-61	Pittsburgh Division
C-2052	3-14-75	Keyser, WV
C-2053	10-27-50	shopped, Du Bois, PA
C-2053	9-6-51	shopped, Du Bois, PA
C-2053	4-3-53	Butler Jct, PA
C-2053	3-3-54	Buffalo Division assigned
C-2053	5-21-54	Punxsutawney, PA
C-2053	10-28-54	assigned New Castle Turn
C-2053	4-13-55	Butler Jct, PA
C-2053	5-13-55	Butler Jct, PA
C-2053	10-14-55	Butler Jct, PA
C-2053	1-13-58	shopped, Du Bois, PA
C-2053	10-28-59	shopped: Du Bois, PA
C-2053	4-13-60	DU shop; from Buffalo Division
C-2053	4-14-60	DU shop to WA shop for St.L.Div
C-2053	8-10-61	Akron Division
C-2053	10-20-61	Akron-Chicago Division
C-2053	7-8-69	Willard to Shelby, OH, local
C-2053	3-14-75	Newark, OH
C-2054	1-13-58	shopped, Du Bois, PA
C-2054	5-5-61	Garrett, IN, operating into Illinois
C-2054	10-20-61	Akron-Chicago Division
C-2054	10-15-64	Garrett, IN assigned
C-2055	4-5-51	Fairmont, WV, extra cab
C-2055	10-3-52	shopped, Gassaway, WV
C-2055	8-18-53	Short Line Pool
C-2055	1-22-54	Clarksburg to Hartzel Dist. Run
C-2055	3-1-54	Clarksburg, WV to Hartzell
C-2055	7-26-61	Benwood, WV
C-2055	12-1-65	BD to Clarksburg, WV, turn
C-2055	7-22-74	Benwood, WV, condemned
C-2056	3-3-54	Buffalo Division assigned
C-2056	4-6-55	Punxsutawney, PA
C-2056	10-14-55	Punxsutawney, PA
C-2056	11-15-55	Glenwood, PA service, extra cab
C-2056	8-27-56	New Castle Pool, PA
C-2056	11-30-56	Trains NC 97 and 94; Buff. Div
C-2056	12-19-56	Elk Run: trains NC 97 and 94
C-2056	1-8-57	Elk Run Jct., PA
C-2056	10-28-59	shopped: Du Bois, PA
C-2056	6-20-60	Du Bois, PA, shopped
C-2056	8-11-61	Du Bois shop; for Buffalo Div
C-2056	8-17-61	Buffalo Division
C-2056	2-27-63	Riker to Glenwood, PA pool
C-2056	4-28-72	Cumberland, MD, for sale
C-2057	3-1-54	Holloway, OH to Benwood pool
C-2057	7-26-61	Benwood, WV
C-2057	10-20-61	Wheeling Division
C-2057	1-12-64	Ohio-Newark Division
C-2057	6-1-66	Chillicothe, OH, freight pool
C-2058	8-16-56	Akron Div, Lake Pool
C-2059	2-10-58	Grafton, WV, extra service
C-2059	1-12-64	Ohio-Newark Division
C-2059	12-1-65	Gassaway, WV, #1 district turn
C-2059	4-28-72	Chillicothe, OH, available for sale
C-2059	7-22-74	Dismantled
C-2060	8-16-56	Akron Div, Lake Pool
C-2060	10-20-61	Akron-Chicago Division
C-2060	4-28-72	Cumberland, MD, for sale
C-2061	2-27-53	PV shop to DU shop for repair
C-2061	8-16-56	Akron Division, B&O Pool
C-2061	1-13-58	shopped, Du Bois, PA
C-2061	4-13-60	DU shop; from Akron Division
C-2061	4-14-60	DU shop to WA shop for St.L.Div
C-2061	7-25-61	Cincinnati to Washington, IN
C-2061	10-20-61	St. Louis Division
C-2061	1-12-64	St. Louis Division
C-2062	9-6-51	shopped, Du Bois, PA
C-2062	2-10-61	Pittsburgh Division
C-2063	6-21-61	Maryland
C-2064	10-20-61	Ohio-Newark Division
C-2064	4-17-63	Sandusky, OH, crew quarters
C-2064	6-22-63	Sandusky, OH, yard
C-2064	1-12-64	Ohio-Newark Division
C-2064	1-18-64	Sandusky, OH, yard service
C-2064	7-8-69	Sandusky, OH, yard turn
C-2065	8-16-56	B&O Pool, AK Div, oper. in PA
C-2065	5-25-61	Akron-Chicago Division
C-2065	7-3-61	Akron Division
C-2065	10-20-61	Akron-Chicago Division
C-2066	1-13-58	shopped, Du Bois, PA
C-2066	5-25-61	Pittsburgh Division
C-2066	9-1-61	Pittsburgh Division
C-2066	4-28-72	Mt. Clare, MD, fire damaged
C-2067	10-27-50	shopped, Du Bois, PA
C-2068	1951	Butler Jct, PA
C-2068	4-22-53	Elk Run Jct., PA
C-2068	3-3-54	Buffalo Division assigned
C-2068	4-6-55	Punxsutawney, PA
C-2068	5-2-55	Elk Run Jct., PA
C-2068	9-15-55	Elk Run Jct (Punxsutawney, PA)
C-2068	10-14-55	Punxsutawney, PA
C-2068	11-15-55	Glenwood, PA service, extra cab
C-2068	8-27-56	Elk Run shop trk, PA
C-2068	9-5-56	Elk Run Jct., PA
C-2068	1957	Punxsutawney, PA
C-2068	5-23-57	Elk Run Jct., PA
C-2068	10-13-59	Punxsutawney, PA, needs replcd.
C-2068	6-21-61	Buffalo Division
C-2068	8-11-61	Kane, PA, switcher
C-2068	2-27-63	Du Bois, PA, shopped
C-2068	10-15-64	Garrett, IN assigned
C-2069	2-20-61	Buffalo Division
C-2069	6-19-61	Northern Sub; Mt. Jewett, PA
C-2069	8-11-61	Trains 87-88, Kane, PA side
C-2069	10-20-61	Ohio-Newark Division
C-2069	2-27-63	Butler, PA, extra cab
C-2069	6-4-63	Washington, IN, shops
C-2069	11-20-63	But Jct to MC for electrification
C-2070	7-25-61	Washington, IN to Cincinnati
C-2070	10-20-61	St. Louis Division
C-2070	1-12-64	St. Louis Division
C-2072	3-1-54	Lorain, OH, extra cab
C-2072	10-20-61	Akron-Chicago Division
C-2072	3-4-59	Akron Division
C-2073	8-15-56	Brunswick, MD, pool
C-2074	5-18-53	Baltimore Div, operating thru DE
C-2074	5-11-54	to MC for I-5D then to Mon. Div
C-2074	2-10-58	Grafton to Cowen, WV, trns 99-90
C-2074	12-1-65	G&B pool, Monongah Division
C-2074	7-22-74	Grafton, WV, G&B pool service
C-2074	3-14-75	Grafton, WV
C-2075	1-31-57	M&K District Run (Sabraton)
C-2075	6-21-61	Maryland
C-2076	2-23-56	DU shop; from Pitts. Division
C-2076	4-7-61	Pittsburgh Division
C-2077	5-5-61	Garrett, IN, operating into Illinois
C-2077	10-20-61	Akron-Chicago Division
C-2077	10-15-64	Garrett, IN assigned
C-2078	2-27-53	PV shop to DU shop for repair
C-2078	8-16-56	B&O Pool, AK Div, oper. in PA
C-2078	10-20-61	Akron-Chicago Division
C-2078	4-28-72	Mt. Clare, MD, available for sale
C-2078	3-14-75	Mt. Clare, Baltimore, MD
C-2079	9-6-56	Millville Digger, Baltimore Division
C-2079	9-10-56	Millville, WV, Digger
C-2079	6-21-61	Maryland
C-2079	7-17-61	BW, MD, Met sub-div local
C-2079	3-14-75	Locust Pt., MD

I-5 Family Assignments

Cab #	Date	Assignment	Cab #	Date	Assignment	Cab #	Date	Assignment
C-2080	10-20-61	Ohio-Newark Division	C-2098	5-5-61	Garrett, IN, operating into Illinois	C-2112	3-1-54	Wheeling Division cab
C-2080	5-19-62	Chillicothe, OH, pool	C-2098	10-20-61	Akron-Chicago Division	C-2113	10-20-61	Ohio-Newark Division
C-2080	6-4-63	Chillicothe, OH, pool	C-2098	10-15-64	Garrett, IN assigned	C-2113	5-19-62	Chillicothe locals 83 and 84
C-2080	1-12-64	Ohio-Newark Division	C-2099	3-1-54	Willard, OH, to Holloway pool	C-2113	6-4-63	Chillicothe locals 83 and 84
C-2080	1-15-64	Chillicothe, OH, pool service	C-2099	8-16-56	Lorain, OH, to New Castle Pool	C-2113	1-12-64	Ohio-Newark Division
C-2080	6-1-66	Chillicothe, OH, freight pool	C-2099	6-21-61	Maryland	C-2113	1-15-64	CE to PR locals 83, 84
C-2080	7-1-67	Ivorydale, OH, transfer service	C-2099	7-17-61	Wilsmere, DE, district switcher	C-2113	6-1-66	Chillicothe, OH, freight pool
C-2081	10-3-52	GRF to Cowen trains 196-197	C-2100	4-5-51	Grafton to Salem, WV, pool	C-2113	7-1-67	Ivorydale, OH, transfer service
C-2081	4-5-51	Grafton to Salem, WV, pool	C-2100	10-3-52	MR Local, Monongah Division	C-2113	7-1-69	Ivorydale, OH, L&N transfer
C-2081	8-18-53	Trains 97-196 Grafton to Benwood	C-2100	8-18-53	Clarksburg mine run	C-2114	8-15-56	Martinsburg, MD
C-2081	1-22-54	Trains 196-197, BD to Grafton	C-2100	1-22-54	Shopped, Gassaway, WV	C-2114	12-1-65	GRF to BD pool, out of Fairmont
C-2081	3-1-54	Trains 196-197 Mon. Div	C-2100	3-1-54	Gassaway, WV, shopped	C-2114	7-22-74	Fairmont, WV, MR pool service
C-2081	5-17-61	Akron Division	C-2100	4-11-55	shopped Gassaway, WV	C-2114	3-14-75	Fairmont, WV
C-2081	10-20-61	Akron-Chicago Division	C-2100	4-11-55	shopped Gassaway, WV	C-2115	4-3-53	Butler Jct, PA
C-2082	4-10-52	Shopped: Mt. Clare, Baltimore	C-2100	2-10-58	Grafton to Benwood, WV pool	C-2115	3-3-54	Buffalo Division assigned
C-2082	8-15-56	Bakerton Digger; E end CU Div	C-2100	12-1-65	MR Pool, Monongah Division	C-2115	10-28-54	assigned between FB and Kane
C-2082	12-1-65	Cowen, WV, 36 district turn	C-2101	8-15-56	Martinsburg, Frog Hollow	C-2115	4-55	Butler Jct, PA
C-2082	7-22-74	Cowen, WV, extra cab	C-2101	6-5-61	Cumberland, MD	C-2115	4-6-55	Butler Jct., PA
C-2082	3-14-75	Benwood, WV	C-2101	7-22-74	Benwood, WV, extra cab	C-2115	8-17-55	Butler Jct, PA
C-2083	5-26-53	DU shop; to I-5C 5-21-53	C-2102	3-1-54	Benwood to Fairmont Pool	C-2115	8-19-55	Butler Jct, PA
C-2083	5-5-61	Garrett, IN, operating into Illinois	C-2102	2-10-58	Paw Paw, WV, mine run	C-2115	9-15-55	Butler Jct, PA
C-2083	10-20-61	Akron-Chicago Division	C-2102	7-26-61	Benwood, WV	C-2115	10-14-55	Butler Jct, PA
C-2083	10-15-64	Garrett, IN assigned	C-2102	6-22-63	Newark to Cincinnati pool	C-2115	1957	Butler Jct, PA
C-2084	4-5-51	Grafton to Cowen service	C-2102	1-12-64	Ohio-Newark Division	C-2115	8-1-57	Butler Jct, PA
C-2084	10-3-52	Grafton to Cowen, WV	C-2102	1-18-64	Newark, OH, unassigned	C-2115	11-13-58	Butler assigned trn. 88 Kane side
C-2084	8-18-53	Trains 91-86, GRF to Cowen, WV	C-2103	5-18-53	Baltimore Div, operating thru DE	C-2115	8-10-59	Northern Sub; Buffalo Division
C-2084	1-22-54	Trains 91-86, GRF to Cowen, WV	C-2103	8-15-56	Brunswick, MD, pool	C-2115	11-3-59	Trains 88-87 Kane, PA, side
C-2084	3-1-54	Trains 91-86 GRF to Cowen, WV	C-2103	12-1-65	Cowen, WV, #8 district turn	C-2115	6-20-60	Trains 87-88, Foxburg, PA side
C-2084	2-10-58	MR Pool, Monongah Division	C-2104	4-5-51	Parkersburg to Grafton pool	C-2115	4-14-61	Buffalo Division
C-2084	12-1-65	Benwood, WV, extra cab	C-2104	10-3-52	Parkersburg, WV, pool	C-2115	6-19-61	Trains 85-86, Butler, PA
C-2084	7-22-74	Brooklyn Jct., WV, district run	C-2104	8-18-53	Parkersburg to Grafton, WV pool	C-2115	8-11-61	Trains 85-86, Buffalo Division
C-2084	3-14-75	Benwood, WV	C-2104	1-22-54	Shopped, Gassaway, WV	C-2115	2-27-63	Trains 85-86, Buffalo Division
C-2086	2-22-48	Brunswick, MD	C-2104	3-1-54	Gassaway, WV, shopped	C-2116	5-25-61	Pittsburgh Division
C-2086	8-19-53	shopped: MC send to Wheel. Div	C-2104	2-10-58	Clarksburg, WV, extra service	C-2116	6-5-61	Pittsburgh Division
C-2086	5-11-54	to MC for I-5D then to Mon. Div	C-2104	12-1-65	Grafton to Salem, WV, pool	C-2119	12-25-55	to Riverside from St. Louis
C-2086	9-6-56	Baltimore, MD, terminal service	C-2104	7-22-74	Clarksburg, WV, yard turn #5	C-2119	12-29-55	used on MX mail train: to E. Reg.
C-2086	9-10-56	Baltimore, MD, terminal	C-2104	3-14-75	Clarksburg, WV	C-2119	12-29-55	Monongah Division
C-2086	6-21-61	Maryland	C-2105	5-13-54	Buff Div or Pitts Div ?	C-2119	12-30-55	GRF for Christmas boxcar specl.
C-2086	7-17-61	Mt. Clare shop, Baltimore, MD	C-2105	2-23-56	DU shop; from Pitts. Division	C-2119	2-10-58	Grafton, WV, stored
C-2088	3-17-48	Brunswick, MD	C-2105	2-23-61	Pittsburgh Division	C-2119	12-1-65	SC&M RR, Monongah Div
C-2089	9-6-56	Brunswick, MD, emergency svc.	C-2106	10-31-45	Riker, PA assigned	C-2120	3-1-54	Lorain to Holloway, OH, pool
C-2089	9-10-56	Brunswick, MD, emergency	C-2106	5-25-61	Pittsburgh Division	C-2120	8-16-56	Lorain, OH, to New Castle Pool
C-2089	5-3-57	Baltimore Div operating thru DE	C-2106	8-14-61	Pittsburgh Division	C-2120	10-20-61	Akron-Chicago Division
C-2089	6-21-61	Maryland	C-2109	1-13-58	shopped, Du Bois, PA	C-2122	3-1-54	Willard to Holloway pool
C-2089	7-17-61	Brunswick, MD, emergency cab	C-2109	5-5-61	Garrett, IN, not assigned	C-2122	8-15-61	Akron Division
C-2090	3-1-54	Lorain, OH, extra cab	C-2109	10-20-61	Akron-Chicago Division	C-2122	10-20-61	Akron-Chicago Division
C-2090	10-20-61	Akron-Chicago Division	C-2109	10-15-64	Garrett, IN, East end local	C-2123	4-10-52	Shopped: Mt. Clare, Baltimore
C-2092	4-24-49	Winchester, VA	C-2110	4-29-48	at DU shop; damaged by fire	C-2123	8-15-56	Brunswick, MD, pool
C-2092	9-6-56	Alexandria Branch Local (Balt Div)	C-2110	9-6-51	Du Bois installed A-1 cab valve	C-2123	1-12-64	Toledo-Indianapolis Division
C-2092	9-10-56	Alexandria Branch Local-Balt Div	C-2110	11-28-51	shopped, Du Bois, PA	C-2123	7-22-74	Grafton, WV, MR pool service
C-2092	6-21-61	Maryland	C-2110	1-16-52	Du Bois, PA	C-2123	3-14-75	Grafton, WV
C-2092	7-17-61	Georgetown district switcher	C-2110	3-3-54	Buffalo Division assigned	C-2124	5-21-53	Fire: Brk Jct; to GS shop for repr.
C-2093	9-6-56	Baltimore, MD, terminal service	C-2110	10-28-54	assigned between Butler and FB	C-2124	3-1-54	Benwood to Fairmont pool
C-2093	9-10-56	Baltimore, MD, terminal	C-2110	4-13-55	Butler Jct, PA	C-2124	7-26-61	Benwood, WV
C-2093	6-21-61	Maryland	C-2110	5-19-55	Butler Jct, PA	C-2124	12-1-65	Benwood to Holloway, OH, pool #2
C-2093	7-17-61	Aberdeen, MD, work train rider	C-2110	6-2-55	Butler Jct, PA	C-2124	7-22-74	Benwood, WV, Solvay district run
C-2094	9-6-56	Brunswick to Winchester, VA	C-2110	8-17-55	Butler Jct, PA	C-2124	3-14-75	Benwood, WV
C-2094	9-10-56	Brunswick, MD, to Winchester	C-2110	8-19-55	Butler Jct, PA	C-2125	9-6-56	Trains 8-9, Keyser, WV
C-2094	6-21-61	Maryland	C-2110	9-15-55	Butler Jct, PA	C-2125	9-10-56	Keyser, WV, train B-9
C-2094	7-17-61	Brunswick, MD	C-2110	10-14-55	Butler Jct, PA	C-2125	2-10-58	Grafton to Salem, WV, pool
C-2095	4-10-52	Shopped: Mt. Clare, Baltimore	C-2110	1-9-56	Butler Jct, PA	C-2125	12-1-65	G&B pool, Monongah Division
C-2095	5-11-54	to MC for I-5D then to Mon. Div	C-2110	1957	Butler Jct, PA	C-2125	7-22-74	Grafton, WV, repair track
C-2095	2-10-58	Grafton to Cowen, WV, trns 99-90	C-2110	3-57	Butler Jct, PA	C-2125	3-14-75	Parkersburg, WV
C-2095	12-1-65	G&B pool, Monongah Division	C-2110	8-1-57	Butler Jct, PA	C-2127	8-16-56	B&O Pool, AK Div, oper. in PA
C-2095	7-22-74	Cowen, WV, #3 district turn	C-2110	11-13-58	Butler assigned trains 85-86	C-2127	8-28-61	Akron Division
C-2096	8-16-56	Cleveland, OH to New Castle run	C-2110	8-10-59	Northern Sub; Buffalo Division	C-2127	10-20-61	Akron-Chicago Division
C-2096	5-25-61	Akron-Chicago Division	C-2110	11-3-59	Trains 85-86, w. end Buffalo Div	C-2128	10-19-55	last repaired KY 6-53
C-2096	10-20-61	Akron-Chicago Division	C-2110	6-20-60	Trains 85-86, w. end Buffalo Div	C-2128	2-10-58	Fairmont, WV, extra cab
C-2097	8-14-56	Eastern Region, oper. In PA	C-2110	5-25-61	Pittsburgh Division	C-2128	12-1-65	Trains 45-46, Grafton to CW turn
C-2097	9-6-56	Riverside, MD (Baltimore)	C-2110	8-7-61	Buffalo Division	C-2128	7-22-74	Condemned; Monongah Div
C-2097	9-10-56	Riverside Yard, Baltimore, MD	C-2110	8-11-61	Riker Yard (PX), PA, extra cab	C-2129	2-10-58	stored at Grafton, WV
C-2097	6-21-61	Maryland	C-2110	2-27-63	Mt. Jewett, PA, switcher	C-2129	12-1-65	Grafton to Salem, WV, pool
C-2097	7-17-61	Washington sub-div, local freight	C-2110	11-20-63	But Jct to MC for electrification	C-2129	7-22-74	Grafton, WV, repair track
C-2097	3-14-75	Mt. Clare, Baltimore, MD	C-2112	11-13-53	to GS shop from Baltimore Div.	C-2129	3-14-75	Buckhannon, WV
C-2098	1-16-59	Garrett, IN, to Robey St, Chicago	C-2112	11-16-53	GRF to Gassaway shop, WV	C-2130	7-26-61	Benwood, WV

I-5 Family Assignments

Cab #	Date	Assignment
C-2130	10-20-61	Akron-Chicago Division
C-2131	5-18-53	Baltimore Div, operating thru DE
C-2131	8-14-56	Eastern Region, oper. In PA
C-2131	9-6-56	Riverside (Balt) emergency svc.
C-2131	9-10-56	Riverside Yard, (Balt), emergency
C-2131	12-1-65	Somerset, PA, shops; to be sold
C-2132	4-5-51	Trains 82-83, Grafton to GS
C-2132	10-3-52	GRF to Gassaway, trains 82-83
C-2132	8-10-53	Trains 82-83, Grafton to GS
C-2132	1-22-54	Shopped, Gassaway, WV
C-2132	3-1-54	Trains 82-83 GRF to Gassaway
C-2132	2-10-58	Gassaway to Grafton, trains 82-83
C-2132	12-1-65	St. Mary's, WV, district run
C-2132	7-22-74	Benwood, WV, extra cab
C-2132	3-14-75	Benwood, WV
C-2133	8-15-56	at Cumberland; released from KY
C-2134	3-6-61	Pittsburgh Division
C-2135	8-15-56	Brunswick, MD, pool
C-2135	10-20-61	Ohio-Newark Division
C-2135	4-17-63	Newark, OH, pool
C-2135	6-22-63	Willard to Benwood pool
C-2135	1-12-64	Ohio-Newark Division
C-2135	1-18-64	Newark, OH, unassigned
C-2135	7-8-69	Zanesville to Parkersburg local
C-2135	4-28-72	Newark, OH, for sale
C-2136	1951	shopped, Du Bois, PA
C-2136	9-6-51	shopped, Du Bois, PA
C-2136	12-7-55	DU shop; sold
C-2137	12-17-58	New Castle, PA
C-2137	2-24-61	Pittsburgh Division
C-2137	4-28-72	Mt. Clare, MD, fire damaged
C-2138	5-5-61	Garrett, IN, operating into Illinois
C-2138	10-20-61	Akron-Chicago Division
C-2139	10-20-61	Toledo-Indianapolis Division
C-2139	1-12-64	Toledo-Indianapolis Division
C-2139	7-1-67	Ivorydale, OH, transfer service
C-2139	7-1-69	Ivorydale, OH, L&N transfer
C-2140	12-17-58	New Castle, PA
C-2140	3-4-59	Pittsburgh Division
C-2140	10-20-61	Toledo-Indianapolis Division
C-2140	1-12-64	St. Louis Division
C-2141	9-6-56	Shopped, Keyser, WV
C-2141	9-10-56	Shopped, Keyser, WV
C-2141	10-20-61	Akron-Chicago Division
C-2141	3-27-69	Winchester, VA
C-2142	9-6-56	Metropolitan Way (Baltimore Div)
C-2142	9-10-56	Metropolitan Way (Balt Division)
C-2142	6-21-61	Maryland
C-2142	7-17-61	Brunswick, MD
C-2143	3-1-54	Lorain, OH, extra cab
C-2143	8-16-56	Lorain, OH, to New Castle Pool
C-2143	5-25-61	Akron-Chicago Division
C-2143	10-20-61	Akron-Chicago Division
C-2144	3-1-54	Parkersburg and Benwood
C-2144	8-29-55	Fairmont, WV
C-2144	7-26-61	Parkersburg, WV
C-2145	3-1-54	Holloway to Benwood pool
C-2145	7-26-61	Benwood, WV
C-2145	10-20-61	Wheeling Division
C-2147	3-1-54	High Car trains 96-97, Whlg. Div
C-2147	7-26-61	Parkersburg, WV
C-2149	11-13-58	Butler assigned trn. 87 Foxburg
C-2149	12-17-58	New Castle, PA
C-2149	3-9-59	Butler Jct, PA
C-2149	11-3-59	Trains 87-88 Foxburg, PA, side
C-2149	6-20-60	Trains 87-88, Kane, PA side
C-2149	5-25-61	Buffalo Division
C-2149	6-19-61	Butler, PA, Coke Run
C-2149	8-11-61	Du Bois shop; for Buffalo Div
C-2149	9-12-61	Buffalo Division
C-2149	2-27-63	Bruin, PA, switcher
C-2150	7-14-55	shopped, Du Bois, PA
C-2150	3-22-61	Akron Division
C-2150	10-20-61	Akron-Chicago Division
C-2150	1-1-68	Portsmouth-Jackson turnaround

Cab #	Date	Assignment
C-2150	7-1-69	Wellston-Edmunds turnaround
C-2151	7-25-61	North Vernon to Sparkville
C-2151	10-20-61	St. Louis Division
C-2151	1-12-64	St. Louis Division
C-2152	10-20-61	Toledo-Indianapolis Division
C-2152	1-12-64	Toledo-Indianapolis Division
C-2152	3-14-75	Indianapolis, IN
C-2154	1951	shopped, Du Bois, PA
C-2154	9-6-51	shopped, Du Bois, PA
C-2154	5-25-61	Pittsburgh Division
C-2154	8-4-61	Pittsburgh Division
C-2155	3-3-54	Buffalo Division assigned
C-2155	4-13-55	Elk Run Jct., PA
C-2155	4-21-55	Butler Jct, PA
C-2155	5-27-55	Butler Jct, PA
C-2155	6-2-55	Butler Jct, PA
C-2155	8-17-55	Butler Jct, PA
C-2155	8-19-55	Butler Jct, PA
C-2155	9-15-55	Butler Jct, PA
C-2155	10-14-55	Butler Jct, PA
C-2155	11-21-56	Butler Jct, PA
C-2155	1957	Butler Jct, PA
C-2155	8-1-57	Butler Jct, PA
C-2155	8-10-59	Northern Sub; Buffalo Division
C-2155	6-20-60	Butler, PA, to New Castle turn
C-2155	5-25-61	Buffalo Division
C-2155	6-19-61	Butler, PA
C-2155	8-11-61	Du Bois shop; for Buffalo Div
C-2155	8-29-61	Akron Division
C-2155	2-27-63	Butler, PA, - New Castle Coke run
C-2155	7-22-74	Parkersburg to Milwood turn
C-2155	3-14-75	Parkersburg, WV
C-2157	10-27-50	shopped, Du Bois, PA
C-2157	5-8-61	Pittsburgh Division
C-2157	5-25-61	Pittsburgh Division
C-2158	1-25-61	Pittsburgh Division
C-2159	1-19-53	loaded in gon: to GS shop
C-2159	3-1-54	Benwood, WV, extra cab
C-2159	8-15-56	Hagerstown, MD, pool
C-2159	10-20-61	Ohio-Newark Division
C-2159	4-17-63	Newark, OH, pool
C-2159	6-22-63	Willard to Benwood pool
C-2159	1-12-64	Ohio-Newark Division
C-2159	1-18-64	Newark Division, pool service
C-2159	7-8-69	Cambridge, OH, district run
C-2160	9-6-56	Riverside (Balt) emergency svc.
C-2160	9-10-56	Riverside (Balt) emergency
C-2160	1-12-64	Toledo-Indianapolis Division
C-2161	5-25-61	Pittsburgh Division
C-2161	6-30-61	Pittsburgh Division
C-2162	2-27-53	PV shop to DU shop for repair
C-2162	5-25-61	Pittsburgh Division
C-2162	6-23-61	Pittsburgh Division
C-2163	6-24-55	shopped, Du Bois, PA
C-2163	5-5-61	Garrett, IN, operating into Illinois
C-2163	10-20-61	Akron-Chicago Division
C-2164	8-5-50	Millville, WV
C-2164	7-26-61	Benwood, WV
C-2164	10-20-61	Wheeling Division
C-2164	12-1-65	Benwood to Holloway, OH, pool #1
C-2164	7-22-74	Benwood, WV, extra cab
C-2164	3-14-75	Benwood, WV
C-2165	1-13-58	shopped, Du Bois, PA
C-2165	1-18-61	Pittsburgh Division
C-2165	7-22-74	Allingdale, WV, SC&M pool
C-2165	3-14-75	Allingdale, WV
C-2166	5-5-61	Garrett, IN, operating into Illinois
C-2166	10-20-61	Akron-Chicago Division
C-2166	10-15-64	Garrett, IN, West end local
C-2168	1-16-59	Garrett, IN, to Robey St, Chicago
C-2168	5-5-61	Garrett, IN, not assigned
C-2168	10-20-61	Akron-Chicago Division
C-2168	10-15-64	Garrett, IN assigned
C-2169	1-16-59	Garrett, IN, to Robey St, Chicago
C-2169	10-20-61	Akron-Chicago Division

Cab #	Date	Assignment
C-2169	10-15-64	Garrett, IN assigned
C-2169	7-8-69	Newark Division pool service
C-2169	3-14-75	Dayton, OH
C-2170	5-5-61	Garrett, IN, operating into Illinois
C-2170	10-20-61	Akron-Chicago Division
C-2170	10-15-64	Garrett, IN assigned
C-2171	1-8-54	sent BW to Grafton for service
C-2171	1-22-54	Grafton to Cowen, WV service
C-2171	3-1-54	Grafton, WV, shopped
C-2171	2-10-58	Grafton, WV, extra service
C-2171	12-1-65	Trains 50-51, Gassaway to GRF
C-2172	5-18-53	Baltimore Div, operating thru DE
C-2172	8-19-53	shopped: MC send to Wheel. Div
C-2172	9-29-53	shopped: GS for Wheeling Div
C-2172	11-13-53	to GS shop from Baltimore Div.
C-2172	11-16-53	GRF to Gassaway shop, WV
C-2172	3-1-54	Gassaway, WV, shopped
C-2172	12-1-65	trains 61-62, GS to Charleston
C-2173	10-20-61	Akron-Chicago Division
C-2173	1-12-64	Toledo-Indianapolis Division
C-2173	7-22-74	Brooklyn Jct., WV, condemned
C-2174	10-20-61	Toledo-Indianapolis Division
C-2174	1-12-64	Toledo-Indianapolis Division
C-2175	10-20-61	Toledo-Indianapolis Division
C-2175	1-12-64	Toledo-Indianapolis Division
C-2175	3-14-75	Buckhannon, WV
C-2176	5-5-61	St. Louis Division
C-2176	1-12-64	St. Louis Division
C-2177	8-15-56	Brunswick, MD, pool
C-2177	6-5-61	Martinsburg, WV
C-2178	7-26-61	Benwood, WV
C-2179	9-6-56	Bay View, MD, to Childs Local
C-2179	9-10-56	Bay View to Childs local
C-2179	5-3-57	Baltimore Div operating thru DE
C-2179	6-21-61	Maryland
C-2179	7-17-61	Baltimore, MD, terminal service
C-2180	4-5-51	Grafton to Salem, WV, pool
C-2180	10-3-52	Grafton to Salem, WV, pool
C-2180	8-10-53	Grafton, WV, to Salem, WV
C-2180	10-27-53	Clarksburg, WV, assigned
C-2180	11-2-53	Clarksburg, WV, assigned
C-2180	1-22-54	Grafton, WV, extra service
C-2180	3-1-54	Grafton, WV, extra cab
C-2180	2-10-58	Cowen to Buckhannon, WV, local
C-2180	12-1-65	Parkersburg to Belpre, OH, turn
C-2181	5-11-54	to MC for I-5D then to Mon. Div
C-2181	10-19-55	last repaired MC 9-54
C-2181	1-13-58	shopped, Du Bois, PA
C-2181	2-10-58	Benwood, WV, assigned
C-2181	4-26-61	Pittsburgh Division
C-2182	4-5-51	Gassaway, WV, shopped
C-2182	10-3-52	Grafton, WV, unassigned
C-2182	8-10-53	G&B Pool, Monongah Division
C-2182	1-22-54	Shopped, Gassaway, WV
C-2182	3-1-54	Gassaway, WV, shopped
C-2182	2-10-58	Fairmont, WV, stored for shop
C-2182	12-1-65	MR Pool, Monongah Division
C-2182	7-22-74	Fairmont, WV, industrial turn
C-2182	3-14-75	Fairmont, WV
C-2183	1-31-57	M&K Local
C-2183	7-25-61	North Vernon to Washington, IN
C-2183	10-20-61	St. Louis Division
C-2183	1-12-64	St. Louis Division
C-2183	7-1-69	Ivorydale (Cincy), roustabout
C-2184	8-15-56	Keyser shop; destroyed Cumbo
C-2185	8-15-56	Cumberland; Kelly Springfield turn
C-2185	6-21-61	Maryland
C-2185	7-17-61	Brunswick, MD
C-2186	5-18-53	Baltimore Div, operating thru DE
C-2186	9-6-56	Millville Digger, Baltimore Division
C-2186	9-10-56	Millville, WV, Digger
C-2186	5-5-61	Indianapolis Division
C-2186	1-12-64	Toledo-Indianapolis Division
C-2186	7-1-67	Ivorydale, OH, transfer service
C-2187	2-27-53	PV shop to DU shop for repair

I-5 Family Assignments

Cab #	Date	Assignment
C-2187	5-10-61	Akron Division
C-2187	10-20-61	Akron-Chicago Division
C-2188	4-5-51	Gassaway, WV, shopped
C-2188	10-3-52	Grafton, WV, unassigned
C-2188	8-10-53	Grafton, WV, shopped
C-2188	1-22-54	G&B Pool, Monongah Division
C-2188	3-1-54	G&B Pool, Monongah Division
C-2188	8-14-56	Eastern Region, oper. In PA
C-2188	9-6-56	Riverside (Balt) emergency svc.
C-2188	9-10-56	Riverside Yard (Balt), emergency
C-2188	6-21-61	Maryland
C-2188	7-17-61	Baltimore, MD, terminal service
C-2189	8-15-56	Released KY shop; to Balt Div
C-2189	9-6-56	Washingtn. Brnch. Locl. (Balt Div)
C-2189	9-10-56	Washington DC branch local
C-2189	6-21-61	Maryland
C-2189	7-17-61	Baltimore, MD, terminal service
C-2189	12-1-65	Trains 43-42, Grafton to CW turn
C-2189	7-22-74	Fairmont, WV, MR pool service
C-2189	3-14-75	Fairmont, WV
C-2190	11-3-47	Millville, WV
C-2190	3-1-54	Benwood, WV, extra cab
C-2190	7-26-61	Parkersburg, WV
C-2190	12-1-65	CL to Fairmont assigned turn
C-2191	1-8-54	sent BW to Grafton for service
C-2191	1-22-54	Short Line Pool
C-2191	3-1-54	Grafton to Salem, WV pool
C-2192	1-31-57	M&K work train
C-2192	6-21-61	Maryland
C-2192	7-17-61	Brunswick, MD
C-2193	8-15-56	Cumberland; Amcelle Turn
C-2193	5-5-61	St. Louis Division
C-2193	1-12-64	St. Louis Division
C-2194	9-6-56	Baltimore Terminal (MD)
C-2194	9-10-56	Baltimore, MD, terminal
C-2194	5-5-61	St. Louis Division
C-2194	1-12-64	St. Louis Division
C-2195	2-10-58	G&B Pool, Monongah Division
C-2195	12-1-65	Grafton, WV, extra cab
C-2196	7-25-61	Washington, IN to Cincinnati
C-2196	10-20-61	St. Louis Division
C-2196	1-12-64	St. Louis Division
C-2196	3-14-75	Cincinnati, OH
C-2198	7-26-61	Benwood, WV
C-2198	12-1-65	Brooklyn Jct., WV, district run
C-2198	7-22-74	Holloway, OH, Egypt Valley svc.
C-2198	3-14-75	Holloway, OH
C-2199	9-6-56	Oella District Switcher (Balt Div)
C-2199	9-10-56	Oella District Switcher-Balt Div
C-2199	6-21-61	Maryland
C-2199	7-17-61	Baltimore, MD, terminal service
C-2200	8-15-56	Brunswick, MD pool
C-2200	12-1-65	Cowen, WV, #5 district turn
C-2202	3-23-48	Millville, WV
C-2202	3-1-54	Trains 81-82, PR to Huntington
C-2202	7-26-61	Parkersburg, WV
C-2202	12-1-65	Parkersburg, WV, city turn
C-2202	7-22-74	Parkersburg, WV, Parmaco turn
C-2202	3-14-75	Parkersburg, WV
C-2202	11-13-53	sending to Wheeling Division
C-2203	9-6-56	Baltimore Terminal (MD)
C-2203	9-10-56	Baltimore, MD, terminal
C-2203	12-1-65	Clarksburg to Parkersburg local
C-2203	1-1-69	Clarksburg, WV, #8 yard turn
C-2203	7-22-74	Fairmont, WV, Hickman Run
C-2203	3-14-75	Gassaway, WV
C-2204	10-20-61	Toledo-Indianapolis Division
C-2204	1-12-64	Toledo-Indianapolis Division
C-2204	3-14-75	Dayton, OH
C-2205	7-25-61	Washington, IN to Cincinnati
C-2205	10-20-61	St. Louis Division
C-2205	1-12-64	St. Louis Division
C-2206	7-25-61	Youngstown, KY, to Cincinnati
C-2206	10-20-61	Ohio-Newark Division
C-2206	5-19-62	shopped, Chillicothe, OH

Cab #	Date	Assignment
C-2206	6-4-63	Washington, IN, shops
C-2206	1-12-64	St. Louis Division
C-2207	7-25-61	Cincinnati to Washington, IN
C-2207	10-20-61	St. Louis Division
C-2207	1-12-64	St. Louis Division
C-2208	7-25-61	Cincinnati to Washington, IN
C-2208	10-20-61	St. Louis Division
C-2208	1-12-64	St. Louis Division
C-2208	7-1-67	Storrs, OH, Holton turn
C-2208	7-1-69	Storrs, OH, St. Joe switcher
C-2210	10-20-61	Toledo-Indianapolis Division
C-2210	1-12-64	Toledo-Indianapolis Division
C-2210	7-22-74	Benwood, WV, extra cab
C-2212	10-17-62	C&O transfer, Cincinnati
C-2212	6-20-63	Ivorydale, OH, transfer service
C-2212	1-12-64	Ohio-Newark Division
C-2212	6-1-66	Chillicothe, OH, freight pool
C-2213	10-20-61	Toledo-Indianapolis Division
C-2213	1-12-64	Toledo-Indianapolis Division
C-2214	4-5-51	Parkersburg to Grafton pool
C-2214	10-3-52	Parkersburg, WV, pool
C-2214	8-10-53	Parkersburg to Grafton, WV, pool
C-2214	1-22-54	Parkersburg to Grafton pool
C-2214	3-1-54	Parkersburg to Grafton pool
C-2214	10-19-55	Keyser, WV
C-2214	2-10-58	MR Pool, Monongah Division
C-2214	12-1-65	MR Pool, Monongah Division
C-2215	9-6-56	Baltimore Terminal (MD)
C-2215	9-10-56	Baltimore, MD, terminal
C-2215	6-21-61	Maryland
C-2215	7-17-61	Baltimore, MD, terminal service
C-2216	5-5-61	Indianapolis Division
C-2216	1-12-64	Toledo-Indianapolis Division
C-2217	8-19-53	shopped: MC send to Wheel. Div
C-2217	9-29-53	shopped: GS for Wheeling Div
C-2217	11-13-53	shopped GS from Baltimore Div
C-2217	3-1-54	Parkersburg, WV, emergency
C-2217	7-26-61	Parkersburg, WV
C-2218	4-10-52	Shopped: Mt. Clare, Baltimore
C-2218	9-6-56	Brunswick, MD, emergency svc.
C-2218	9-10-56	Brunswick, MD, emergency
C-2218	2-10-58	Benwood - Grafton trains 197-196
C-2218	12-1-65	Trains 49-40, Grafton to CW turn
C-2218	7-22-74	Brooklyn Jct., 10 PM Distr. Run
C-2221	5-18-53	Baltimore Div, operating thru DE
C-2221	9-6-56	Baltimore Terminal (MD)
C-2221	9-10-56	Baltimore, MD, terminal
C-2221	6-21-61	Maryland
C-2221	7-17-61	Old Main Line local freight
C-2222	5-18-53	Baltimore Div, operating thru DE
C-2222	9-6-56	Trains 8-22, Keyser, WV
C-2222	9-10-56	Keyser, WV, trains 8-22
C-2222	2-10-58	Parkersburg to Grafton, WV, pool
C-2222	12-1-65	GRF to BD pool, out of Fairmont
C-2222	7-22-74	Fairmont, WV, Underwood Pool
C-2223	6-5-61	Martinsburg, WV
C-2223	9-7-61	Pittsburgh Division
C-2223	9-7-61	Pittsburgh Division assigned
C-2224	9-6-56	Trains 6-25, Keyser, WV
C-2224	9-10-56	Keyser, WV, trains 6-25
C-2224	2-10-58	Grafton to Cowen, WV, trns 99-90
C-2224	12-1-65	MR Pool, Monongah Division
C-2225	8-15-56	Hagerstown, MD, pool
C-2226	4-5-51	Grafton to Salem, WV, pool
C-2226	10-3-52	Grafton, WV, unassigned
C-2226	8-10-53	Gassaway, WV, shopped
C-2226	1-22-54	Grafton to Salem, WV pool
C-2226	3-1-54	Grafton to Salem, WV pool
C-2226	2-10-58	Shopped, Keyser, WV
C-2226	5-5-61	St. Louis Division
C-2226	1-12-64	St. Louis Division
C-2226	7-8-69	Shopped, Newark, OH
C-2227	4-5-51	G&B Pool, Monongah Division
C-2227	10-3-52	G&B pool, Monongah Division
C-2227	1-22-54	G&B Pool, Monongah Division

Cab #	Date	Assignment
C-2227	3-1-54	G&B Pool, Monongah Division
C-2227	2-10-58	G&B Pool, Monongah Division
C-2227	12-1-65	Grafton to Salem, WV, pool
C-2227	7-22-74	Grafton, WV, Ozie Turn
C-2228	9-6-56	Baltimore Terminal (MD)
C-2228	9-10-56	Baltimore, MD, terminal
C-2228	5-5-61	Indianapolis Division
C-2228	1-12-64	Toledo-Indianapolis Division
C-2229	4-5-51	Parkersburg to Grafton pool
C-2229	10-3-52	Grafton to Cowen, WV
C-2229	8-10-53	G&B Pool, Monongah Division
C-2229	1-22-54	Trains 99-92 GRF to Cowen, WV
C-2229	3-1-54	Trains 99-92, GRF to Cowen
C-2229	2-10-58	Grafton to Cowen trains 91-86
C-2229	12-1-65	Cowen, WV, #7 district turn
C-2229	7-22-74	Gassaway, WV, work train svc.
C-2230	8-16-56	B&O Pool, AK Div, oper. in PA
C-2230	5-25-61	Akron-Chicago Division
C-2230	8-4-61	Akron Division
C-2230	10-20-61	Akron-Chicago Division
C-2231	9-6-56	Baltimore Terminal (MD)
C-2231	9-10-56	Baltimore, MD, terminal
C-2231	6-21-61	Maryland
C-2231	7-17-61	Baltimore, MD, terminal service
C-2231	12-1-65	Somerset, PA, shops, 9-13-65
C-2232	3-1-54	Gassaway, WV, shopped
C-2232	7-26-61	Parkersburg, WV
C-2232	12-1-65	Holloway, OH, mine run
C-2232	1-1-69	Parkersburg, WV, Industrial Turn
C-2232	7-22-74	Grafton, WV, on repair track
C-2233	1951	shopped, Du Bois, PA
C-2233	9-6-56	shopped, Du Bois, PA
C-2233	5-3-61	Pittsburgh Division
C-2233	10-20-61	Akron-Chicago Division
C-2233	7-22-74	Clarksburg, WV, extra cab
C-2234	5-5-61	Garrett, IN, operating into Illinois
C-2234	10-20-61	Akron-Chicago Division
C-2234	10-15-64	Garrett, IN assigned
C-2235	2-3-44	Punxsutawney, PA
C-2235	1951	Elk Run Jct., PA
C-2235	5-2-51	Riker, PA assigned
C-2235	9-6-51	Punxsutawney, PA
C-2235	4-22-53	Elk Run Jct., PA
C-2235	6-4-53	Glenwood, PA
C-2235	3-3-54	Buffalo Division assigned
C-2235	4-13-55	Du Bois, PA assigned
C-2235	5-19-55	shopped, Du Bois, PA
C-2235	10-14-55	shopped, Du Bois, PA
C-2235	5-25-61	Pittsburgh Division
C-2235	9-14-61	Pittsburgh Division
C-2236	10-27-50	Butler Jct, PA
C-2236	4-3-53	Butler Jct, PA
C-2236	3-3-54	Buffalo Division assigned
C-2236	10-28-54	extra cab at Butler Jct, PA
C-2236	4-13-55	Du Bois, PA assigned
C-2236	5-19-55	shopped, Du Bois, PA
C-2236	10-14-55	shopped, Du Bois, PA
C-2236	4-13-60	DU shop; from Pittsburgh Division
C-2236	4-14-60	DU shop to WA shop for St.L.Div
C-2236	10-20-61	Ohio-Newark Division
C-2236	5-19-62	Chillicothe, OH, pool
C-2236	6-4-63	Chillicothe, OH, pool
C-2236	1-12-64	Ohio-Newark Division
C-2236	1-15-64	Chillicothe, OH, pool service
C-2236	3-25-65	Chillicothe, OH
C-2236	6-1-66	Chillicothe, OH, freight pool
C-2236	7-8-69	Newark Division pool service
C-2237	6-27-44	Punxsutawney, PA
C-2237	5-2-51	Riker, PA assigned
C-2237	9-6-51	Punxsutawney, PA
C-2237	3-3-54	Buffalo Division assigned
C-2237	5-21-54	Punxsutawney, PA
C-2237	3-7-55	Buffalo Division
C-2237	4-13-55	Elk Run Jct., PA
C-2237	10-14-55	Punxsutawney, PA

I-5 Family Assignments

Cab #	Date	Assignment
C-2237	11-15-55	Glenwood, PA pool
C-2237	5-25-61	Pittsburgh Division
C-2237	6-14-61	Pittsburgh Division
C-2238	4-13-60	DU shop; from Pittsburgh Division
C-2238	4-14-60	DU shop to WA shop for St.L.Div
C-2238	10-20-61	St. Louis Division
C-2238	1-12-64	Toledo-Indianapolis Division
C-2239	10-20-61	Ohio-Newark Division
C-2239	5-19-62	Newark, OH, pool
C-2239	4-17-63	Southwest Pool, Newark, OH
C-2239	6-4-63	Newark, OH, pool
C-2239	6-22-63	Newark to Cincinnati pool
C-2239	1-12-64	Ohio-Newark Division
C-2239	1-15-64	Newark to Cincinnati pool
C-2239	1-18-64	NE to Cincinnati pool service
C-2239	7-8-69	Shopped, Du Bois, PA
C-2240	10-20-61	Ohio-Newark Division
C-2240	10-17-62	Oakley Job, Cincinnati
C-2240	6-20-63	Oakley, OH (Cincinnati)
C-2240	1-12-64	Ohio-Newark Division
C-2241	5-25-61	Pittsburgh Division
C-2241	6-19-61	Pittsburgh Division
C-2242	4-28-61	Pittsburgh Division
C-2242	7-22-74	Pt. Pleasant, WV, district turn
C-2243	8-15-56	Hagerstown, MD, pool
C-2243	9-29-61	Cumberland Division
C-2244	5-25-61	Pittsburgh Division
C-2244	7-14-61	Pittsburgh Division
C-2245	10-20-61	Ohio-Newark Division
C-2245	5-19-62	Chillicothe to Portsmouth switcher
C-2245	1-12-64	Toledo-Indianapolis Division
C-2245	7-1-67	Ivorydale, OH, transfer service
C-2245	7-1-69	Storrs, OH, to Sedamsville Job
C-2246	3-8-61	Pittsburgh Division
C-2246	1-13-58	shopped, Du Bois, PA
C-2247	3-31-61	Pittsburgh Division
C-2248	4-5-51	Gassaway, WV, shopped
C-2248	10-3-52	Fairmont to Benwood turn
C-2248	8-10-53	Parkersburg to Grafton, WV, pool
C-2248	9-20-53	FR to BD; to Gassaway shop
C-2248	1-22-54	Parkersburg to Grafton pool
C-2248	3-1-54	Parkersburg to Grafton pool
C-2248	11-16-55	derailed in Grafton, WV yard
C-2248	2-10-58	Parkersburg to Grafton, WV, pool
C-2248	12-1-65	Grafton to BD pool out of FR
C-2248	1-1-69	GRF to BD pool working out of FR
C-2248	7-22-74	Fairmont, WV, MR pool service
C-2249	5-25-61	Pittsburgh Division
C-2249	7-5-61	Pittsburgh Division
C-2250	2-10-58	Grafton, WV, stored
C-2250	12-1-65	Trains 41-48, GRF to Cowen turn
C-2250	1-1-69	Clarksbg, WV, - Weston dist run
C-2251	4-5-51	Day Gypsy Dist. Run (Mon Div)
C-2251	10-3-52	Fairmont to Benwood turn
C-2251	8-10-53	Benwood, WV, to Fairmont pool
C-2251	1-22-54	Clarksburg mine run
C-2251	3-1-54	Clarksburg, WV, Mine Run
C-2251	10-19-55	last repaired GS 4-55
C-2251	2-10-58	Shopped, Keyser, WV
C-2251	12-1-61	CL to Weston Merchandise Turn
C-2251	1-1-69	Parkersburg to Millwood distr. run
C-2252	12-2-55	Forest Hill, Chicago, IL
C-2252	5-5-61	Garrett, IN, operating into Illinois
C-2252	10-20-61	Akron-Chicago Division
C-2252	10-15-64	Garrett, IN assigned
C-2253	1951	Butler Jct, PA
C-2253	4-28-53	DU shop; billed to Punxsutawney
C-2253	3-3-54	Buffalo Division assigned
C-2253	5-21-54	Punxsutawney, PA
C-2253	4-13-55	Du Bois, PA assigned
C-2253	5-19-55	shopped, Du Bois, PA
C-2253	8-28-55	DU shop; released as an I-5D
C-2253	10-14-55	Punxsutawney, PA
C-2253	11-15-55	Glenwood, PA pool
C-2253	8-27-56	Glenwood, PA, pool
C-2253	12-4-56	Elk Run Jct., PA
C-2253	1957	Punxsutawney, PA
C-2253	5-23-57	Elk Run Jct, PA
C-2253	8-10-59	New Castle, PA, to Riker yard
C-2253	2-12-60	Riker to New Castle, PA
C-2253	6-20-60	Du Bois, PA, shopped
C-2253	2-3-61	Buffalo Division
C-2253	6-19-61	Trains 87-88; Buffalo Division
C-2253	11-1-61	Foxburg, PA
C-2253	2-27-63	Trains 87-88, Foxburg, PA side
C-2254	4-5-51	Short Line Pool
C-2254	10-3-52	Short Line Pool, Monongah Div
C-2254	8-10-53	Benwood, WV, to Fairmont pool
C-2254	1-22-54	Benwood to Fairmont Pool
C-2254	1-26-54	Benwood to Fairmont pool
C-2254	3-1-54	Grafton, WV
C-2254	8-31-54	Benwood to Fairmont pool
C-2254	10-19-55	last repaired GS 12-53
C-2254	2-10-58	Fairmont, WV, extra cab
C-2255	10-20-61	Ohio-Newark Division
C-2255	5-19-62	Chillicothe, OH, pool
C-2255	6-4-63	Chillicothe, OH, pool
C-2255	1-12-64	Ohio-Newark Division
C-2255	1-15-64	Chillicothe, OH, pool service
C-2255	6-1-66	Chillicothe, OH, freight pool
C-2256	10-20-61	Ohio-Newark Division
C-2256	10-17-62	Park Place Job, Cincinnati
C-2256	6-4-63	Washington, IN, shops
C-2256	6-20-63	Ivorydale, OH, transfer service
C-2256	1-12-64	Ohio-Newark Division
C-2256	12-1-65	Ivorydale, OH, transfer service
C-2257	3-1-54	Trains 96-97, Benwood to GRF
C-2257	7-26-61	Parkersburg, WV
C-2257	12-1-65	Huntington to Mile Post 165
C-2257	1-1-69	Trains 204-203 PR to BD, WV
C-2258	3-1-54	Benwood to Fairmont Pool
C-2258	7-26-61	Benwood, WV
C-2258	12-1-65	Benwood, WV
C-2258	1-1-69	Brooklyn Jct., WV, PM district run
C-2258	7-22-74	Brooklyn Jct., WV, district turn
C-2260	5-18-53	Baltimore Div, operating thru DE
C-2260	2-10-58	G&B Pool, Monongah Division
C-2260	12-1-65	Trains 45-46, Grafton to CW turn
C-2260	1-1-69	Du Bois, PA, shopped
C-2260	7-22-74	Grafton, WV, on repair track
C-2261	3-1-54	Gassaway, WV, shopped
C-2261	7-26-61	Parkersburg, WV
C-2261	12-1-65	Parkersburg, Parmaco turn
C-2261	1-1-69	Benwood, WV, pool service
C-2261	7-22-74	Brooklyn Jct., WV, Brk. Jct. Turn
C-2262	5-19-61	Akron Division
C-2262	10-20-61	Akron-Chicago Division
C-2263	8-16-56	Lorain, OH to New Castle pool
C-2263	10-20-61	Akron-Chicago Division
C-2264	3-1-54	Cleveland, OH to Holloway pool
C-2264	10-20-61	Akron-Chicago Division
C-2264	10-15-64	Garrett, IN assigned
C-2265	3-1-54	Willard, OH to Holloway pool
C-2265	10-20-61	Akron-Chicago Division
C-2266	2-17-61	Pittsburgh Division
C-2266	4-28-72	Connellsville, PA, for sale
C-2267	5-25-61	Akron-Chicago Division
C-2267	8-2-61	Akron Division
C-2267	10-20-61	Akron-Chicago Division
C-2268	8-16-56	New Castle, PA, extra cab
C-2268	5-25-61	Pittsburgh Division
C-2268	8-16-61	Pittsburgh Division
C-2269	8-16-56	B&O Pool, AK Div, oper. in PA
C-2269	5-25-61	Akron-Chicago Division
C-2269	7-17-61	Akron Division
C-2269	10-20-61	Akron-Chicago Division
C-2270	8-16-56	Cleveland, OH to New Castle run
C-2270	1-13-58	shopped, Du Bois, PA
C-2270	5-25-61	Akron-Chicago Division
C-2270	7-12-61	Akron Division
C-2270	10-20-61	Akron-Chicago Division
C-2271	1-13-58	shopped, Du Bois, PA
C-2271	4-13-60	DU shop; from Akron Division
C-2271	4-14-60	DU shop to WA shop for St.L.Div
C-2271	8-21-61	Akron Division
C-2271	10-20-61	Akron-Chicago Division
C-2272	5-5-61	Garrett, IN, operating into Illinois
C-2272	10-20-61	Akron-Chicago Division
C-2272	10-15-64	Garrett, IN assigned
C-2274	10-20-61	Akron-Chicago Division
C-2274	4-28-72	Chillicothe, OH, fire damaged
C-2275	8-16-56	B&O Pool, AK Div, oper. in PA
C-2275	5-25-61	Akron-Chicago Division
C-2275	10-20-61	Akron-Chicago Division
C-2276	8-16-56	B&O Pool, AK Div, oper. in PA
C-2276	4-24-61	Akron Division
C-2276	10-20-61	Akron-Chicago Division
C-2276	4-28-72	Mt. Clare, MD, available for sale
C-2277	8-16-56	B&O Pool, AK Div, oper. in PA
C-2277	5-12-61	Akron Division
C-2277	10-20-61	Akron-Chicago Division
C-2278	1-16-59	Garrett, IN, to Robey St, Chicago
C-2278	5-5-61	Garrett, IN, operating into Illinois
C-2278	10-20-61	Akron-Chicago Division
C-2278	10-15-64	Garrett, IN assigned
C-2279	1-13-58	shopped, Du Bois, PA
C-2279	5-5-61	Garrett, IN, operating into Illinois
C-2279	10-20-61	Akron-Chicago Division
C-2279	10-15-64	Garrett, IN assigned
C-2279	6-1-66	Chillicothe, OH, freight pool
C-2280	5-5-61	Garrett, IN, operating into Illinois
C-2280	10-20-61	Akron-Chicago Division
C-2280	10-15-64	Garrett, IN assigned
C-2281	5-5-61	Garrett, IN, operating into Illinois
C-2281	10-20-61	Akron-Chicago Division
C-2281	10-15-64	Garrett, IN assigned
C-2281	6-1-66	Ivorydale, OH, pool cab
C-2281	9-1-66	Ivorydale, OH, pool cab
C-2282	1-16-59	Garrett, IN, to Robey St, Chicago
C-2282	5-5-61	Garrett, IN, operating into Illinois
C-2282	10-20-61	Akron-Chicago Division
C-2283	4-17-63	Newark, OH, pool
C-2283	6-22-63	Willard to Benwood pool
C-2283	1-12-64	Ohio-Newark Division
C-2283	1-18-64	Newark Division, pool service
C-2283	7-8-69	Newark Division pool service
C-2284	10-20-61	Ohio-Newark Division
C-2284	4-17-63	Central Ohio local, Newark, OH
C-2284	6-22-63	Central OH Local, rear caboose
C-2284	1-12-64	Ohio-Newark Division
C-2284	1-18-64	Central Ohio local (Newark, OH)
C-2285	10-20-61	Ohio-Newark Division
C-2285	5-19-62	Newark, OH
C-2285	6-4-63	Washington, IN, shops
C-2285	1-12-64	Ohio-Newark Division
C-2286	5-5-61	Indianapolis Division
C-2286	1-12-64	Toledo-Indianapolis Division
C-2287	10-20-61	Toledo-Indianapolis Division
C-2287	1-12-64	Toledo-Indianapolis Division
C-2288	10-20-61	Toledo-Indianapolis Division
C-2288	1-12-64	Toledo-Indianapolis Division
C-2289	7-25-61	North Vernon, IN to Cincinnati
C-2289	1-12-64	St. Louis Division
C-2289	7-1-67	St. Joe switcher, Storrs, OH
C-2290	10-20-61	Ohio-Newark Division
C-2290	4-17-63	O&LK rider, Newark, OH
C-2290	6-22-63	O&LK Local (NE)
C-2290	1-12-64	Ohio-Newark Division
C-2290	1-18-64	O&LK local, rider car
C-2290	7-8-69	Newark Division pool service
C-2290	3-14-75	Newark, OH
C-2291	10-20-61	Toledo-Indianapolis Division
C-2291	1-12-64	Toledo-Indianapolis Division
C-2291	1-15-64	Chillicothe to Portsmouth local
C-2291	6-1-66	Chillicothe, OH, freight pool

I-5 Family Assignments

Cab #	Date	Assignment
C-2292	1-12-64	Toledo-Indianapolis Division
C-2293	10-20-61	St. Louis Division
C-2293	1-12-64	St. Louis Division
C-2293	12-1-65	Grafton, WV, extra cab
C-2293	1-1-69	Fairmont, WV, MR Pool
C-2293	7-22-74	Fairmont, WV, extra cab
C-2293	3-14-75	Fairmont, WV
C-2294	10-20-61	Toledo-Indianapolis Division
C-2294	1-12-64	Toledo-Indianapolis Division

Cab #	Date	Assignment
C-2295	1-12-64	Toledo-Indianapolis Division
C-2296	5-5-61	St. Louis Division
C-2296	1-12-64	St. Louis Division
C-2296	3-14-75	Indianapolis, IN
C-2297	5-5-61	St. Louis Division
C-2297	7-25-61	Washington, IN to Cincinnati
C-2297	1-12-64	St. Louis Division
C-2297	7-1-68	Stock Yards, trains 83, 84 (Cincy)

Cab #	Date	Assignment
C-2297	7-1-69	Ivorydale, OH, C&O transfer
C-2298	7-25-61	Cincinnati to Washington, IN
C-2298	10-20-61	St. Louis Division
C-2298	1-12-64	St. Louis Division
C-2298	7-1-69	Oakley (Cincy), OH transfer
C-2299	7-25-61	Washington, IN to Cincinnati
C-2299	10-20-61	St. Louis Division
C-2299	1-12-64	St. Louis Division

A visit to the Chillicothe shops on June 12, 1977, found class I-5 C-2064 repainted and ready for return to service. After photographing the cab we visited the shop offices where car forman Ora Sheets was working on some paperwork. "What do you think of that caboose?", Ora asked. "It looks great" we said. "Too bad you have the wrong class stenciled on it." Ora looked surprised. "What do you mean?" he asked. "That's a short wheelbase I-5. But you have it stencilled as an I-5D!". He never corrected it. The car had been in service at Indianapolis. Plywood sides were added during this shopping (this side only). The car was

painted yellow with silver roof and handrails, black underframe and steps and Enchantment Blue (not black) lettering. And the red side stripe returned on this car. <u>This was the last wood caboose painted by the B&O</u>. It first was sent to Philadelphia for local service. Appropriately this last repaint ended up in Baltimore for local service. In 1980 it was damaged by fire and was out of service at Riverside. *Dwight Jones*

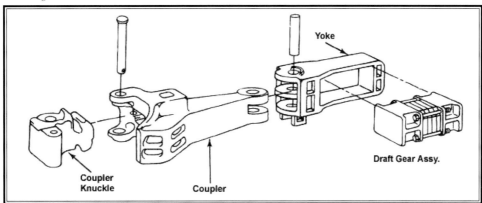

Older B&O cabooses began to receive the "R" stencil (for Restricted service) in 1975 in accordance with Federal Railroad Administration (FRA) rule 215.303. The "R" was to be stencilled just below or to the right of the car number, be the same color as the car number, and be the same size as the car number. Following the "R" stencil, in 1" size figures was to be listed the reasons a car was in Restricted service. Reasons could be: Age, Coupler, Draft, Bearings, Trucks, Underframe, Wheels and/or Yoke. Requirements for each of those items could be found defined in the FRA rule.

Before the steel-bodied wagon-tops took over on the west end of the Cumberland Division, I-5 family cabooses held the assignment. This is a prolific B&O company photo of a coal train rounding Salt Lick curve just west of Terra Alta, West Virginia, a favorite spot for company photographers. The end of this train, shown in the blowup at left, shows the single helper shoving on the caboose.

Caboose C-2139 is shown at Hamilton, Ohio, on April 26, 1987. This was the last I-5 family cab left on the railroad—no longer technically used as a caboose but rather as a rider car for MofW service. Six months later it was scrapped by a contractor in northern Kentucky. *Dwight Jones*

CHAPTER 4

Quick History

Original Numbers:	C-2300 to C-2374	Cars Built:	175
Original Numbers:	C-2700 to C-2799	In Service (2013):	0
Year Built: 1942 and 1943 (modified)		Chessie Class:	C-19
Weight: 47,760 lbs		Preserved:	6 (now 5)
Built by: B&O Shops: MTC, DU, WA (see roster)			

The I-16 caboose boxcar conversions continued the idea initiated by the B&O with the I-13 stock car conversions (covered in volume 3). Difficulty in obtaining steel for new cabooses is one reason cited for conversion of these older wood cars to cabooses.

The I-13 cars were modified in 1941. The I-16 conversions started 16 months later.

In the case of the I-16 cabooses, box cars of classes M-12, M-13, M-13A, M-13B and M-14A provided the cores for the work which was assigned to three different B&O car shops.

In November 1942 the shops at Mount Clare (Baltimore), Du Bois, Pennsylvania, and Washington,

Indiana, simultaneously modified 25 cars each for a total of 75 new cabooses (C-2300 to C-2374).

Eight months later these same shops completed an additional 100 cabooses with the shops at Washington doing 50 cars compared to the 25 completed at the other two shops (C-2700 to C-2799).

Two unusual prototype cars were first completed, one at Washington and one at Mount Clare. Photos of these two cars are showm in this chapter. So unusual were these two cars that the shops apparently felt the need to stencil the word CABOOSE on the cars so it would be clearly understood as to their purpose! As noted in this chapter these two early cars were returned to the shops and further modified

This B&O builder's photo of "new" caboose C-2306 was made on October 17, 1942, after conversion at Mt. Clare. Note the arch-bar trucks. Modelers may be interested in the pole lying on the ground beside the caboose, used to push cars with an engine which were on an adjacent track, a dangerous practice later eliminated. This particular pole has stenciling on it to identify its track location (although we can only read the word TRACK). It also is sitting on risers to keep it off the ground and help preserve its life. Cars had "poling pockets" to help secure the pole during movements (they show on the corners between the coupler and step). *B&O Photo / collection of Dwight Jones*

Baltimore, Md., August 31, 1942.
MP&E 7456

Mr. C. W. Van Horn,
Vice-President.

Dear Sir:

Referring to Mr. Becherer's conversation with Mr. L. C. Sauerhammer, attached are four photographs, two side and two end views of 36-ft. box car converted into caboose 180482 at Mt. Clare shop recently, which car is now in service at Baltimore. Also B&O 181200 was converted at Washington, Ind. Both of these cars were converted on 940 authority C-48922, which was held up as per your letter of May 14, 1942.

Also attached is print Z-69264-A covering bay window construction of proposed caboose car converted from class M-13 box car. We do not have any cars built in accordance with this print.

Also attached is one photograph, No. 2127, covering side and end view of caboose car C-1800. These cars were converted from old CI&W stock cars, and we now have 36 in service. Your particular attention is called to the fact this has the bay window in it.

It is my recommendation that we complete the remaining 18 cabooses on form 940 authority C-48922, in accordance with print Z-69264-A referred to above, and also that we return B&O 180482 and 181200 to the shops to have bay windows applied.

Will you please advise if we have your authority to do this?

Yours truly,

[signature]

akg -

to match the final class I-16 configuration.

Interior Arrangement (1942)

Drawing Y-69342 was prepared to document the interior arrangement of these cars and is dated September 16, 1942. A revision dated January 19, 1951, changed the style and location of the torpedo rack and showed a floor block at the door.

End Construction (1942)

B&O drawing V-69362, dated September 21, 1942,

documented the end construction of the I-16 cars. Significant revisions to this drawing included changing the marker light bracket location to the end post with a revision date of June 29, 1943. With a revision date of May 23, 1946, an extra handhold was added to the end posts near the marker light bracket. This new handhold does not show it was adopted on all I-16 cabooses.

Marker Lamp Bracket Location Change (1943)

A B&O neo-style letter dated June 4, 1943, indicated the following:

"There has been some complaint as to the location of marker lamps on Caboose Cars, Class I-16, Series C-2300 to C-2374, and C-2700 to C-2799.

"The markers are now placed on the body of caboose at platform, and it has been decided to change the location to platform corner posts as illustrated on print S-70190-A, copies attached.

"These changes to be made when cars are available and the work can be performed without interfering with their operation."

Although not noted in the letter the complaint was that the engine crew could not see the markers because they were blocked by the side bay. Moving the markers farther back on the caboose helped to remedy this.

Bay Seats Improved (1943)

As shown by interior photos in this chapter, the I-16 cars, as built, had a wood seat on one side of the bay and a bunk on the opposite side. It must have been uncomfortable to sit on the edge of the bunk since there was no back to rest against. And it likewise must have been uncomfortable to sit on the bunk side of the side bay to observe the train due to a large gap between the edge of the bunk and wall of the side bay.

A B&O neo-style letter was issued under date of June 14, 1943, indicating that a permanent seat cushion was to be manufactured and installed in this gap area which would allow a trainman to sit close to the bay wall.

The cushions were to be applied to both sides of the cars whenever the cabooses were available and the work could be performed without interfering with the operation of the cars.

The shops at Washington, Indiana, were instructed to manufacture a sufficient number of cushions to equip all of the class I-16 caboose cars.

An additional B&O neo-style letter was issued on November 9, 1943, with applicable drawings, indicating that a removable back rest was to be added to the bunk seat. Quoting from the letter:

I-16 Retirements by Year

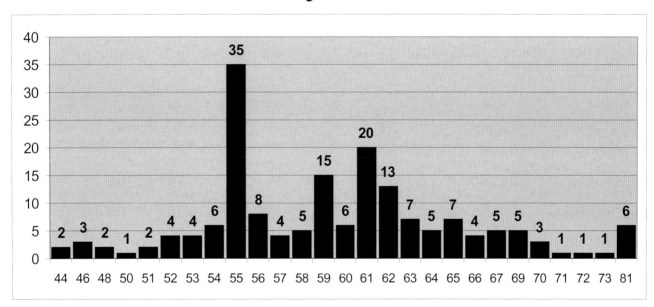

The chart above shows the quantity of I-16 cabooses that were retired each year. It appears the B&O got their money's worth from the class for a good solid 12 years. The large number of retirements in 1955 correspond to specific cars being renumbered for MofW service as can be seen from our detailed roster listings. Those renumberings and conversions were completed at Mount Clare, Washington, Indiana, and Du Bois, Pennsylvania. The arrival of more diesels, running of longer trains, and newer all-steel cabooses reduced the need for these war-time conversions. The last car to be retired, C-2356, in 1973, was traded to a steel company for some scrap. The six cars retired in 1981 had left the roster years earlier but had not been properly reported as such and were arbitrarily removed in 1981 to clean up the series.

It almost seemed like a competition—Mt. Clare submitted the version shown above and the shops at Washington, Indiana, converted the car shown below. Both cars retained their revenue box-car numbers and therefore the purpose of the car was stencilled on the side. The car above has a windshield on a side window. Below, the storekeeper has supplied two mis-matched marker lights. The one on the right is one of the older style with four cage-style external mounting brackets while the one on the left is the next version which has four brackets only along the bottom.
Two B&O Photos collection of Dwight Jones

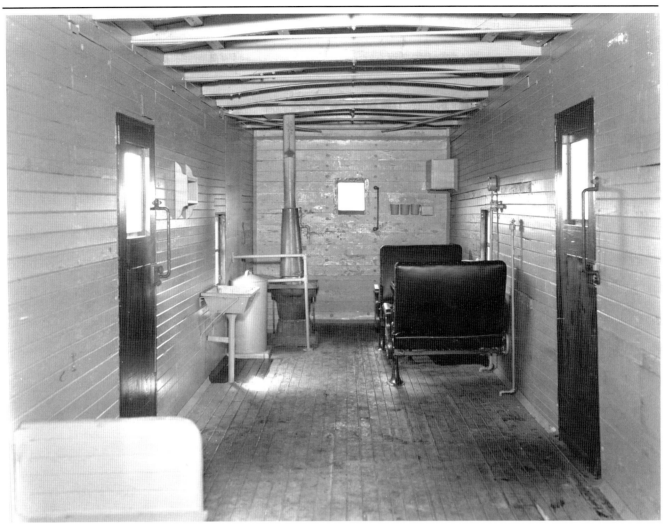

This inside view of the 181220 shows the spartan interior furnishings. Washington, Indiana, was a key passenger train car repair shop which likely accounts for the two passenger car walkover seats shown at right. A conductor's table was installed between the two seats at a window location. Mounted to the wall above the seats are a forms box, three holders for globes and a first aid kit. On the left is a water can and simple wash basin with a torpedo rack mounted on the wall near the door. Part of a bunk shows on the left near the photographer. No coal box shows in this single interior view. We suspect it would be near the side doors. *B&O photo, collection of Dwight Jones*

"Application of back rests will facilitate the observation of freight trains by their crews, through the bay windows when using end of bunks as a seat." This would be considered understatement!

When not in use the back rests were to be stored in brackets provided under bay window arm rests.

The letter further stated: "Back rests and attachments to be manufactured at Mt. Clare for I-16 Caboose Cars operating in the Eastern Region, and by Washington, Ind. for cars in the Central and Western Regions."

Rain Shield at Bay Window (1945)

Drawing S-72927 documented a rain shield (gutter)

that was to be applied above the bay window. A note on the drawing indicated that the shields were to be made from reclaimed roof sheets. The same item applied to both I-13 and I-16 cabooses. The drawing was issued to the field with a neo-style letter dated November 27, 1945. See a copy of this neo-style letter reproduced in this chapter.

Second Lives

Because of their roomy interiors and the caboose equipment (bunks, stove, wash facilities), the I-16 cars found second lives in the Maintenance of Way department as living quarters for workers such as crane operators. The rosters in this chapter document the various non-revenue numbers that were assigned to these cars after conversions.

File 2-608 - Conversion of box cars into caboose cars

Baltimore, August 13, 1942

Mr. C. W. Van Horn:-

     Provisions were made for the rebuilding of 20 Class
M-13 steel underframe box cars into caboose cars and understand
you deferred consideration of this project.

     Have now been advised that B. & O. 181220 at Washington,
Ind. was converted, also that B. & O. 180482 was converted and is
now being used in the Baltimore District. Inasmuch as these cars
have been converted you will, no doubt, desire to grant authority
to have them restencilled in the regular caboose car series.

     If agreeable, would suggest C-2300 for B. & O. 180482
and C-2301 for B. & O. 181220.

               W. C. BAKER.

Copy to:

Mr. A. K. Galloway.
Mr. F. H. Einwaechter.

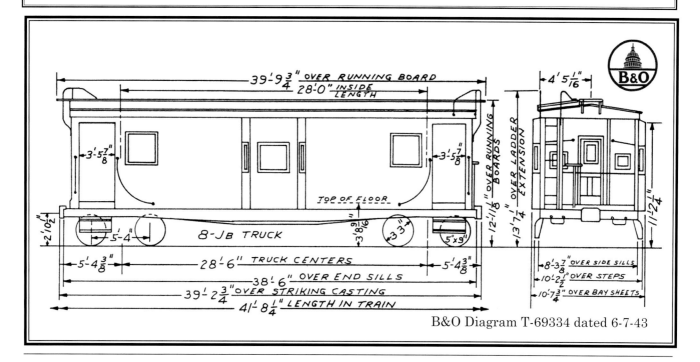

B&O Diagram T-69334 dated 6-7-43

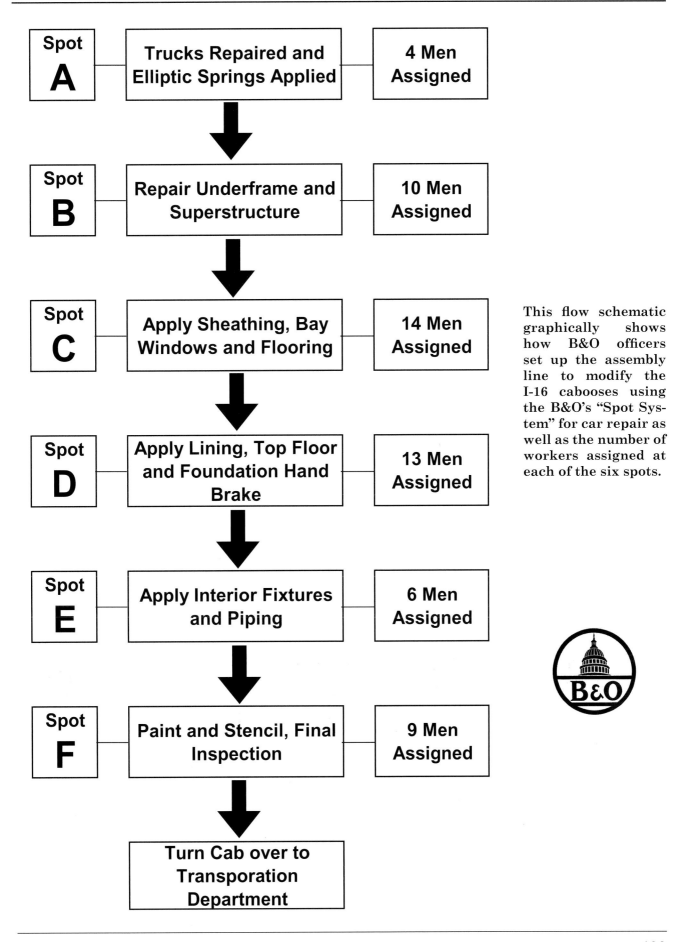

Spot **A**	Trucks Repaired and Elliptic Springs Applied	4 Men Assigned
Spot **B**	Repair Underframe and Superstructure	10 Men Assigned
Spot **C**	Apply Sheathing, Bay Windows and Flooring	14 Men Assigned
Spot **D**	Apply Lining, Top Floor and Foundation Hand Brake	13 Men Assigned
Spot **E**	Apply Interior Fixtures and Piping	6 Men Assigned
Spot **F**	Paint and Stencil, Final Inspection	9 Men Assigned

Turn Cab over to Transporation Department

This flow schematic graphically shows how B&O officers set up the assembly line to modify the I-16 cabooses using the B&O's "Spot System" for car repair as well as the number of workers assigned at each of the six spots.

B&O photo of the desk end of a newly converted I-16. Marker lights were always hung inside the caboose when not in use. Window shades were many times reclaimed from those removed from passenger train cars. *B&O Photo, collection of Dwight Jones*

Likely still wearing its original paint and lettering the C-2791, one of the last I-16 cabooses built, was photographed at Smithfield, Pennsylvania, on July 5, 1948. The car still retains its arch-bar type trucks. Hinged access panels on the steps provide access to journals. *Paul B. Dunn collection*

This photo of C-2306 shows the original configuration of the interior. Four bunks are located in the photographer's end of the car. The wooden seats at the bay look a bit uncomfortable and likely would later get some kind of cushion covering. The conductor's desk is located at the far end, left, behind the lockers. A window at that location provides extra light at the desk. Across the aisle are located the coal box, coal stove, overhead water tank and porcelain sink, not visible behind the bay bench. *B&O photo, collection of Dwight Jones*

This October 17, 1942, B&O builders photo, taken at the Mt. Clare shops, documents the end configuration of the C-2306. *B&O Photo, collection of Dwight Jones*

The graph at right documents the classes of the various boxcars that were used as cores for the I-16 caboose program. These older boxcars were determined to be obsolete due primarily to their smaller cubical capacity. In 1940 B&O reported a total of 449 boxcars from these classes still on the roster.

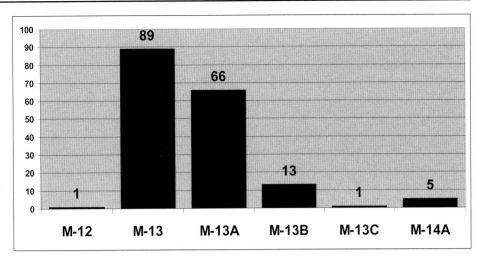

Baltimore, Md., June 2, 1952. Hlh-Drs

102 - Caboose Cars - Used in Glenwood-Punxsutawney Service -

Mr. A. H. Keys:-

Referring to your letter of May 21 and returning attached from Mr. R. B. Fisher, regarding complaint of Trainmen against putting two helpers behind caboose cars in the Glenwood-Punxsutawney Service.

In our opinion, neither the class I-16 or I-10 Caboose Cars are strong enough to be placed in front of two S-1 type engines used as helpers in pusher service.

The class I-16 Caboose Cars were converted from Box Cars class M-13 and M-13a, which were built in 1906 and 1910 and are over 42 years of age. The class I-10 Cars were built in 1918 and have a 15" 30 Lb. channel as center sills. The sills on both the class I-16 and I-10 Cars were not designed for heavy pusher service.

If possible, we would recommend that some of our class I-12 Caboose Cars be transferred to the Glenwood Service, as they have a stronger center sill and will hold up in this service.

If impossible to obtain any of the class I-12 Cars, the only alternative would be to switch the Caboose Car to the rear of the two Helpers.

Copy -
Mr. A. B. Lawson

Enc.

S. G. Hoshor captured this C-2700-series I-16 caboose rolling through Athens, Ohio, in 1941. This view provides a good look at the roof details and running boards on an as-built I-16. Yellow handholds were still five years in the future. Also in the future was a change to the Ohio caboose law allowing bay-window cars in the state (1945). B&O officers obviously were pushing their luck with this Ohio I-16 assignment.
collection of Si DeBolt

Not one but two I-16s get shoved on by an EL helper engine in this Wayne Brumbaugh view. The C-2779 wears the 1945 lettering scheme.
collection of Dwight Jones

I-16 cabooses were not allowed to be used in any type of helper service, heavy or light. Of course it was necessary for someone to know this. Whoops!

On August 23, 1926, the company photographer was called on to record 40-ton boxcar 181619 because it had been converted to class M-13C at Mt. Clare by adding steel sheathing to its sides. It originally was a class M-13 car built in 1906 at South Baltimore Car & Foundry. The addition of the steel sheathing increased the car weight from 44,300 pounds to 46,600 pounds. It was the only class M-13C car rostered by B&O. This car was converted to I-16 caboose C-2754. Did the caboose retain the steel sheathing? No photos have yet turned up to answer the question. The caboose was retired in April 1961 and was condemned on certificate #5 at the Washington, Indiana, shops on May 5, 1961. *B&O photos, collection of Dwight Jones*

The C-2766 is shown with an unorthodox small "Great States" emblem in this photo. If you look closely you can see the old mounting holes for the marker light brackets, which have been moved to the end post. *Paul B. Dunn collection / collection of Dwight Jones*

Caboose C-2363 is shown on the caboose track at Newark, Ohio, ca. 1960 wearing the lettering scheme adopted by the railroad in 1955. The car last was painted at the Washington, Indiana, shops in 1958. *Paul B. Dunn collection / collection of Dwight Jones*

Last painted at the Washington, Indiana, shops in May 1965, the C-2355 wears the last lettering scheme applied to the I-16 cabooses featuring the simplified Capitol Dome emblem. The car had been placed into Dismantle category at Flora, Illinois, on February 10, 1970, before being dispatched to the shops at Chillicothe, where it is shown in mid-1970. It was sold in July 1970 to a private owner who moved the car to his farm east of Chillicothe. *Paul B. Dunn / collection of Dwight Jones*

As can be seen from our rosters, a number of I-16 cabooses were converted to non-revenue service and given "X" or "XM" prefix numbers. Because of their interior furnishings they were ideal candidates for this service conversion. The X-2131 is stenciled "MofW Dept, Camp Service". The yellow triangle in the upper left corner was the only paint many received. *Paul B. Dunn / collection of Dwight Jones*

Encyclopedia of B&O Cabooses Volume 4

The X-2773 (C-2710) wears fresh paint in this view, likely repainted at Newark and shown at Zanesville, Ohio. Considerable overspray shows around the stencils and the "X" is upside down. The drawing for application of the yellow triangle is in the painting chapter.
Paul B. Dunn / collection of Dwight Jones

The X-2773, above, was retired at the Chillicothe shops and subsequently was sold to E. H. Castle, owner of the Cool Springs Park museum/convenience store located near Rowlesburg, West Virginia. Mr. Castle also purchased one I-10 and three I-5 family cabooses for his display which also features several narrow gauge cars and engines and various farm implements from years past.

Some of the I-16 conversions to MofW service received aluminum/silver paint with black lettering, a scheme adopted by the road in 1960 for camp service cars. The X-2855, devoid of its steel side bay, was photographed by Julian Barnard at Connellsville, Pennsylvania, on February 19, 1966. It had been converted from caboose C-2761 in 1956.

Robert Selle photographed the X-4117 at Cincinnati in September of 1964. Not only have the steel side bay and side windows been removed but an additional window has been added. This car was changed from caboose C-2302 in 1956 at the Lorain, Ohio, car shops.

Baltimore, Md., June 4, 1943.

102 - Caboose Cars - Class I-16 - Location of Marker Lamps -

Messrs.
W.S.Eyerly	W.H.Longwell	F.J.Crockett
H.M.Sherrard	W.B.Nolan	R.B.Fisher
R.A.Conner	G.H.Rosenberg	A.H.Keys
C.W.Esch	E.Stimson,Jr.	A.J.Larrick
F.M.Galloway	J.W.Schad	H.A.Harris
F.R.Gelhausen	C.H.Spence	T.H.Hollen
L.R.Haase	W.J.Baumiller	W.P.Hollen
F.L.Hall	E.L.Brown	E.H.Meckstroth
W.F.Harris	W.A.Bender	G.O.Prosser
J.P.Hines	E.B.Cox	

There has been some complaint as to the location of marker lamps on Caboose Cars, Class I-16, Series C-2300 to C-2374, and C-2700 to C-2799.

The markers are now placed on the body of caboose at platform, and it has been decided to change the location to platform corner posts as illustrated on print S-70190-A,   copies attached.

These changes to be made when cars are available and the work can be performed without interfering with their operation.

Portions of two neo-style letters documenting marker light bracket relocation.

Baltimore, Md., August 30, 1948.

102 - Caboose Cars - Classes I-13 and I-16 - Location of Marker Lamps -
(SUPERSEDING LETTER OF JUNE 4th, 1943)

Messrs.
C.H.Spence	L.R.Haase	E.Stimson,Jr.	H.A.Harris
H.M.Sherrard	J.P.Hines	H.W.Chew	T.H.Hollen
W.J.Baumiller	A.E.McCafferty	C.E.Gainer	E.F.Gross
A.E.Beckman	J.S.Major	F.J.Crockett	B.C.Fouch
J.T.Connelly	F.J.Rosenberg	A.L.Kerr	B.J.Mangan
R.A.Conner	G.H.Rosenberg	R.B.Fisher	G.O.Prosser
F.M.Galloway	T.I.Schachtele	A.J.Larrick	W.C.Reister
A.W.Gibson	G.W.Short	A.F.Pugh	

This letter embodies previous instructions on location of marker lamps for class I-16 caboose cars, with revision covering relocation of marker lamps on class I-13 caboose cars.

The class I-13 and I-16 Caboose Cars, having marker lamp brackets located on body corner post, should have brackets relocated to platform corner post, as shown on print S-70190-B,   copies attached.

Change to be made when cars are available and the work performed without interfering with their operation.

Baltimore, Md., July 26, 1948.

102 - Caboose Cars   ) Application of End Handrail and Handhold - Class
127 - Safety Appliances   )   I-16 Caboose Cars -

Messrs.
  C.H.Spence   L.R.Haase   E.Stimson,Jr.   H.A.Harris
  H.M.Sherrard   J.P.Hines   H.W.Chew   T.H.Hollen
  W.J.Baumiller   A.E.McCafferty   C.E.Geiner   E.F.Gross
  A.E.Beckman   J.S.Major   F.J.Crockett   B.C.Fouch
  J.T.Connelly   F.J.Rosenberg   A.L.Kerr   B.J.Mangan
  R.A.Conner   G.H.Rosenberg   R.B.Fisher   G.O.Prosse
  A.W.Gibson   T.I.Schachtele   A.J.Larrick   W.C.Reiste
  F.M.Galloway   G.W.Short   A.F.Pugh

        When class I-16 caboose cars, series C-2700 to C-2799, are on shop
tracks for repairs, or when handrails need renewal, arrange to apply new design as shown on the following prints,   copies attached:-

            S-69379-B - Platform End Rail and Connection
            V-69362-E - End construction

        The end rails, both side and center, can be fabricated from angles
now on car, if in good condition, and proper size. All new parts required
should be furnished by the Cumberland Bolt and Forge Shop.

        Handhold No. 72 should also be applied, as shown on print V-69362-E,
to all four corner posts, to assist trainmen when mounting or dismounting
caboose cars.

        Application of end handrails and handhold, to be reported on
Form 2404-A to Office of Mechanical Engineer.

Copy - Messrs.
  A.B.Lawson   H.Rees   D.M.Lohr   L.G.Kohler
  A.H.Keys   C.W.Esch   F.H.Becherer,Jr.   G.H.Flagg
  F.A.Baldinger   R.W.Eves   H.P.McQuilkin   W.H.Gordon
  H.J.Burkley   G.F.Patten   V.N.Dawson

kp/e
enc.

Groups 102, 127 -

143

Baltimore, Md., November 27, 1945.

102 - Caboose Cars - Class I-13 and I-16 - Application of Rain Shield to
End Bay Windows -

Messrs.

W.S.Eyerly	J.T.Connelly	C.H.Spence	A.J.Larrick
K.L.Sherrard	J.P.Hines	E.Stimson,Jr.	A.F.Pugh
R.A.Conner	W.H.Longwell	E.L.Brown	F.C.Crockett
F.M.Kalloway	L.L.Robinson,Jr.	P.L.Hofstetter	T.R.Mollen
L.R.Haase	F.J.Rosenberg	F.C.Gimbel	E.H.Heckstroth
F.L.Hall	G.H.Rosenberg	E.B.Cox	G.O.Prosser
	T.I.Schachtele	R.B.Fisher	W.C.Reister

When Caboose Cars, Class I-13 and I-16 are on shop tracks for
repairs and where facilities are available at layover periods, arrange to
apply rain shields, over end bay windows, both sides of car as shown on the
Print S-72927-A, copies attached.

Rain Shield to be manufactured locally from reclaimed roof sheets.

Report application on Form 2404-A to Office of Mechanical Engineer.

APPROVED:

Cy.Messrs.

F.H.Becherer	H.Rees	J.T.Staab
H.L.Holland	W.H.Gordon	H.F.McQuilkin
F.A.Baldinger	A.H.Keys	V.H.Dawson
H.J.Burkley	R.W.Eves	W.M.Hinkey
	E.F.Gross	E.R.Ricker

kp/fbg
enc.

Group No. 102 -

Engineer Ambrose Miller receiving train order in the cab of Diesel switching locomotive via radio

The antenna of the mobile transmitter-receiver is shown mounted on the roof over the locomotive headlight

B&O DEMONSTRATES

TRAIN CONTROL COMMUNICATION

Baltimore and Ohio Magazine ran an article on the use of early radio on the B&O with their issue of September 1944. Extracts from that article follow:

Eastern Railroad History was made on July 27 when the first Baltimore and Ohio train controlled by radio pulled out of Camden Station, with orders to pick up a string of freight cars loaded with essential war materials and deliver them to the Bethlehem-Fairfield Shipyards.

Engine and caboose both were equipped with Bendix Radio Company VHF mobile transmitters and receivers. A substantial number of B&O officers, press representatives, radio engineers and radio representatives were on hand to witness the event. Passenger cars were sandwiched to house all of the dignitaries.

At the appointed time the dispatcher relayed the ap-

propriate train order instructions to the conductor in the caboose. Upon receiving them the conductor then called the engineer in yard engine 404 who responded "Yes, what is it?" Of course he also had heard the instructions from the dispatcher over his radio. With that the "Radio Special" as the train had been dubbed moved out of Camden.

Earlier President R. B. White had indicated that success of this experiment would not mean that passenger trains would move by radio tomorrow, "But", he added, "it will come".

The article stated that power for the radio equipment in the caboose was obtained from a set of batteries that had been installed for that purpose.

One special point noted in the article was that the B&O had obtained a license for the use of the radio

continued on page 150

The caption for the above magazine cover read as follows: "The picture on our cover this month might really be termed a historic one. It shows Conductor E. T. Howard receiving, in Caboose No. C2702, the first official train orders issued by radio on the B&O. Conductor Howard is talking with Dispatcher C. A. Gosnell in Camden Station. Looking on is Flagman Wade Hammett. B&O photo by Staff Photographer F. C. Dixon."

This montage of the new radio installation was prepared by the B&O to show the various aspects of the new fangled contraption including a closeup of the whirlybird antenna in the center photo.
collection of Dwight Jones

Radio equipped C-2702 was photographed above by Carl Gerber.
Baltimore NRHS collection

B&O officers made a number of photos of the test radio equipment installed in the C-2702. Photographed on July 1, 1944, this closeup image likely was made to record the installation of the two side vents for venting the interior battery compartment. *B&O Photo / collection of Dwight Jones*

On the following page are two interior views of the C-2702 photographed on July 1, 1944. The photos indicate that the bunks were removed in one end of the caboose being replaced by the extensive radio equipment and electrical generation parts. The photos show that electric lights have also been added to the car. Some reports on early caboose radio equipment indicated that the electrical generation equipment was so noisy that one could hardly hear anything on the radio! *B&O Photos, collection of Dwight Jones*

Left, C-2702 was assigned around Grafton in the early 1950s. This photo "may" show an official thanking a retiree and have nothing to do with radios. We have no information for this photo.

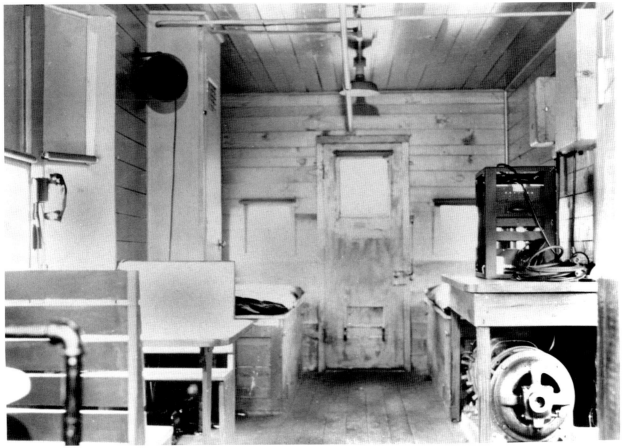

This closeup view provides a good look at the whirlybird radio antenna mounted to the roof of both the caboose and the yard engine.

Nothing like a little pressure when you are trying to copy a train order! This may represent the actual event while the photo on the cover of the B&O magazine, shown earlier, may have been a public relations "recreation".

continued from page 145

equipment from the FCC, which stated that B&O could use radio equipment "anywhere on the B&O system for experimental and developmental purposes." It was also anticipated that the B&O would be able to obtain a permanent license after conclusion of the war.

Although just an experiment at the time B&O communications engineers and radio manufacturing experts were continuing their research seeking ways to improve the equipment to withstand the heat, moisture and periodic shocks to which they are certain to be subjected to in the railroad environment.

At the time of the article it was stated that obtaining new radio equipment was nearly impossible due to the demands of the war.

The B&O article concluded with this paragraph:

"In this one hundredth anniversary year of the invention of the electric telegraph, it is particularly appropriate that the B&O, the railroad which granted to the inventor, Morse, use of its right-of-way for erection of his first telegraph line, should again be pioneering in the development of the newest form of electric communications—radio."

Perhaps the last I-16 body left on the railroad was this car, renumbered to X-2208 and shown at Aurora, Indiana, on May 9, 1981. The car had been here for at least 10 years when this photo was made. The steel bay had been removed and replaced with plywood when the car was converted for MofW service.

Dwight Jones

Baltimore, March 2, 1953.

File PC-5.6 – Lighting for caboose cars – Report on Lighting Measurements.

        At 9:00 PM, February 26th, 1953, measured the lighting in
caboose #C-2313 at Riverside, Md.

        This caboose is as shown on C.E.MP&E Dwg. Y-69342, except that
an additional oil lamp is installed over the table slightly below and
toward the "A" end from the lamp shown on the plan. Also, an oil lamp
is installed adjacent to the air gauge.

        With all lanterns lighted, glassware very clean, and lamp
wicks adjusted to almost the smoking point readings were taken as marked
in yellow on print of Dwg. Y-69342 attached. It will be noted that 2.5
footcandles was the maximum practical value measured on the table.

        On the air gauge it will be noted that a vertical value of 0.1
footcandle is shown. The air gauge was actually masked by glare, and
was not readable by light from the oil lamp; a flashlight was necessary
to read the gauge.

        In other areas except where readings are indicated the lighting
level was below 0.1 footcandle, and not measurable.

                                        W. R. Preece,
                                        E. W. Bultman.

Lighting is measured in units called "foot-candles" as
noted in the B&O memo reproduced above. It is interesting to note that the measured value at the conductor's desk was only 2.5 foot-candles. The latest recommended value in 2016 for work at a desk is a value
between 20 and 50 foot-candles.

At right is a typical oil lamp
from an I-16 caboose, this one
mounted over the conductor's
desk.

Original Number	Photo?	Date Built (Modified)	Built (Modified) By	Modified From	Previous Number	Class, Type	Box Car Built	Box Car Built By	Applied 'AB' Brakes	Date Retired	Disposition	Comments
C-2300		11-42	B&O shops, Mt. Clare (Baltimore), MD	180482		M-13 Box Car	11-06	Western Stl. Car & Fdry.		4-53	Condemned on Certificate #3, 4-13-53 at Gassaway, WV	also reported: Condemned: Lorain, OH, 6-5-53
C-2301	Photo	11-42	B&O shops, Mt. Clare (Baltimore), MD	181220		M-13 Box Car	2-06	S. Baltimore Car & Fdry.	3-51	4-62	Condemned: Washington, IN 4-3-62	
C-2302	Photo	11-42	B&O shops, Mt. Clare (Baltimore), MD	183418		M-13A Box Car	4-10	American Car & Fdry.	5-53	1-57	Renumbered X-4117 at Lorain, OH, 12-31-56	retired mid-1960s
C-2303		11-42	B&O shops, Mt. Clare (Baltimore), MD	X-6155	180112	M-13 Box Car	12-05	Western Stl. Car & Fdry.		4-46	Retired; collision with engine 6168 at East Side (Philly); fire	Damaged: Fire: 3-3-46 (Philadelphia)
C-2304		11-42	B&O shops, Mt. Clare (Baltimore), MD	183538		M-13A Box Car	4-10	American Car & Fdry.	MTC 8-14-51	5-66	Leased to B&OCT; Dismantled: Barr Yard, Chicago, 5-66	
C-2305	Photo	11-42	B&O shops, Mt. Clare (Baltimore), MD	X-6374	190088	M-13B Box Car	4-10	American Car & Fdry.	7-53	10-64	Leased to B&OCT; Fire: East Chicago, IN, 7-64;	Dismantled: Barr Yard, Chicago
C-2306	Yes	11-42	B&O shops, Mt. Clare (Baltimore), MD	X-6207	182460	M-13A Box Car	5-10	Standard Stl. Car Co.	6-51	8-63	Sold: 7-65 at Du Bois, PA, to Orville Marshall	Mr. Marshall actually received C-2159 per telcon June 2016
C-2307		11-42	B&O shops, Mt. Clare (Baltimore), MD	X-6000	165644	M-12 Box Car	11-02	American Car & Fdry.	10-51	9-57	Fire: E. Chicago, IN, 9-19-57; underframe and sides corroded;	written up as scrap at East Chicago, 10-25-56
C-2308		11-42	B&O shops, Mt. Clare (Baltimore), MD	X-6164	180431	M-13 Box Car	1-06	Western Stl. Car & Fdry.	1-55	4-59	Fire: Pine Junction, 1-24-59; car destroyed;	Destroyed: Fire: Barr Yard, 6-59
C-2309	Yes	11-42	B&O shops, Mt. Clare (Baltimore), MD	X-6227	183360	M-13A Box Car	3-10	American Car & Fdry.	6-52	3-56	Renumbered X-2857	Dismantled: Brunswick, MD 2-29-68
C-2310	Photo	11-42	B&O shops, Mt. Clare (Baltimore), MD	X-6159	180172	M-13 Box Car	12-05	Western Stl. Car & Fdry.	6-53	3-65	Leased to B&OCT; Dismantled: Barr Yard 12-65	
C-2311	Photo	11-42	B&O shops, Mt. Clare (Baltimore), MD	X-6158	180154	M-13 Box Car	12-05	Western Stl. Car & Fdry.	12-49	12-65	Dismantled: Washington, IN	
C-2312	Photo	11-42	B&O shops, Mt. Clare (Baltimore), MD	X-6373	190055	M-13B Box Car	4-10	American Car & Fdry.	7-49	7-62	Condemned 6-29-62; MTC 1-30-51	Damaged: fire: Mt. Clare, MD 1-30-51
C-2313		11-42	B&O shops, Mt. Clare (Baltimore), MD	X-6232	183508	M-13A Box Car	4-10	American Car & Fdry.	5-51	10-56	Renumbered X-2858 at Keyser, WV, 10-19-56	retired 9-57
C-2314	Photo	11-42	B&O shops, Mt. Clare (Baltimore), MD		190063	M-13B Box Car	4-10	American Car & Fdry.	6-53	9-67	Leased to B&OCT	Sold 9-5-67 as scrap to Indiana Metals Co. sales order #5012
C-2315	Photo	11-42	B&O shops, Mt. Clare (Baltimore), MD	181103		M-13 Box Car	1-06	S. Baltimore Car & Fdry.	10-52	11-81	Damaged: fire: Mt. Clare, 9-26-53; Limbo: 12-77;	Retired 11-20-81 car could not be found (see photo this book)
C-2316		11-42	B&O shops, Mt. Clare (Baltimore), MD	X-6173	180878	M-13 Box Car	2-06	Western Stl. Car & Fdry.	7-50	5-55	Renumbered X-2143 at Mt. Clare, 3-28-55	retired 9-57
C-2317		11-42	B&O shops, Mt. Clare (Baltimore), MD	X-6222	182971	M-13A Box Car	7-10	Standard Stl. Car Co.	11-49	4-59	Condemned on Certificate #1, at KY, 4-29-59;	Condemned: Keyser 6-2-59 Dismantled: Barr Yard 1-65
C-2318		11-42	B&O shops, Mt. Clare (Baltimore), MD	X-6195	181949	M-13 Box Car	10-06	S. Baltimore Car & Fdry.	6-53	5-66	Leased to B&OCT; Dismantled at Barr Yard, Chicago 5-66	
C-2319	Photo	11-42	B&O shops, Mt. Clare (Baltimore), MD	180531		M-13 Box Car	1-06	Western Stl. Car & Fdry.	6-48	11-63	Sold from Du Bois to A.H. Bochert	telcon with his widow June 2016 she knows nothing about this
C-2320		11-42	B&O shops, Mt. Clare (Baltimore), MD	X-6157	180147	M-13 Box Car	12-05	Western Stl. Car & Fdry.	7-53	11-81	Retired; car could not be found	Retired 11-20-81 per agreement with Gen. Mgr.-Car Department
C-2321		11-42	B&O shops, Mt. Clare (Baltimore), MD	182798		M-13A Box Car	6-10	Standard Stl. Car Co.		2-46	Retired	Damaged: Fire: BW to Philly pool, destroyed 12-17-45
C-2322		11-42	B&O shops, Mt. Clare (Baltimore), MD	181392		M-13 Box Car	3-06	S. Baltimore Car & Fdry.	12-48	12-57	Condemned on Certificate #5, 12-9-57 at Wilsmere, DE	Cond: Wilsmere 6-30-59; to Wicomico Steel, Baltimore, MD
C-2323		11-42	B&O shops, Mt. Clare (Baltimore), MD	X-3117	182635	M-13A Box Car	5-10	Standard Stl. Car Co.	11-52	8-56	Condemned on Certificate #3, 8-9-56 at Keyser, WV	
C-2324		11-42	B&O shops, Mt. Clare (Baltimore), MD	X-6167	180506	M-13 Box Car	1-06	Western Stl. Car & Fdry.		11-48	Retired	Destroyed: fire: Hancock, WV 10-25-48; cab sent to Keyser
C-2325	Photo	11-42	B&O shops, Du Bois, PA	X-6223	183036	M-13A Box Car	2-10	American Car & Fdry.	1-53	3-64	Dismantled: Willard, OH	
C-2326		11-42	B&O shops, Du Bois, PA	X-6154	180072	M-13 Box Car	12-05	Western Stl. Car & Fdry.	7-52	5-58	Destroyed: Fire: Barr Yard 2-9-58; Fire: Barr Yard 3-5-58	
C-2327		11-42	B&O shops, Du Bois, PA	180173		M-13 Box Car	12-05	Western Stl. Car & Fdry.	10-51	11-54	Condemned on Certificate #9, 12-9-54 at Keyser, WV;	Condemned at Keyser, WV 12-9-54
C-2328	Photo	11-42	B&O shops, Du Bois, PA	181993		M-13 Box Car	11-06	S. Baltimore Car & Fdry.	8-52	3-56	Renumbered X-2859	retired mid-1960s
C-2329		11-42	B&O shops, Du Bois, PA	X-6181	181333	M-13 Box Car	3-06	S. Baltimore Car & Fdry.	7-52	12-55	Renumbered X-2764 at Keyser, WV, 12-23-55	
C-2330		11-42	B&O shops, Du Bois, PA	X-6375	190140	M-13B Box Car	5-10	American Car & Fdry.	4-53	5-65	Dismantled: Lorain, OH	
C-2331	Photo	11-42	B&O shops, Du Bois, PA	X-3307	180814	M-13 Box Car	2-06	Western Stl. Car & Fdry.		4-55	Condemned on Certificate #3, 4-19-55 at Du Bois, PA	Condemned at Du Bois, PA 5-31-55
C-2332		11-42	B&O shops, Du Bois, PA	X-6200	182224	M-13A Box Car	3-10	Standard Stl. Car Co.	DU 2-29-52	4-63	Dismantled: Willard, OH	
C-2333		11-42	B&O shops, Du Bois, PA	X-6211	182601	M-13A Box Car	5-10	Standard Stl. Car Co.	9-49	4-55	Condemned on Certificate #3, 4-19-55 at Du Bois, PA	Condemned: DU 6-6-55 Condemned: KY 9-27-56
C-2334	Photo	11-42	B&O shops, Du Bois, PA	180441		M-13 Box Car	1-06	Western Stl. Car & Fdry.	9-50	10-57	Wrecked: Fostoria, OH, 10-18-57, train #102, eng. 710	Written up: scrap at Willard, OH, 10-21-57
C-2335		11-42	B&O shops, Du Bois, PA	X-6216	182708	M-13A Box Car	6-10	Standard Stl. Car Co.	12-48	4-55	Condemned on Certificate #3, 4-19-55 at Glenwood, PA	Condemned at DU 6-6-55 on Certificate #3
C-2336		11-42	B&O shops, Du Bois, PA	X-6186	181483	M-13 Box Car	4-06	S. Baltimore Car & Fdry.	9-51	4-61	Dismantled: Du Bois, PA, 6-1-61	
C-2337	Photo	11-42	B&O shops, Du Bois, PA	X-6460	190168	M-13B Box Car	5-10	American Car & Fdry.	8-50	12-61	Wrecked and Dismantled at Willard, OH, 11-27-61	Damaged: fire: 1-25-48
C-2338		11-42	B&O shops, Du Bois, PA	X-6203	182306	M-13A Box Car	4-10	Standard Stl. Car Co.		11-52	Retired	Wrecked: Du Bois, PA 11-4-52
C-2339		11-42	B&O shops, Du Bois, PA	X-6210	182598	M-13A Box Car	5-10	Standard Stl. Car Co.		12-61	Dismantled: Du Bois, PA, 12-7-61	
C-2340		11-42	B&O shops, Du Bois, PA	X-6187	181485	M-13 Box Car	4-06	S. Baltimore Car & Fdry.		6-48	Retired	Damaged: fire Butler Jct., PA 3-20-48
C-2341		11-42	B&O shops, Du Bois, PA	X-6234	183604	M-13A Box Car	4-10	American Car & Fdry.	10-50	4-55	Condemned on Certificate #3 Du Bois, PA, 4-19-55	Condemned: Du Bois, PA 5-31-55
C-2342	Photo	11-42	B&O shops, Du Bois, PA	X-6160	180246	M-13 Box Car	12-05	Western Stl. Car & Fdry.	10-49	10-55	Condemned on Certificate #7, 10-14-55 at Benwood, WV	fire: Benwood, 2-24-47 Condemned: DU 11-21-55
C-2343	Photo	11-42	B&O shops, Du Bois, PA	X-6454	190232	M-13B Box Car	5-10	American Car & Fdry.	6-53	10-66	Dismantled: 9-14-66, Barr Yard, Chicago	Some records show this cab as "B&OCT"

Original Number	Photo?	Date Built (Modified)	Built (Modified) By	Modified From	Previous Number	Class, Type	Box Car Built	Box Car Built By	Applied 'AB' Brakes	Date Retired	Disposition	Comments
C-2344	Photo	11-42	B&O shops, Du Bois, PA	X-6170	180651	M-13 Box Car	1-06	Western Stl. Car & Fdry.	4-51	12-62	Condemned: Willard, OH, 11-21-62	
C-2345		11-42	B&O shops, Du Bois, PA	X-6194	181903	M-13 Box Car	9-06	S. Baltimore Car & Fdry.	6-53	12-61	Dismantled: Du Bois, PA, 12-7-61	
C-2346		11-42	B&O shops, Du Bois, PA	X-6197	182064	M-13A Box Car	2-10	Standard Stl. Car Co.	7-53	12-61	Dismantled: Du Bois, PA, 12-12-61	
C-2347		11-42	B&O shops, Du Bois, PA	X-6420	181118	M-13 Box Car	1-06	S. Baltimore Car & Fdry.	3-50	7-59	Renumbered X-4184 at Du Bois, PA, 7-15-59	retired mid-1960s
C-2348		11-42	B&O shops, Du Bois, PA	X-6199	182127	M-13A Box Car	3-10	Standard Stl. Car Co.		8-59	Renumbered X-4185 at DU Bois, PA, 7-29-59	retired mid-1960s
C-2349		11-42	B&O shops, Du Bois, PA	X-6224	183057	M-13A Box Car	3-10	American Car & Fdry.	DU 11-20-53	4-61	Condemned on Certificate #5 Du Bois, PA, 5-16-61	
C-2350		11-42	B&O shops, Washington, IN	183172		M-13A Box Car	3-10	American Car & Fdry.	10-50	12-62	Condemned: Washington, IN 11-23-62	
C-2351		11-42	B&O shops, Washington, IN	180152		M-13 Box Car	12-05	Western Stl. Car & Fdry.	10-49	2-58	Condemned: Certificate #1, Washington, IN, 2-19-58	Condemned: Washingon, IN 4-16-58
C-2352	Photo	11-42	B&O shops, Washington, IN	182807		M-13A Box Car	6-10	Standard Stl. Car Co.	7-52	12-65	Condemned: Washington, IN	
C-2353		11-42	B&O shops, Washington, IN	183687		M-13A Box Car	5-10	American Car & Fdry.	6-53	4-55	Renumbered X-2134 at Keyser, WV, 3-31-55	
C-2354		11-42	B&O shops, Washington, IN	183518		M-13A Box Car	4-10	American Car & Fdry.	7-53	4-61	Condemned on Certificate #5, approved 1961;	Dismantled: Keyser, WV 5-2-61
C-2355	Yes	11-42	B&O shops, Washington, IN	X-6376	180364	M-13 Box Car	12-05	Western Stl. Car & Fdry.	12-50	7-70	Sold: Fred J. Heinzelman 7-8-70 on sales order #4703	see photo: (see Vol V) scrapped February 2006
C-2356		11-42	B&O shops, Washington, IN	X-6162	180354	M-13 Box Car	12-05	Western Stl. Car & Fdry.	2-53	1-73	Sold: U.S.R.E. Co. sales order 4730	sold 1-9-73 at no charge in exchange for scrap
C-2357		11-42	B&O shops, Washington, IN	X-6403	181992	M-13 Box Car	11-06	S. Baltimore Car & Fdry.	3-51	6-70	Dismantled: Chillicothe, OH, 6-10-70	
C-2358		11-42	B&O shops, Washington, IN	X-6040	181388	M-13 Box Car	3-06	S. Baltimore Car & Fdry.	2-53	4-55	Renumbered X-2130 at Washington, IN, 4-4-55	Damaged: fire: Olney, IL ($200) 2-18-55, retired 4-60
C-2359		11-42	B&O shops, Washington, IN	X-6412	182692	M-13A Box Car	6-10	Standard Stl. Car Co.	11-50	11-63	Retired	
C-2360		11-42	B&O shops, Washington, IN	X-6033	180202	M-13 Box Car	12-05	Western Stl. Car & Fdry.	10-50	11-63	Dismantled: Washington, IN	
C-2361		11-42	B&O shops, Washington, IN	183674		M-13A Box Car	4-10	American Car & Fdry.		4-61	Cond. on Certificate #5, 1961;	Dismantled: Washington, IN 5-5-61
C-2362		11-42	B&O shops, Washington, IN	X-6031	180179	M-13 Box Car	12-05	Western Stl. Car & Fdry.	5-50	2-62	Renumbered X-4194 at Washington, IN, 2-1-62	Retired 10-71; car not located in inventory
C-2363	Photo	11-42	B&O shops, Washington, IN	X-6438	190011	M-13B Box Car	4-10	American Car & Fdry.	7-51	5-69	Dismantled: Chillicothe, OH, 5-13-69	
C-2364		11-42	B&O shops, Washington, IN	X-6030	180074	M-13 Box Car	12-05	Western Stl. Car & Fdry.	9-50	1-55	Condemned on Certificate #1 at Washington, IN, 1-21-55;	Condemned: Washington, IN 2-2-55
C-2365	Photo	11-42	B&O shops, Washington, IN	X-6204	182316	M-13A Box Car	4-10	Standard Stl. Car Co.	12-49	4-55	Renumbered X-2131 at Washington, IN, 3-31-55	Sold: scrap from CE 7-19-77 sales order 4797
C-2366		11-42	B&O shops, Washington, IN	X-6394	190157	M-13B Box Car	5-10	American Car & Fdry.		11-44	Wrecked	
C-2367	Photo	11-42	B&O shops, Washington, IN	182985		M-13A Box Car	7-10	Standard Stl. Car Co.	10-50	8-69	Dismantled: Du Bois, PA, 8-7-69	
C-2368	Photo	11-42	B&O shops, Washington, IN	X-6044	181766	M-13 Box Car	6-06	S. Baltimore Car & Fdry.	10-50	7-70	Dismantled: Chillicothe, OH, 7-27-70	
C-2369		11-42	B&O shops, Washington, IN	X-6054	183038	M-13A Box Car	3-10	American Car & Fdry.	12-49	4-55	Renumbered X-2132 at Washington, IN, 3-31-55	retired mid-1960s
C-2370	Photo	11-42	B&O shops, Washington, IN	X-6056	183428	M-13A Box Car	4-10	American Car & Fdry.	7-51	7-58	Condemned on Certificate #3 at WA 6-25-58;	Condemned: Washington, IN 7-11-58
C-2371	Yes	11-42	B&O shops, Washington, IN	X-6034	180220	M-13 Box Car	12-05	Western Stl. Car & Fdry.	12-49	1-69	Sold: Lauren C. Ansley Rochester, NY; arrived 2-69	sold sales order #4367, 1-30-69; for restaurant; (see Vol III)
C-2372		11-42	B&O shops, Washington, IN	X-6057	183669	M-13A Box Car	4-10	American Car & Fdry.	6-51	4-59	Condemned on Certificate #1 at Wilsmere, DE, 4-29-59;	Condemned: Wilsmere, DE, 4-29-59
C-2373	Photo	11-42	B&O shops, Washington, IN	X-6050	182675	M-13A Box Car	6-10	Standard Stl. Car Co.	6-53	4-55	Renumbered X-2139 at Mt. Clare (Baltimore), MD, 4-7-55	retired mid-1960s
C-2374	Photo	11-42	B&O shops, Washington, IN	X-6053	182933	M-13A Box Car	6-10	Standard Stl. Car Co.	10-51	4-55	Renumbered X-2140 at Mt. Clare (Baltimore), MD, 4-1-55	Dismantled: Somerset, PA 3-31-67

A B&O trainman is on the rear platform of this I-16 caboose eye-balling his train as the run nears the west end of Willard yard in May of 1957. The location is Attica Junction, 4.2 miles west of the Willard Yard Limit Board on the Chicago Division. *collection of Dwight Jones*

Original Number	Photo?	Date Built (Modified)	Built (Modified) By	Modified From	Previous Number	Class, Type	Box Car Built	Box Car Built By	Applied 'AB' Brakes	Date Retired	Disposition	Comments
C-2700		7-43	B&O shops, Mt. Clare (Baltimore), MD	X-6192	181770	M-13 Box Car	6-06	S. Baltimore Car & Fdry.	10-52	4-54	Fire: destroyed: Wicomico Street, Baltimore, MD, 4-5-54	2404 form made out at Mt. Clare also fire: Ellicott City, 1-21-54
C-2701	Photo	7-43	B&O shops, Mt. Clare (Baltimore), MD	X-6188	181517	M-13 Box Car	5-06	S. Baltimore Car & Fdry.	7-53	9-67	Leased to B&OCT	Sold: 9-8-67 to Indiana Metals sales order #5012
C-2702	Photo	7-43	B&O shops, Mt. Clare (Baltimore), MD	X-6189	181564	M-13 Box Car	5-06	S. Baltimore Car & Fdry.	1-53	9-67	Sold as scrap	Sold: 9-8-67 to Indiana Metals on sales order #5012
C-2703		7-43	B&O shops, Mt. Clare (Baltimore), MD	X-6456	183582	M-13A Box Car	4-10	American Car & Fdry.	11-49	11-81	Retired; car cannot be found	Retired 11-20-81 per Gen. Mgr - Car Department
C-2704		7-43	B&O shops, Mt. Clare (Baltimore), MD	X-6235	183622	M-13A Box Car	4-10	American Car & Fdry.		2-44	Wrecked	
C-2705	Photo	7-43	B&O shops, Mt. Clare (Baltimore), MD	X-6219	182776	M-13A Box Car	6-10	Standard Stl. Car Co.	7-49	4-69	Dismantled: B&O shops, Du Bois, PA, 4-21-69	
C-2706		7-43	B&O shops, Mt. Clare (Baltimore), MD	X-6196	181960	M-13 Box Car	10-06	S. Baltimore Car & Fdry.	11-49	4-55	Renumbered X-2144 at Mt. Clare, 4-12-55	retired 4-61
C-2707	Photo	7-43	B&O shops, Mt. Clare (Baltimore), MD	X-6217	182726	M-13A Box Car	6-10	Standard Stl. Car Co.	9-50	6-59	Wrecked 1-12-59 at Gassaway, WV; accident with engine 5642	
C-2708		7-43	B&O shops, Mt. Clare (Baltimore), MD	X-6161	180335	M-13 Box Car	12-05	Western Stl. Car & Fdry.	7-48	11-54	Condemned on Certificate #9, 11-17-54, at Gassaway, WV	Condemned: Gassaway, WV 8-15-55
C-2709		7-43	B&O shops, Mt. Clare (Baltimore), MD		180423	M-13 Box Car	1-06	Western Stl. Car & Fdry.	12-49	5-55	Renumbered X-2142 at Mt. Clare, 3-28 55	
C-2710	Photo	7-43	B&O shops, Mt. Clare (Baltimore), MD	X-6180	181239	M-13 Box Car	2-06	S. Baltimore Car & Fdry.		12-55	Renumbered X-2773 at Keyser, 12-23-55; Retired Chillicothe	Sold: E. Castle, Rowlesburg, WV, 8-8-73, s.o. #4789, (see Vol IV)
C-2711		7-43	B&O shops, Mt. Clare (Baltimore), MD	X-6156	180134	M-13 Box Car	12-05	Western Stl. Car & Fdry.	9-52	11-54	Condemned on Certificate #9, 11-17-54 at Gassaway, WV	Condemned: Gassaway, WV 8-15-55
C-2712		7-43	B&O shops, Mt. Clare (Baltimore), MD	X-6214	182655	M-13A Box Car	5-10	Standard Stl. Car Co.	11-49	4-59	Condemned on Certificate #1, 4-29-59, at Keyser, WV	Condemned: Keyser, WV 6-2-59
C-2713		7-43	B&O shops, Mt. Clare (Baltimore), MD	X-6205	182330	M-13A Box Car	4-10	Standard Stl. Car Co.	6-53	5-65	Leased: B&OCT; Dismantled Barr Yard, Chicago, 2-65	
C-2714		7-43	B&O shops, Mt. Clare (Baltimore), MD	X-6043	181754	M-13 Box Car	6-06	S. Baltimore Car & Fdry.		9-50	Retired	
C-2715		7-43	B&O shops, Mt. Clare (Baltimore), MD	X-6184	181403	M-13 Box Car	3-06	S. Baltimore Car & Fdry.	9-52	4-55	Renumbered X-2138 at Mt. Clare, 4-7-55	retired 10-60
C-2716		7-43	B&O shops, Mt. Clare (Baltimore), MD		182935	M-13A Box Car	6-10	Standard Stl. Car Co.	5-53	7-59	Renumbered X-2862 at Keyser 6-30-59 at a cost of $500	for 1-2 man living quarters for MofW operators; retired mid-1960s
C-2717		7-43	B&O shops, Mt. Clare (Baltimore), MD	X-6212	182708	M-13A Box Car	5-10	Standard Stl. Car Co.	6-53	3-65	Leased to B&OCT	
C-2718	Photo	7-43	B&O shops, Mt. Clare (Baltimore), MD		181943	M-13 Box Car	10-06	S. Baltimore Car & Fdry.	10-50	2-58	Sold to SIRT	Destroyed: Fire. Arlington, Staten Island, NY, 4-15-65
C-2719		7-43	B&O shops, Mt. Clare (Baltimore), MD	X-6208	182481	M-13A Box Car	5-10	Standard Stl. Car Co.	6-53	4-66	Leased: B&OCT; Dismantled Barr Yard, Chicago 4-66	
C-2720	Photo	7-43	B&O shops, Mt. Clare (Baltimore), MD	X-6190	181692	M-13 Box Car	6-06	S. Baltimore Car & Fdry.		7-59	Renumbered X-2864 at Keyser 6-30-59 at a cost of $500	sold: Whitewater Valley RR 11-74 then to priv. owner (see Vol III)
C-2721		7-43	B&O shops, Mt. Clare (Baltimore), MD	X-6166	180457	M-13 Box Car	1-06	Western Stl. Car & Fdry.	MTC 2-1-52	3-56	Renumbered X-2856	retired mid-1960s
C-2722		7-43	B&O shops, Mt. Clare (Baltimore), MD		186526	M-14A Box Car	3-10	Ralston Steel Car Co.	11-50	4-61	Condemned on Certificate #5, 1961, at Keyser, WV	Dismantled: Keyser, WV 5-2-61
C-2723	Photo	7-43	B&O shops, Mt. Clare (Baltimore), MD	X-6231	183454	M-13A Box Car	4-10	American Car & Fdry.	6-53	9-63	Leased to B&OCT; Wrecked, dismantled: Barr Yard, Chicago	
C-2724		7-43	B&O shops, Mt. Clare (Baltimore), MD	X-6182	181363	M-13 Box Car	3-06	S. Baltimore Car & Fdry.	1-53	12-55	Renumbered X-2788 at Keyser, WV, 12-23-55	retired 7-62
C-2725	Photo	7-43	B&O shops, Du Bois, PA	X-6041	181421	M-13 Box Car	3-06	S. Baltimore Car & Fdry.	1-49	11-81	Retired; car cannot be found	Retired 11-20-81 per Gen. Mgr.- Car Department
C-2726		7-43	B&O shops, Du Bois, PA	X-6169	180631	M-13 Box Car	1-06	Western Stl. Car & Fdry.		10-52	Retired	Damaged: fire 8-31-48 Wrecked: Du Bois 10-16-52
C-2727	Photo	7-43	B&O shops, Du Bois, PA	X-6171	180711	M-13 Box Car	1-06	Western Stl. Car & Fdry.	10-50	12-61	Dismantled: B&O shops, Du Bois, PA, 12-7-61	
C-2728	Photo	7-43	B&O shops, Du Bois, PA	X-6249	186851	M-14A Box Car	8-10	Ralston Steel Car Co.	1-51	12-51	Retired	Damaged: fire: Keller, 12-16-51 "2404" completed at Willard, OH
C-2729		7-43	B&O shops, Du Bois, PA	X-6229	183440	M-13A Box Car	4-10	American Car & Fdry.	12-48	12-58	Wrecked: Gratztown, PA, 3-5-58, extra east 4464	Form 2404 made out at Washington, IN
C-2730		7-43	B&O shops, Du Bois, PA	X-6226	183120	M-13A Box Car	3-10	American Car & Fdry.	10-50	3-55	Renumbered X-2125 at Du Bois, PA, 3-29-55	retired mid-1960s
C-2731		7-43	B&O shops, Du Bois, PA	X-2096	186939	M-14A Box Car	9-10	Ralston Steel Car Co.	10-50	7-59	Renumbered X-2863 at Keyser 6-30-59 at a cost of $500	for 1-2 man living quarters for MofW operators; retired mid-60s
C-2732		7-43	B&O shops, Du Bois, PA	Ice Box X-4734	183494	M-13A Box Car	4-10	American Car & Fdry.	9-50	2-62	Dismantled: Du Bois, PA, 1-22-62	
C-2733	Photo	7-43	B&O shops, Du Bois, PA	X-6165	180432	M-13 Box Car	1-06	Western Stl. Car & Fdry.	DU 8-10-53	3-62	Condemned: Du Bois, PA, 2-27-62	
C-2734	Photo	7-43	B&O shops, Du Bois, PA		181822	M-13 Box Car	8-06	S. Baltimore Car & Fdry.	4-50	10-63	Sold: private owner in Pennsylvania (see Vol V)	car in poor condition in woods photographed by author 6-2016
C-2735		7-43	B&O shops, Du Bois, PA	X-6209	182522	M-13A Box Car	5-10	Standard Stl. Car Co.		4-54	Destroyed: Fire: Layton, PA, 1-9-54	2404 form made out at Glenwood, PA, 4-3-54
C-2736		7-43	B&O shops, Du Bois, PA	X-6178	181176	M-13 Box Car	1-06	S. Baltimore Car & Fdry.	12-52	4-54	Condemned on Certificate #4 Willard, OH, 4-27-54	Condemned: Willard, OH 5-10-54
C-2737		7-43	B&O shops, Du Bois, PA	X-6202	182254	M-13A Box Car	4-10	Standard Stl. Car Co.		10-52	Destroyed: Fire	Fire: Versailles, PA, 9-4-52
C-2738	Photo	7-43	B&O shops, Du Bois, PA		180841	M-13 Box Car	2-06	Western Stl. Car & Fdry.		3-55	Renumbered X-2127 at Du Bois, PA, 3-31-55	Dismantled: Brunswick, MD 3-4-67
C-2739		7-43	B&O shops, Du Bois, PA	X-3108	182526	M-13A Box Car	5-10	Standard Stl. Car Co.	DU 8-4-55	DU 12-6-60	Renumbered XM-4188 12-6-60	retired mid-1960s
C-2740		7-43	B&O shops, Du Bois, PA	X-2088	182547	M-13A Box Car	5-10	Standard Stl. Car Co.	5-51	12-61	Dismantled at Du Bois, PA, 12-11-61	
C-2741	Photo	7-43	B&O shops, Du Bois, PA		181556	M-13 Box Car	5-06	S. Baltimore Car & Fdry.	8-49	12-62	Condemned at Willard, OH, 11-21-62	
C-2742	Photo	7-43	B&O shops, Du Bois, PA	X-6253	186931	M-14A Box Car	9-10	Ralston Steel Car Co.	GW 12-30-53	1-62	186931 reported renumbered to dup. X-1518 then C-2742 7-43	Condemned: Du Bois, PA 12-22-61
C-2743		7-43	B&O shops, Du Bois, PA	X-6450	181865	M-13 Box Car	8-06	S. Baltimore Car & Fdry.	3-50	10-64	Fire: East Chicago, IN, 7-64; Dismantled Barr Yard, Chicago	Damaged: fire. 8-31-48

Roster Copyright © 2016 by Dwight Jones **DO NOT COPY**

Original Number	Photo?	Date Built (Modified)	Built (Modified) By	Modified From	Previous Number	Class, Type	Box Car Built	Box Car Built By	Applied 'AB' Brakes	Date Retired	Disposition	Comments
C-2744		7-43	B&O shops, Du Bois, PA	X-2097	186950	M-14A Box Car	9-10	Ralston Steel Car Co.	10-50	3-55	Renumbered X-2126 at Du Bois, PA, 3-30-55	retired 4-61
C-2745		7-43	B&O shops, Du Bois, PA	183310		M-13A Box Car	3-10	American Car & Fdry.	11-51	12-61	Dismantled: Du Bois, PA, 12-12-61	
C-2746		7-43	B&O shops, Du Bois, PA	183497		M-13A Box Car	4-10	American Car & Fdry.	12-50	4-55	Condemned on Certificate #3, 4-19-55, at Du Bois, PA	Condemned: Du Bois, PA 5-31-55
C-2747		7-43	B&O shops, Du Bois, PA	181356		M-13 Box Car	3-06	S. Baltimore Car & Fdry.	4-53	3-56	Renumbered X-2860	retired mid-1960s
C-2748	Photo	7-43	B&O shops, Du Bois, PA	182140		M-13A Box Car	3-10	Standard Stl. Car Co.	7-49	3-55	Renumbered X-2141 at Mt. Clare, MD, 3-25-55	retired 12-62
C-2749		7-43	B&O shops, Du Bois, PA	181771		M-13 Box Car	6-06	S. Baltimore Car & Fdry.	3-51	DU 12-6-60	Renumbered X-4189 at Du Bois, PA, 2-6-60	retired mid-1960s
C-2750		7-43	B&O shops, Washington, IN	182036		M-13A Box Car	2-10	Standard Stl. Car Co.	5-53	4-59	Condemned on Certificate #1, 4-29-59 at Washington, IN	Condemned: Washington, IN 2-12-60
C-2751		7-43	B&O shops, Washington, IN	183086		M-13A Box Car	3-10	American Car & Fdry.	4-51	9-59	Condemned on Certificate #5, 9-10-59, at Washington, IN	Condemned: Washington, IN 9-23-59
C-2752		7-43	B&O shops, Washington, IN	190188		M-13B Box Car	5-10	American Car & Fdry.	WA 1-6-54	WA 4-13-60	Renumbered X-4196	sold: scrap: M.D. Freidman 4-30-70 on sales order 6313
C-2753	Photo	7-43	B&O shops, Washington, IN	182972		M-13A Box Car	7-10	Standard Stl. Car Co.	WA 8-20-51	8-69	Dismantled: Du Bois, PA, 8-7-69	
C-2754		7-43	B&O shops, Washington, IN	181619 Steel		**M-13C Box Car**	5-06	S. Baltimore Car & Fdry.	12-49	4-61	Condemned on Certificate #5, 5-6-61, at Washington, IN	**only class M-13C car (steel sheathing added)**
C-2755	Photo	7-43	B&O shops, Washington, IN	183396		M-13A Box Car	4-10	American Car & Fdry.	7-52	3-53	Condemned on Certificate #2, 3-9-53, at Keyser, WV	Also reported Condemned: KY 4-24-53
C-2756		7-43	B&O shops, Washington, IN	X-6039	181099	M-13 Box Car	1-06	S. Baltimore Car & Fdry.	10-50	4-61	Condemned on Certificate #5, 1961, at Washington, IN	Condemned: Washington, IN 5-5-61
C-2757		7-43	B&O shops, Washington, IN	X-6047	182206	M-13A Box Car	3-10	Standard Stl. Car Co.	7-51	1-55	Condemned on Certificate #1, 1-21-55, at Keyser, WV	Condemned: Keyser, WV 7-20-55
C-2758	Photo	7-43	B&O shops, Washington, IN	X-6029	180039	M-13 Box Car	12-05	Western Stl. Car & Fdry.	7-50	1-61	Destroyed by fire at Indianapolis, IN, 12-24-60	
C-2759		7-43	B&O shops, Washington, IN	181105		M-13 Box Car	1-06	S. Baltimore Car & Fdry.		4-53	Condemned on Certificate #3, 4-13-53, at Gassaway, WV	Also reported Condemned: Lorain, OH, 5-28-53
C-2760	Photo	7-43	B&O shops, Washington, IN	181419		M-13 Box Car	3-06	S. Baltimore Car & Fdry.	WA 8-3-54	4-59	Condemned on Certificate #1, 4-29-59, at Washington, IN	Renumbered X-2208 at Washington, IN, 1-60
C-2761		7-43	B&O shops, Washington, IN	X-6037	180520	M-13 Box Car	1-06	Western Stl. Car & Fdry.	KY 8-13-51	3-56	Renumbered X-2855	Dismantled: Somerset, PA 3-30-67
C-2762		7-43	B&O shops, Washington, IN	X-6028	180038	M-13 Box Car	12-05	Western Stl. Car & Fdry.		6-52	Leased to B&OCT; Dismantled at Barr Yard, Chicago, 2-65	
C-2763	Photo	7-43	B&O shops, Washington, IN	X-6427	180101	M-13 Box Car	12-05	Western Stl. Car & Fdry.	7-52	4-55	Renumbered X-2135 at Keyser, WV 3-31-55	retired 9-57
C-2764		7-43	B&O shops, Washington, IN	X-6185	181414	M-13 Box Car	3-06	S. Baltimore Car & Fdry.	12-51	9-59	Condemned on Certificate #5, 9-10-59, at Washington, IN	Condemned: Washington, IN 9-22-59
C-2765		7-43	B&O shops, Washington, IN	X-6440	190162	M-13B Box Car	5-10	American Car & Fdry.	1-55	10-55	Condemned on Certificate #7, 10-14-55, at Keyser, WV	Condemned: Keyser, WV 1-21-56
C-2766	Photo	7-43	B&O shops, Washington, IN	X-6390	183035	M-13A Box Car	3-10	American Car & Fdry.	12-51	4-61	Dismantled at Washington, IN, on Certificate #5 for 1961	
C-2767		7-43	B&O shops, Washington, IN	X-6055	183226	M-13A Box Car	3-10	American Car & Fdry.	1-55	5-65	Leased to B&OCT	
C-2768		7-43	B&O shops, Washington, IN	X-6042	181720	M-13 Box Car	6-06	S. Baltimore Car & Fdry.	12-49	12-62	Condemned: Washington, IN, 11-23-62	
C-2769	Photo	7-43	B&O shops, Washington, IN	X-6428	182289	M-13A Box Car	4-10	Standard Stl. Car Co.	12-51	9-67	Leased to B&OCT	Sold scrap sales order #5012, 9-8-67 to Indiana Metals
C-2770		7-43	B&O shops, Washington, IN	X-6035	180330	M-13 Box Car	12-05	Western Stl. Car & Fdry.	5-52	12-64	Wrecked and destroyed at Lebanon, IL	
C-2771		7-43	B&O shops, Washington, IN	X-6032	180189	M-13 Box Car	12-05	Western Stl. Car & Fdry.	2-53	12-56	Renumbered X-2861 at Keyser, WV, 10-19-56	retired 9-57
C-2772		7-43	B&O shops, Washington, IN	X-6446	181124	M-13 Box Car	6-06	S. Baltimore Car & Fdry.	6-50	2-55	Condemned on Certificate #2, 2-24-55, at Washington, IN	Condemned: Washington, IN 3-18-55
C-2773		7-43	B&O shops, Washington, IN	X-6445	180318	M-13 Box Car	12-05	Western Stl. Car & Fdry.	12-52	4-59	Condemned on Certificate #1, 4-29-59, at Wilsmere, DE	Condemned: Wilsmere, DE, 4-29-59;
C-2774	Photo	7-43	B&O shops, Washington, IN	X-6444	180266	M-13 Box Car	12-05	Western Stl. Car & Fdry.		8-62	Condemned: at Washington, IN, 8-6-62;	sold to Maryland Construction Company (a B&O paper co.)
C-2775		7-43	B&O shops, Washington, IN	X-6418	180969	M-13 Box Car	2-06	Western Stl. Car & Fdry.		10-46	Retired	Destroyed: Green Springs, WV 9-19-46 wreck
C-2776		7-43	B&O shops, Washington, IN	X-6027	180020	M-13 Box Car	11-05	Western Stl. Car & Fdry.	8-50	4-61	Condemned on Certificate #5, 1961 at Washington, IN	Condemned: Washington, IN 5-2-61
C-2777		7-43	B&O shops, Washington, IN	X-6430	182587	M-13A Box Car	5-10	Standard Stl. Car Co.	1-53	4-55	Renumbered X-2136 at Keyser, WV, 3-31-55	retired 4-60
C-2778	Photo	7-43	B&O shops, Washington, IN	X-6408	181739	M-13 Box Car	6-06	S. Baltimore Car & Fdry.	1-53	4-72	Destroyed by fire, Ridgeley, IL, 4-9-72	
C-2779	Photo	7-43	B&O shops, Washington, IN	X-6388	181175	M-13 Box Car	1-06	S. Baltimore Car & Fdry.	6-53	9-67	Leased to B&OCT	Sold: 9-8-67 to Indiana Metals on sales order 5012
C-2780	Photo	7-43	B&O shops, Washington, IN	X-6045	181889	M-13 Box Car	8-06	S. Baltimore Car & Fdry.	6-53	WA 4-13-60	Renumbered X-4197	sold: scrap at Washington, IN 1-8-75 on sales order #4547
C-2781		7-43	B&O shops, Washington, IN	X-6046	181979	M-13 Box Car	11-06	S. Baltimore Car & Fdry.	5-51	4-55	Renumbered X-2137 at Keyser, WV, 3-31-55	retired 12-57
C-2782	Photo	7-43	B&O shops, Washington, IN	X-6387	180163	M-13 Box Car	12-05	Western Stl. Car & Fdry.	11-51	4-61	Condemned on Certificate #5, 1961, Washington, IN	Damaged: fire: Moorefield, IN 10-13-51; Cond: WA 5-2-61
C-2783	Photo	7-43	B&O shops, Washington, IN	X-6389	182579	M-13A Box Car	5-10	Standard Stl. Car Co.	3-52	11-81	Retired; car cannot be found	Retired 11-20-81 per Gen. Mgr - Car Department
C-2784	Photo	7-43	B&O shops, Washington, IN	X-6426	180000	M-13 Box Car	11-05	Western Stl. Car & Fdry.	WA 8-12-55	2-62	Renumbered X-4198 at Washington, IN, 2-1-62	retired mid-1960s
C-2785		7-43	B&O shops, Washington, IN	X-6400	183432	M-13A Box Car	4-10	American Car & Fdry.	8-50	12-61	Dismantled: B&O shops, Du Bois, PA, 12-12-61	
C-2786	Photo	7-43	B&O shops, Washington, IN	X-6036	180456	M-13 Box Car	1-06	Western Stl. Car & Fdry.	6-51	4-71	Sold: Barr Yard, to Industrial Salv. & Wrecking 4-19-71	Sold on sales order #4767
C-2787		7-43	B&O shops, Washington, IN	X-6049	182671	M-13A Box Car	5-10	Standard Stl. Car Co.		4-55	Condemned on Certificate #3, 4-19-55, at Du Bois, PA	Condemned: Du Bois, PA 5-31-55

Roster Copyright © 2016 by Dwight Jones **DO NOT COPY**

Original Number	Photo?	Date Built (Modified)	Built (Modified) By	Modified From	Previous Number	Class, Type	Box Car Built	Box Car Built By	Applied 'AB' Brakes	Date Retired	Disposition	Comments
C-2788	Photo	7-43	B&O shops, Washington, IN	X-6038	180807	M-13 Box Car	2-06	Western Stl. Car & Fdry.	12-49	3-55	Renumbered X-2133 at Washington, IN, 3-30-55	retired mid-1960s
C-2789		7-43	B&O shops, Washington, IN	X-6451	190051	M-13B Box Car	4-10	American Car & Fdry.		4-53	Condemned on Certificate #3, 4-13-53, at Gassaway, WV	Also reported Condemned: Lorain, OH, 5-28-53
C-2790		7-43	B&O shops, Washington, IN	X-6447	181532	M-13 Box Car	5-06	S. Baltimore Car & Fdry.	11-50	12-62	Condemned at Washington, IN, 11-23-62	
C-2791	Photo	7-43	B&O shops, Washington, IN	182660		M-13A Box Car	5-10	Standard Stl. Car Co.	6-50	12-61	Dismantled at B&O shops, Du Bois, PA, 12-7-61	
C-2792		7-43	B&O shops, Washington, IN	181409		M-13 Box Car	3-06	S. Baltimore Car & Fdry.	6-53	4-55	Condemned on Certificate #3, 4-19-55, at Glenwood, PA	Condemned: Du Bois, PA 5-31-55
C-2793		7-43	B&O shops, Washington, IN	X-6439	190126	M-13B Box Car	5-10	American Car & Fdry.	1-51	3-55	Renumbered X-2128 at Du Bois, PA, 3-29-55	retired mid-1960s
C-2794		7-43	B&O shops, Washington, IN	X-6048	182629	M-13A Box Car	5-10	Standard Stl. Car Co.	11-52	7-64	Wrecked, Dismantled at B&O shops, Washington, IN	
C-2795	Photo	7-43	B&O shops, Washington, IN	X-6452	190114	M-13B Box Car	5-10	American Car & Fdry.	5-50	11-81	Retired; car cannot be found	Retired 11-20-81 per Gen. Mgr.- Car Department
C-2796		7-43	B&O shops, Washington, IN	X-6051	182821	M-13A Box Car	6-10	Standard Stl. Car Co.	11-51	DU 12-9-60	Renumbered XM-4192	Sold: scrap Midwest Steel from Glenwood, 4-82; s.o. # 4727
C-2797		7-43	B&O shops, Washington, IN	X-6448	181703	M-13 Box Car	6-06	S. Baltimore Car & Fdry.		10-51	Wrecked, collision, Tippecanoe, OH, 8-15-51	2404 form written at Lorain, OH 10-17-51
C-2798		7-43	B&O shops, Washington, IN	X-6191	181721	M-13 Box Car	6-06	S. Baltimore Car & Fdry.		3-55	Renumbered X-2129 at Du Bois, PA, 3-31-55	retired mid-1960s
C-2799		7-43	B&O shops, Washington, IN	X-6449	181763	M-13 Box Car	6-06	S. Baltimore Car & Fdry.	12-51	5-60	Wrecked 3-19-60 at Wildwood, PA	

Notes:

1. Many of the I-16 cabooses were converted to "X" and "XM" cars for non-revenue service. When the retirement date is known for those non-revenue cars it is shown in the "Comments" column.

2. The "XM" prefix on non-revenue equipment identifies a car qualified for use in mainline trains with no restrictions on speed, etc.

3. Some disposition data references a "2404 form". See pages 52 and 76 for examples and definitions for this form. See also page 21 of Volume 3 in this series.

Class I-16 caboose C-2758 brings up the markers (notice they have been moved to the end posts) on this eastbound train headed from Springfield, Illinois, to Decatur and Indianapolis. The long trestle is about three miles east of Springfield across Sugar Creek and has been described as the longest, or at least one of the longest, trestles in Illinois. This part of the line was abandoned in 1963 from just east of the bridge back into Springfield. *caption information and photo courtesy Duane Carrell*

I-16 Assignments, C-2300 / C-2700-series

Cab #	Date	Assignment	Cab #	Date	Assignment	Cab #	Date	Assignment
C-2300	4-5-51	Benwood to Fairmont, WV, pool	C-2343	5-5-61	Chicago Div. operating into IL	C-2716	8-10-53	Cowen, WV, extra cab
C-2302	3-1-54	Wheeling Division	C-2343	10-20-61	Akron-Chicago Division	C-2716	1-22-54	Buckhannon, WV, district run
C-2306	8-14-56	Eastern Region, oper. In PA	C-2344	1-16-59	Garrett, IN, to Robey St, Chicago	C-2716	3-1-54	Buckhannon District Run
C-2306	9-6-56	East Side to Wilsmere, DE, local	C-2344	5-5-61	Garrett, IN, operating into Illinois	C-2716	8-15-56	Hancock, MD, work train rider
C-2306	9-10-56	East Side to Wilsmere Local	C-2344	10-20-61	Akron-Chicago Division	C-2716	2-10-58	Shopped, Keyser, WV
C-2306	5-2-57	Operating In state of Delaware	C-2345	6-22-60	Pittsburgh Div. for MofW use	C-2717	4-5-51	Grafton, WV, extra cab
C-2306	5-3-57	Baltimore Div operating thru DE	C-2347	3-21-57	Butler Jct, PA	C-2718	8-14-56	Assigned to SIRT, Staten Isl., NY
C-2306	6-21-61	Maryland	C-2347	1-13-58	Shopped: Du Bois, PA	C-2718	6-12-61	SIRT, Staten Island, NY
C-2306	7-7-61	Baltimore Division	C-2348	1-26-45	Shopped: Du Bois, PA	C-2719	1-13-58	Shopped: Du Bois, PA
C-2306	7-17-61	Brunswick, MD	C-2348	1-13-58	Shopped: Du Bois, PA	C-2721	9-6-56	Millville Digger, Baltimore Div.
C-2307	4-10-52	Shopped: Mt. Clare, Baltimore	C-2349	1-16-59	Willard to Toledo pool	C-2721	9-10-56	Millville, WV, Digger
C-2307	5-18-53	Baltimore Div, operating thru DE	C-2349	5-5-61	Garrett, IN, not assigned	C-2722	5-18-53	Baltimore Div, operating thru DE
C-2309	4-5-51	Cowen, WV, extra cab	C-2349	10-20-61	Akron-Chicago Division	C-2722	8-15-56	Martinsburg - Cumbo roustabout
C-2309	8-10-53	Clarksburg Industrial Turn	C-2352	5-5-61	St. Louis Division	C-2722	9-6-56	Silver Spring, MD, distr. switcher
C-2309	1-22-54	Gassaway, WV, extra cab	C-2352	1-12-64	St. Louis Division	C-2722	9-10-56	Silver Spring, MD, Dist. Switcher
C-2309	3-1-54	Gassaway, extra service	C-2354	8-15-56	Martinsburg, WV; work train rider	C-2723	4-5-51	Cowen to Buckhannon, WV, local
C-2310	4-5-51	Trains 97-196, Monongah Div.	C-2355	5-5-61	St. Louis Division	C-2724	4-5-51	Brooklyn Jct., WV, to CL Local
C-2311	3-1-54	Sent to Huntington, WV	C-2355	1-12-64	St. Louis Division	C-2724	8-10-53	Parkersburg, WV, Industr. Turn
C-2312	9-6-56	Shopped, Keyser, WV	C-2356	5-5-61	St. Louis Division	C-2724	1-22-54	Viscose turn & Parmaco run
C-2312	9-10-56	Keyser, WV, shopped	C-2356	1-12-64	St. Louis Division	C-2724	3-1-54	Parkersburg Industrial Turn
C-2312	5-2-57	Operating In state of Delaware	C-2357	5-5-61	St. Louis Division	C-2725	6-22-60	Pittsburgh Division: MofW use
C-2312	5-3-57	Baltimore Div operating thru DE	C-2357	1-12-64	St. Louis Division	C-2725	5-25-61	Pittsburgh Division
C-2312	6-21-61	Maryland	C-2359	5-5-61	St. Louis Division	C-2726	9-6-51	Shopped: Du Bois, PA
C-2312	7-7-61	Baltimore Division	C-2359	1-12-64	St. Louis Division	C-2727	10-27-50	Shopped: Du Bois, PA
C-2312	7-17-61	Keyser, WV, shopped	C-2360	5-5-61	St. Louis Division	C-2727	6-22-51	Shopped: Du Bois, PA
C-2314	4-5-51	Gassaway, WV, shopped	C-2363	7-25-61	Washington, IN to Cincinnati	C-2727	1-13-58	Shopped: Du Bois, PA
C-2315	5-18-53	Baltimore Div, operating thru DE	C-2363	10-20-61	St. Louis Division	C-2727	6-22-60	Pittsburgh Div. for MofW use
C-2315	9-6-56	East Side to Wilsmere, DE, local	C-2363	1-12-64	St. Louis Division	C-2728	10-27-50	Shopped: Du Bois, PA
C-2315	9-10-56	East Side to Wilsmere Local	C-2367	5-5-61	St. Louis Division	C-2728	1-2-52	Keller, OH
C-2315	5-2-57	Operating In state of Delaware	C-2367	1-12-64	St. Louis Division	C-2729	9-6-51	Shopped: Du Bois, PA
C-2315	5-3-57	Baltimore Div operating thru DE	C-2368	1-12-64	St. Louis Division	C-2730	10-27-50	Shopped: Du Bois, PA
C-2315	6-21-61	Maryland	C-2371	5-5-61	St. Louis Division	C-2731	10-27-50	Shopped: Du Bois, PA
C-2315	7-7-61	Baltimore Division	C-2371	1-12-64	St. Louis Division	C-2732	1-13-58	Shopped: Du Bois, PA
C-2315	7-17-61	Bay View, MD, work train	C-2372	9-6-56	Wilsmere, DE, district switcher	C-2732	6-22-60	Pittsburgh Div. for MofW use
C-2319	5-18-53	Baltimore Div, operating thru DE	C-2372	9-10-56	Wilsmere District Switcher	C-2733	5-2-51	Riker Yard, PA
C-2319	9-6-56	Baltimore, MD, terminal service	C-2372	5-2-57	Operating In state of Delaware	C-2733	9-6-51	Punxsutawney, PA
C-2319	9-10-56	Baltimore, MD, terminal	C-2372	5-3-57	Baltimore Div operating thru DE	C-2733	3-3-54	Buffalo Division assigned
C-2319	6-21-61	Maryland	C-2372	7-7-61	Baltimore Division	C-2733	5-11-54	Buffalo Division assigned
C-2319	7-7-61	Baltimore Division	C-2372	7-17-61	Keyser, WV	C-2733	5-5-55	Butler Jct, PA
C-2319	7-17-61	Brunswick, MD	C-2700	4-10-52	Shopped: Mt. Clare, Baltimore	C-2733	6-2-55	Butler Jct, PA
C-2320	8-15-56	Cumberland work train rider	C-2700	5-18-53	Baltimore Div, operating thru DE	C-2733	8-17-55	Butler Jct, PA
C-2322	9-6-51	Punxsutawney, PA	C-2701	5-18-53	Baltimore Div, operating thru DE	C-2733	9-15-55	Butler Jct, PA
C-2322	5-18-53	Baltimore Div, operating thru DE	C-2702	4-5-51	Grafton, WV, extra cab	C-2733	10-14-55	Punxsutawney, PA
C-2322	8-14-56	Eastern Region, oper. In PA	C-2702	8-10-53	Grafton, work train rider	C-2733	9-24-56	Butler Jct, PA
C-2322	9-6-56	East Side (Philly.) tramp svc.	C-2702	1-22-54	Shopped, Gassaway, WV	C-2733	1-2-57	Butler Jct, PA
C-2322	9-10-56	East Side (Philly) Tramp cab	C-2702	3-1-54	Gassaway, shopped	C-2733	8-1-57	Butler Jct, PA
C-2322	6-21-61	Maryland	C-2703	4-10-52	Shopped: Mt. Clare, Baltimore	C-2733	11-13-58	Butler Jct, PA, assigned
C-2322	7-7-61	Baltimore Division	C-2703	6-21-61	Maryland	C-2733	7-10-59	Shopped: Du Bois, PA
C-2322	7-17-61	East Side, PA (Philadelphia)	C-2703	7-7-61	Baltimore Division	C-2733	11-3-59	Butler, PA, extra cab
C-2323	3-1-54	Parkersburg emergency service	C-2703	7-17-61	Wilsmere, DE, yard service	C-2733	12-15-59	Punxsutawney, PA
C-2325	5-5-61	Garrett, IN, not assigned	C-2705	5-18-53	Baltimore Div, operating thru DE	C-2733	6-20-60	Northern sub; xtra svc., Buf Div
C-2325	10-20-61	Akron-Chicago Division	C-2705	9-6-56	Shopped, Keyser, WV	C-2733	5-25-61	Buffalo Division
C-2327	8-15-56	Condemned; E end CU Div	C-2705	9-10-56	Shopped, Keyser, WV	C-2733	6-19-61	Butler, PA, emergency service
C-2328	8-15-56	Cumberland work train rider	C-2707	4-5-51	Gassaway, WV, shopped	C-2733	8-11-61	Butler, PA, extra cab
C-2330	3-1-54	Lorain, OH, extra cab	C-2707	8-10-53	Fairmont, work train rider	C-2734	5-18-53	Baltimore Div, operating thru DE
C-2330	10-20-61	Akron-Chicago Division	C-2707	1-22-54	Fairmont, WV, industrial turn	C-2734	8-15-56	Hancock, MD, night dist. Switchr
C-2331	9-6-56	Georgetown dist. (Baltimore Div)	C-2707	3-1-54	Fairmont Industrial Turn	C-2739	9-6-51	Punxsutawney, PA
C-2331	9-10-56	Georgetown District Run	C-2707	10-20-58	Grafton, WV, work train rider	C-2739	7-25-56	Shopped: Du Bois, PA
C-2332	1951	shopped: Du Bois, PA	C-2708	4-5-51	Grafton to Fairmont district run	C-2739	6-22-60	Pittsburgh Div. for MofW use
C-2332	9-6-51	Shopped: Du Bois, PA	C-2708	8-10-53	Buckhannon District Turn	C-2740	5-4-44	Punxsutawney, PA
C-2332	5-5-61	Garrett, IN, not assigned	C-2708	1-22-54	Shopped, Gassaway, WV	C-2740	6-22-60	Pittsburgh Division
C-2332	10-20-61	Akron-Chicago Division	C-2708	3-1-54	Gassaway, WV, shopped	C-2740	5-25-61	Pittsburgh Division
C-2335	3-19-45	Shopped: Du Bois, PA	C-2709	5-18-53	Baltimore Div, operating thru DE	C-2741	1-16-59	Fostoria, OH, switch run to WR
C-2336	9-6-51	Shopped: Du Bois, PA	C-2710	4-5-51	Fairmont to CL district turn	C-2741	10-20-61	Akron-Chicago Division
C-2336	7-12-55	Shopped: Du Bois, PA	C-2710	8-10-53	Parkersburg, WV, extra cab	C-2742	6-22-60	Pitts. Div; at DU for repairs
C-2336	6-22-60	Pittsburgh Division	C-2710	1-22-54	Fairmont, work train rider	C-2743	5-5-44	Elk Run Jct, PA
C-2337	1-16-59	Willard to Toledo pool	C-2710	3-1-54	Baltimore Division	C-2743	1-13-58	Shopped: Du Bois, PA
C-2337	10-20-61	Akron-Chicago Division	C-2711	3-1-54	Gassaway, shopped	C-2743	3-27-59	Shopped: Du Bois, PA
C-2338	10-27-50	Shopped: Du Bois, PA	C-2712	4-10-52	Shopped: Mt. Clare, Baltimore	C-2744	10-27-50	Shopped: Du Bois, PA
C-2338	9-6-51	Shopped: Du Bois, PA	C-2712	1-22-54	Frederick, MD, yard	C-2744	5-11-54	Buffalo Division assigned
C-2339	7-11-55	Shopped: Du Bois, PA	C-2712	9-10-56	Frederick, MD, yard	C-2744	10-14-55	Punxsutawney, PA
C-2339	1-13-58	Shopped: Du Bois, PA	C-2713	4-5-51	Grafton, WV, extra cab	C-2745	10-27-50	Shopped: Du Bois, PA
C-2339	6-22-60	Pittsburgh Div. for MofW use	C-2715	4-10-52	Shopped: Mt. Clare, Baltimore	C-2745	3-3-54	Buffalo Division assigned
C-2341	10-27-50	shopped: Du Bois, PA	C-2715	5-18-53	Baltimore Div, operating thru DE	C-2745	5-11-54	Buffalo Division assigned
C-2343	1-16-59	Garrett, IN to Barr Yard, Chicago	C-2716	4-5-51	Cowen, WV, #7 district turn	C-2745	10-14-55	Punxsutawney, PA

I-16 Assignments, C-2300 / C-2700-series (continued)

Cab #	Date	Assignment
C-2745	11-15-55	Riker, PA, work train rider
C-2745	8-12-59	Shopped: Du Bois, PA
C-2745	10-28-59	Shopped: Du Bois, PA
C-2745	6-20-60	Du Bois, PA, shopped
C-2745	8-11-61	Du Bois, PA, shopped
C-2746	10-27-50	Shopped: Du Bois, PA
C-2746	9-6-51	Punxsutawney, PA
C-2747	4-5-51	Clarksburg to Brk. Jct., Local
C-2747	8-10-53	Clarksburg to Brooklyn Jct. Local
C-2747	1-22-54	Clarksburg to Brooklyn Jct., local
C-2747	3-1-54	CL to Brk. Jct. Local
C-2748	4-10-52	Shopped: Mt. Clare, Baltimore
C-2749	10-27-50	Shopped: Du Bois, PA
C-2749	6-22-60	Pitts. Div; at DU for repairs
C-2753	5-5-61	St. Louis Division
C-2753	1-12-64	St. Louis Division

Cab #	Date	Assignment
C-2761	9-6-56	Washington DC
C-2761	9-10-56	Washington DC
C-2765	1-31-57	M&K work train rider
C-2770	1-12-64	St. Louis Division
C-2771	8-15-56	Hancock, MD, work train rider
C-2773	4-10-52	Shopped: Mt. Clare, Baltimore
C-2773	5-18-53	Baltimore Div, operating thru DE
C-2773	8-14-56	Eastern Region, oper. In PA
C-2773	9-6-56	East Side (Philly) work train
C-2773	9-10-56	East Side (Philly) work train
C-2773	5-2-57	Oper. In state of Delaware
C-2773	5-3-57	Baltimore Div operating thru DE
C-2778	10-20-61	St. Louis Division
C-2783	5-18-53	Baltimore Div, operating thru DE
C-2783	9-6-56	Baltimore, MD, terminal service
C-2783	9-10-56	Baltimore, MD, terminal

Cab #	Date	Assignment
C-2783	6-21-61	Maryland
C-2783	7-7-61	Baltimore Division
C-2783	7-17-61	Baltimore, MD, terminal service
C-2785	1-13-58	Shopped: Du Bois, PA
C-2785	6-22-60	Pittsburgh Div. for MofW use
C-2786	5-5-61	Washington, IN, shopped
C-2786	1-12-64	St. Louis Division
C-2789	4-5-51	CL to FR, WV, assigned turn
C-2790	5-5-61	Washington, IN, shopped
C-2791	1-13-58	Shopped: Du Bois, PA
C-2794	5-5-61	St. Louis Division
C-2794	1-12-64	St. Louis Division
C-2795	1-16-59	Seymour, IN
C-2795	7-25-61	Bunk room at Shoals, IN
C-2795	10-20-61	St. Louis Division
C-2795	1-12-64	St. Louis Division
C-2796	6-22-60	Pittsburgh Div. for MofW use

Before the implementation of caboose pooling, which began in August 1965, cabooses on the B&O were assigned to specific conductors and typically did not change their assignment often, sometimes remaining on a specific run for years. These assignment listings are documented to assist modelers who wish to assign accurate caboose numbers to regions they model. All of our assignment information has been compiled from a number of sources from the Transportation, Mechanical, Labor Relations and other official railroad sources.

I-16 cabooses make good lineside buildings as shown by this car at Worthington, West Virginia, photographed on June 29, 1975, and painted yellow/tan. The plywood covering the door is an indication it no longer is in use. Close inspection revealed the old number C-2315. That car was retired in 1981 because it could not be found on the system, an indication it was placed here without proper paperwork and authority. *Dwight Jones*

We first got the "heads up" about this car from a Bob Reid photo that appeared in the January-February 1975 *B&O Railroader* magazine. To learn more about this car we consulted with area B&O authority Terry Arbogast, who advised that the car was located at Anabelle Junction (note the high-target switch stand in the photo), just across the river and to the east from Worthington, West Virginia. Terry believed the car was used by local track men or carmen. He did further checking with one of his local contacts who had been inside the car and indicated that there was a phone inside and extra parts such as air hoses. Terry's contact indicated that the car burned up, possibly by railroad personnel, during July/August 1982. The date was well established as the contact was attending a ball game across the road and he noted the remains still were smoldering. Today the B&O rails are gone and the right-of-way is the West Fork River Trail, a nearly 15 mile long trail which is part crushed stone and part paved asphalt.

Markers

If you are a caboose fan you may have entertained the thought at some point of having your own caboose, perhaps placed on a piece of panel track in your yard or on your weekend getaway property as others have done. For most that is not practical. Almost as good is to collect a piece of that caboose history. Marker lights are a way to do just that.

Over the years the B&O has used a number of different marker types as have most railroads. In this book series we are presenting the history of these markers which may peek the readers' interest to start their own collection.

In this volume, we continue that coverage showcasing the markers that were used on B&O cabooses during the 1960s, along with various company documents that help shed light on marker history.

Like most railroad collectibles, the price of markers has risen in recent years with the proliferation of on-line auction sites and the bidding competition they bring. Good values can still be found at local auctions and estate sales.

Reflectorized markers show on C-2018 photographed at B&O's Willard, Ohio, yard on February 27, 1965. *two photos by Julian W. Barnard, Jr.*

An upgrade over the reflectorized markers were the Star battery operated markers shown on the C-2277 at Willard on February 27, 1965.

Reflector Markers

A B&O letter dated August 9, 1962, from F. R. Geiselman, B&O Mechanical Engineer, indicated that B&O should order 128 cast aluminum brackets (enough to make 32 reflector sets at two pair per caboose) from a Davenport, Iowa, foundry. The brackets and markers had been designed by the Rock Island and Pacific Railroad Company which had given their permission for B&O to order the brackets.

A B&O letter dated August 13, 1962, indicated that the quantity was to be increased to 168 sets to equip 41 cabooses with four spare brackets. The letter also authorized purchasing the aluminum plates for these markers with red Scotchlite on one side and green Scotchlite on the opposite side. All parts were to be shipped to Mount Clare for assembly.

The B&O drawing for these reflectorized markers is dated August 10, 1962, and is copied in this chapter. These markers became the primary markers for wood cupola cabooses operating in states that did not require electrical markers on cabooses (Maryland, Pennsylvania and New York required electric markers on cabooses).

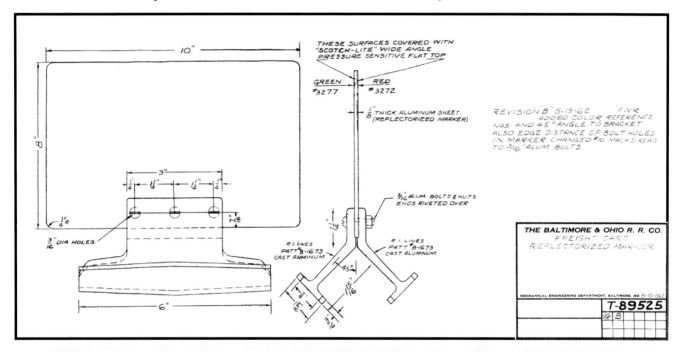

From the author's collection, two reflector markers, above, and a pair of the battery-operated markers on the following page. The above photo shows the red side on the left and the green side on the right marker. They fit perfectly into the B&O cast marker brackets.

The early sixties correspondence indicates that the components for the reflector markers were to be shipped to Mount Clare for assembly. With down-grading of those shops the work for assembling these reflector markers was transferred to the shops at Martinsburg, West Virginia, by December of 1965.

Instructions for the use of markers was found in both the operating rules book and in division timetables.

The information at right is from the C&O/B&O Operating Rules book dated April 27, 1969.

The T-19 paragraph below is extracted from Baltimore Division timetable #1 dated April 27, 1969. Timetables for divisions located on the western part of the B&O stated only that the use of reflectorized markers was permitted without the restriction about the states of Pennsylvania and Maryland.

T-19.—MARKERS.

The use of reflectorized markers is permitted except in the states of Pennsylvania and Maryland.

Markers

19. The following markers will be displayed, one on each side of the rear of every train, to indicate the rear of the train:

By Day—Marker lamps not lighted.

By Night—Marker lamps lighted showing red to rear.

Engines and cars equipped with fixed electric markers will display marker lamps lighted showing red to rear by day and night.

A train not equipped to display the prescribed markers will display a red flag and a white light by night to indicate the rear of the train.

Markers do not indicate the track on which a train is standing or moving.

Reflectorized markers may be used in territory designated by special instructions.

Trains of other railroads may display markers as prescribed by that railroad when operating on C&O-B&O rails.

19-A. Markers will not be displayed for yard movements, unless required by special instructions.

Battery-Operated Markers

These are two of the Star brand of battery-operated marker lights, each one powered by a pair of 6-volt lantern batteries. The marker on the right is an older style with stenciled "B&O" markings in black and an older style of latches on the sides. The marker on the left is a slightly more modern version with different side latches and "B&O" markings applied as a stamp in black. The tops of these markers had a red lens on one side and a green lens on the opposite side. The tops can be rotated to display either color to the rear.

STAR

Introduces:
ELECTRONIC FLASHING MARKER LAMPS

Specifically designed for the safety of trains and crews, Star Headlight & Lantern Company's Electronics Division now offers its new transistorized Electronic Flashing Marker Lamp.

Model 805-RR is a heavy duty, dependable lamp for rear end protection of Caboose and passenger cars. Unit can also be adapted to Blue Light Service for Car Inspectors.

Lenses are available in 4¼", 5³⁄₁₆", and 7" O.D. Colors are red, yellow, green and blue.

The twin-lens housing allows the combination of two colors such as red and yellow. By merely turning the housing 180 degrees the opposite color may be displayed, and without intermixing of colors. The 5³⁄₁₆" Lens (Model 805-RR) and the 7" Lens (Model 810-RR) feature a ½" band of reflecting area around the periphery of the lens. This area reflects light from a locomotive headlight giving a fixed reference point to the flashing light.

The use of our Electronic Marker Lamps will provide safer train operation; in addition, your lamp costs, and maintenance costs will be drastically reduced. The automatic ON and OFF function of our indestructible photocell yields large savings in battery costs. The flashing light is there *only* when needed! Our efficiently designed circuit utilizes all the electrical energy of a battery—not just half. It is necessary to change the two batteries only four or five times a *year!* You're safer by far with Star!

Model 805-RR
5³⁄₁₆" Lens—Reflecting type

SPECIFICATIONS
(Of Model 805-RR)

Flashing Rate: 60 per minute
Flash Duration: .1 second
Lamp: Star 8045. Clip included for holding spare lamp
Lens: 5³⁄₁₆" OD Reflecting type; colors as ordered.
Approx. Beam Candlepower: 9
Battery: One or two six-volt (lantern type)
Switch: Inside of case, tamperproof; optional Outside
Service Life: 2000 hours plus, with two batteries
Daylight Controlled: Photocell allows unit to operate only at dusk, night, dawn, gray stormy days; and when going through tunnels.
Case: Heavy drawn steel, electro zinc coated.

Mounting: ½-13 Button Head tamper proof screw. Optional: Bracket mounted to Railroad specifications
Finish: Baked enamel, traffic yellow
Weight: Less Batteries: 2½ lbs and 5¼ lbs.
Size of Case, Outside: 5½" wide x 2⅞" deep x 5" high
Overall Height: 10¾"
Operating Temperature Range: Minus 20° F. to 135° F. Temperature compensated circuit maintains uniform flashing rate throughout entire range.
Flashing Unit: Transistorized circuit; close-tolerance combined with two printed circuit boards gives military reliability.

Punxsutawney, Pa., Sept. 4, 1963

Messrs: V. H. Freygang
       L. O. Robinson
       R. L. Myers
       W. D. Luzier
       B. H. Peterson

        Following is quoted letter dated August 26, 1963
from RMG Rayburn:

        "Referring to my letter March 25, 1963 and other
correspondence, concerning the use of reflectorized caboose markers
in freight service.

        According to our records we have approximately
302 sets of these markers in service on the System, including the
following on the Central Region.

                B&OCT   41 sets
                Bflo. Div 15 "
                Ak-Chgo" 78 "

        All information available indicates that the use
of these reflectorized markers has been eminently satisfactory and
of course, has resulted in a considerable saving of money — see my
letter Dec. 17, 1962.

        Understand we have also had in service for a
considerable period of time, four electric blinking battery type
markers on Trains 53, 54, 57 and 58 between Cincinnati, Ohio and
Detroit, Mich., at a substantial saving.

        Wish you would again canvass the situation to
determine what the opportunities are for expanding the use of
reflectorized markers in freight service where we can legally use
them and the electric blinking type marker in passenger service,
letting me have your further advice promptly."

        Give this consideration promptly and advise.

                                O. H. Fletcher

Motive Power Department Shop Bulletin No. 94-G
Stores Department Circular No. D-12-G
(Superseding Shop Bulletin No. 94-F and Stores Department No. D-12-G)
Repairs and Reclamation of Tinware, Oil Lanterns, Marker and
Classification Lamps, and Electric Trainmen's Lanterns   -

Messrs.
H. M. Dowling
P. L. Hofstetter   O. M. Dorsey
C. E. Howdyshell   P. R. Lewis
J. A. Lyons   W. S. Furlow
W. A. Barrick   B. J. Borgman
C. W. Sears   K. F. Mewshaw
L. L. Frye   J. N. Minns
R. A. Shields, Jr.   G. B. Kirwan
J. A. F. Craig   C. R. Haskins

        Above joint circular letter is cancelled. No more items of tinware,
lanterns, etc. will be shipped to Keyser in the future. Items of this nature
should be turned over to your storekeeper who will scrap locally, except
for oil marker lamps and kerosene lanterns which have a possible resale
value in the museum at Mt. Clare.

        Demand for oil marker lamps is decreasing rapidly and this item
should be ordered from Mt. Clare in the future.

                                        G. M. Beischer

As was noted in volume 3, the shops at Keyser was
a major repair point for kerosene marker lights and
other lanterns. The shops at Keyser were reported
closed in May of 1965, which ties in to this June 2
memo indicating that no more of those lights were
to be sent to Keyser for repair. The above memo also
signals the start of sales of those cherished marker
lights at the B&O Museum in Baltimore.

At right, a trainman prepares to remove
the reflectorized marker on a recently
arrived caboose at North Lima, Ohio,
on August 8, 1964. Caboose C-2049 has
a stencil on the steps stating the pro-
verbial WATCH YOUR STEP. *Eileen J. Wolford*

B&O R.R. CO.

Baltimore, Md., December 22, 1965
File: Circulars A-227 and A-431

Circular A-227. Electric Trainmen's Lanterns
Circular A-431. Equipment and Supplies for Caboose Cars

ALL STOREKEEPERS:

In the near future a revised circular will be issued covering caboose supplies. The new circular will completely eliminate oil markers and oil lanterns.

Replacing the two red kerosene lanterns now listed will be:

2 - Item 250-0096345 Electric Hand Lanterns, Star No. 204/BR Red
(Blanket Orders; B&O 15167 - B&O C.T. 15168 - S.I.R.T. T-1946)

Replacing the two oil marker lamps now listed will be:

A) In electrified cabooses - nothing. The marker lamps are a permanent part of the caboose.

OR

B) For use in non-electrified cabooses not operating in Maryland, Pennsylvania or New York.
2 - Item No. 361-0009496 Reflectorized Markers, B&O BP-89525.
(Order from Martinsburg)

OR

C) For use in non-electrified cabooses operating in Maryland, Pennsylvania, or New York.
1 - Item No. 361-0006572 L.H. Electronic Flasher Marker Model 805/RR
1 - Item No. 361-0006573 R.H. "   "   "   "   "
(Order on Purchase)

Existing supplies of oil markers and kerosene lanterns should be issued and continued in service as long as they are usable. Since the anticipated circular change will eventually eliminate the use of all oil lanterns and markers in train service, effective immediately no additional oil markers or kerosene lanterns should be purchased for this service. When necessary to replace your stock, order the new items indicated above. It will not be necessary to secure Form 745-A when furnishing the red electric lanterns as a replacement for the red kerosene lanterns as a caboose supply.

A few kerosene lanterns should be held in stock for miscellaneous uses other than train service. Limited quantities to be ordered on Mount Clare in future. Mount Clare only to order on purchase in lots of five dozen.

T. R. Grady
Manager Materials

cc: All Staff - Materials Department
    All Division Superintendents - 50
    Mr. R. J. Burns
    Mr. J. T. Collinson

Mr. J. H. Grozinger
Mr. T. P. Hackney
Mr. R. J. Hollingsworth
Mr. T. J. Klauenberg
Mr. W. A. Mullen

Mr. W. C. Reister-100
Mr. C. R. Wheeler
Mr. E. C. Whipp
Mr. H. M. Wyant

Whistles

The use of whistles on cabooses is a key safety item for backup moves where the caboose leads. While not supplying the sound volume of a bell or diesel horn it can be used effectively for crossing protection and to alert individuals walking across or near tracks. They typically are operated by a trainman standing on the end platform and observing the path ahead.

B&O's own design of an air-operated whistle dates at least to August 1, 1911, when drawing S-26080 was issued.

A B&O drawing also was prepared for the Sherburne whistle (S-38370) dated March 16, 1920.

The B&O whistle was operated by opening the valve (or cut out cock). The air could also be dumped to stop the train in case of emergency by a separate cut out cock which was Tee'd off the whistle post a few inches below the whistle.

The Sherburne whistle was operated by a push button on the side of the cut out cock. The handle could be rotated to dump the air.

The large Westinghouse Clarion whistle was typically mounted to an end of the cupola and protruded slightly above the cupola roof. It used so much air that it would automatically dump the air on the train if it was used. To prevent this a separate air reservoir was provided in the upper part of the interior toilet compartment.

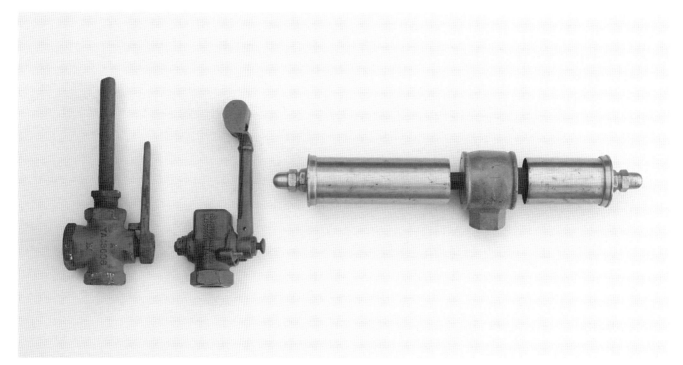

From the author's collection the three types of whistles found on B&O cabooses. At left is one of the home-made B&O whistles. In the middle is a Sherburne purchased whistle and at right is one of the Westinghouse Clarion whistles found only on I-10 cabooses and a few I-5 cars assigned on the Buffalo Division.

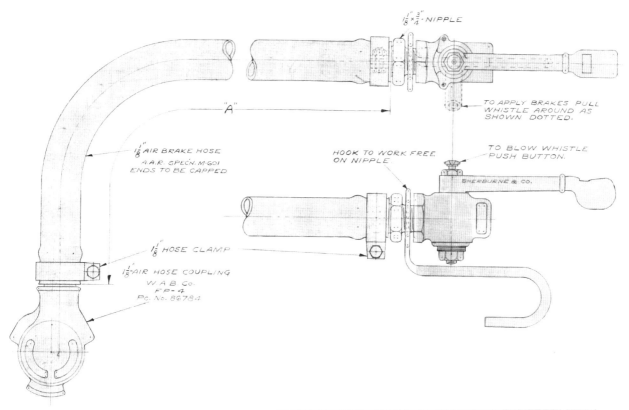

$1\frac{1}{8}" \times \frac{3}{4}"$ NIPPLE

"A"

$1\frac{1}{8}"$ AIR BRAKE HOSE
A.A.R. SPEC'N. M·601
ENDS TO BE CAPPED

HOOK TO WORK FREE
ON NIPPLE

TO APPLY BRAKES PULL
WHISTLE AROUND AS
SHOWN DOTTED.

TO BLOW WHISTLE
PUSH BUTTON.

SHERBURNE & CO.

$1\frac{1}{8}"$ HOSE CLAMP

$1\frac{1}{8}"$ AIR HOSE COUPLING
W A B Co.
FP-4
Pc. No. 86784

A	WHERE USED	LINE No.
11'-0"	STANDARD FOR FREIGHT CARS FREIGHT YARD SHIFTERS, MINE, DISTRICT, INDUSTRIAL AND TRANSFER RUNS.	1
5'-8"	STANDARD FOR PASSENGER AND WORK TRAINS.	2

Questions arose from the photo of C-2500 which showed a backup hose (conductor's hose or "pig tail") shown draped over the end railing. The hose in the photo is attached to the whistle post but typically would be coupled to the end of the air hose and would provide a trainman standing on the end platform a whistle and a way to dump the air and apply the brakes from the caboose.

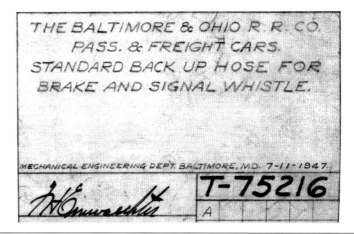

THE BALTIMORE & OHIO R. R. CO.
PASS. & FREIGHT CARS.
STANDARD BACK UP HOSE FOR
BRAKE AND SIGNAL WHISTLE.

MECHANICAL ENGINEERING DEPT. BALTIMORE, MD. 7-11-1947.

T-75216

A

Paint & Lettering

What color B&O cabooses were painted throughout the years is a key question of both modelers and historians. In the last volume we provided the information that Devil's Red was re-implemented in July 1941, replacing Freight Car Brown which had previously replaced Devil's Red at an unknown date.

We "believe" that the Freight Car Brown was not used very long. Although we have yet to discover the exact date, the following information is supplied as evidence:

1. Painting Circular F-60-H was revised several times in the late 1930s and was reissued on May 1, 1940. The next revision prior to those dates was four years earlier. Taken alone these revision dates mean nothing. But consider also the following:

2. A July 1936 article in *Baltimore and Ohio Magazine* (see page 42 of volume 3) is titled The Little Old <u>RED</u> Caboose Has Gone Modern" (our emphasis on the word RED). If Freight Car Brown was the prevalent color in 1936 then we would assume the title of the article would have been different.

3. On the same page of volume 3, left column, third paragraph, is a description of the color of C-2502 which stated "...the caboose on exhibition was painted gray instead of the usual "Devil's Red"." This must have meant that the prevalent caboose color in 1939 was Devil's Red.

4. Refer to the bottom photo on page 25 of volume 3 which depicts C-2500 in fresh paint coupled to a freshly painted boxcar. If it is assumed that the boxcar is painted Freight Car Brown, it is interesting to note that the steps and end platform of the caboose appear to be the same color as the boxcar but the body of the caboose appears in a lighter shade in the black-and-white photo. It is known that caboose steps were specified to be painted Freight Car Brown

for a time (refer to the verbiage on page 198 of volume 3). It is our belief that the body of C-2500 is painted Devil's Red.

5. Painting drawing T-66156, reproduced in this chapter, was completed on April 4, 1940, and originally documented how to paint cabooses in the freight car brown colors. The creation date of this drawing ties in with some of our above evidence.

Much of the above is intelligent speculation. Perhaps more hard documentation can be uncovered in the future to help nail down just when Freight Car Brown superseded Devil's Red as the caboose body color.

Green Window Frames and Doors

There is confusion, even among B&O officials, regarding window sash and window frames and their colors. The window sash is the wood frame that the glass is installed in. The sash goes up and down with the movement of the window. The window frame is stationary and is attached to the caboose body.

During the years that color images are available, cabooses can be found with green end doors and window sashes, a few can be found also with green window frames (but these are a minority and not common). And some can be found with red window sashes and end doors. Two examples can be seen by examining the two photos on the top of page 202 in Volume 3 as well as color photos in this edition.

A B&O memo dated February 10, 1956, indicated this:

"I talked to L.M. Schalk [Superintendent of the Du Bois car shop] about painting cabooses and asked him where the instructions were regarding painting the exterior of window sashes and outside of door green. He said it was in the Circular, but after looking at the Circular (F-60-I) he agreed that there was nothing about green paint on the exterior.

"He says they have been painting them with the green on outside as long as they have been painting cabooses, and if they are wrong then everyone else is. He cannot find any instructions and says so far as he knows, it is just common sense. However, I told him we were not carrying out the intent of the circular, and he agreed that we were not, but did not intend to make any change."

A B&O memo issued about a month later on the Buffalo division, dated February 13, 1956, is reproduced below:

"A recent inspection of cabooses being painted at various points in accordance with our caboose painting program reveals that at some points they are painting the entire exterior of the caboose with red paint.

"It should be understood that the standard for painting cabooses on the outside is to have the window frames [the writer should have said "sash"] and doors on the outside painted green.

"Please be governed accordingly in the future when painting cabooses on the Buffalo Division.

"All interior painting of cabooses should be as outlined in Circular F-60-I." [this circular is reproduced in Volume 3 in this book series].

This memo implies that there must have been some discussion or research and it was determined that green was the correct standard for window sash and doors.

Although Superintendent Schalk could not answer the question about the green color for the doors and window sash, B&O specifications indicated the following:

Painting drawing T-66156, issued April 4, 1940, specifically identified doors and window sash on the exterior to be painted green (B&O stock number 311). This drawing is reproduced on page 175.

However, the above drawing was superseded by drawing T-83278, dated December 28, 1953, (see pages 128-129 in volume 3). This drawing specified that all exterior surfaces be painted caboose car red, stock number F-151. So it would appear that the intent of Baltimore officials was to eliminate the green on the end doors and window sash. Indeed this did happen on the I-17A cars completed at Washington, Indiana.

Memos of this era, quoted on page 16 of volume 2 in this series specifically state that the original I-17 scheme was that the sash be painted (inside and outside) with Olive Green paint, stock # F-103. When the new interior scheme was developed in 1953 it was noted that "The window sash on the outside of the caboose should be painted bright red, stock number F-151, same as exterior of caboose."

The practice varied at B&O shops. The Washington and Chillicothe shops did not use green in the sixties. Du Bois did green window sash to 1969 with red doors. Brunswick did green sash and doors into the early 1970s with their final caboose repaints.

B&O drawing T-86584 (rev A) is dated 11-14-56 and specifies the yellow triangle to be painted on the left corner for those I-16s assigned to MofW service.

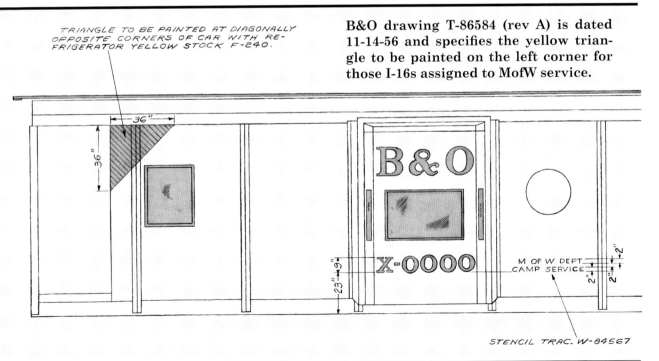

TRIANGLE TO BE PAINTED AT DIAGONALLY OPPOSITE CORNERS OF CAR WITH REFRIGERATOR YELLOW STOCK F-240.

STENCIL TRAC. W-84567

Painting & Lettering Timeline

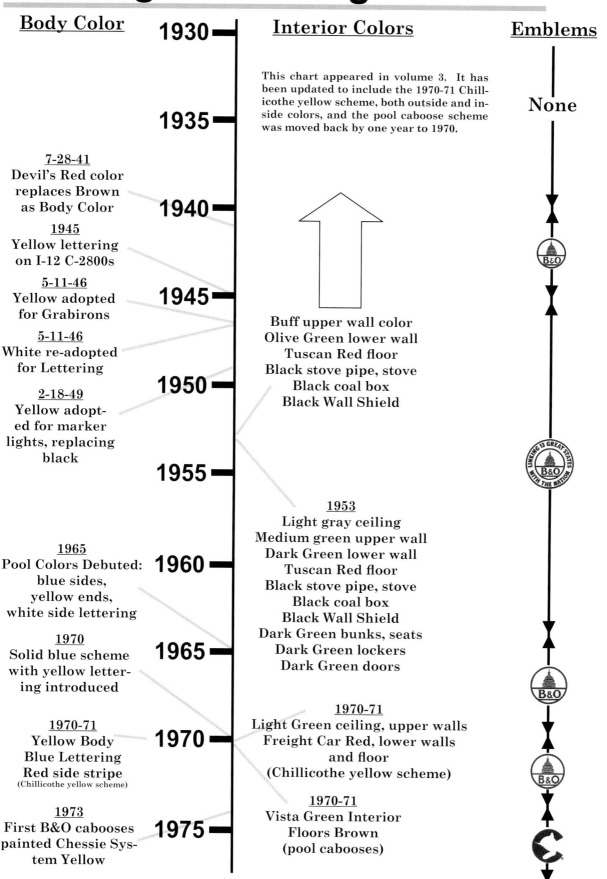

Body Color

7-28-41
Devil's Red color
replaces Brown
as Body Color

1945
Yellow lettering
on I-12 C-2800s

5-11-46
Yellow adopted
for Grabirons

5-11-46
White re-adopted
for Lettering

2-18-49
Yellow adopt-
ed for marker
lights, replacing
black

1965
Pool Colors Debuted:
blue sides,
yellow ends,
white side lettering

1970
Solid blue scheme
with yellow letter-
ing introduced

1970-71
Yellow Body
Blue Lettering
Red side stripe
(Chillicothe yellow scheme)

1973
First B&O cabooses
painted Chessie Sys-
tem Yellow

Interior Colors

1930

1935

This chart appeared in volume 3. It has
been updated to include the 1970-71 Chillicothe yellow scheme, both outside and inside colors, and the pool caboose scheme
was moved back by one year to 1970.

1940

1945

Buff upper wall color
Olive Green lower wall
Tuscan Red floor
Black stove pipe, stove
Black coal box
Black Wall Shield

1950

1955

1953
Light gray ceiling
Medium green upper wall
Dark Green lower wall
Tuscan Red floor
Black stove pipe, stove
Black coal box
Black Wall Shield
Dark Green bunks, seats
Dark Green lockers
Dark Green doors

1960

1965

1970

1970-71
Light Green ceiling, upper walls
Freight Car Red, lower walls
and floor
(Chillicothe yellow scheme)

1970-71
Vista Green Interior
Floors Brown
(pool cabooses)

1975

Emblems

None

126 – Lettering and Marking – Application of Continental Car Cement
        System Cars–

                                    Baltimore,Md. Sept.17, 1927

Messrs: H.J.Burkley   C.E.McGann   C.G.Slagle
  T.R.Stewart   R.H.Cline   T.E.Mewshaw   R.A.Conner
  F.E.Cooper   F.R.Gelhausen F.K.Moses   W.J.Dixon
  W.K.Gonnerman M.A.Gleeson   T.C.O'Brien   J.F.Bowden
  J.P.Quinn   W.F.Harris   W.B.Porterfield W.A.Bonder
  C.M.Scott   J.J.Herlihy   Harry Rees   W.W.Calder
  F.A.Baldinger J.P.Hines   J.W.Schad   C.M.Hitch
                                J.M.Shay   T.H.Hollen
                                                 E.B.Miller

        The following instructions will cover the repainting of all
freight car equipment belonging to the Baltimore and Ohio Railroad and
Subsidiary Lines, superseding instructions covered in circular F-60-F
regarding the kind of paint and number of coats applied to car.

        Whenever any cars are on shop tracks for repainting,they
should be painted as follows,with one coat of Continental Car Cement
with a consistency that two gallons of the cement will be applied to
each 100 sq.ft.of surface.

                       All Metal Parts of Underframes
BOX CARS: Roofs
                       All Metal Parts of Trucks

                       All Metal parts of Underframes,
GONDOLA & HOPPER   Body,interior and exterior,metal parts
    CARS   All metal parts of trucks

                       All Metal Parts of Body
FLAT CARS: All Metal Parts of Trucks

                       Eaves Molding and Roofs
CABOOSE CARS: All Metal Parts of Underframe
                       All Metal Parts of Trucks

        When new metal parts are applied to car, the Continental Car
Cement must be applied between the joints.

        When parts of car are in a rusty condition,they should be
thoroughly scraped with steel scrapers,and brushed with wire brush in
order to remove the accumulation of rust and rust pockets.

        After cement has been applied and before stenciling, one
coat of shellac should be applied directly under the letters and
figures,and in no case, should the stenciling be painted over cement.

                                             W B Whitsitt
hlh-s
Cy.Messrs:
    G.H.Emerson   G.R.Galloway   W.S.Galloway
    C.A.Gill   A.H.Hodges   E.W.Walther
    A.K.Galloway   W.D.Johnston   H.Shoemaker
    J.J.Tatum   A.E.McMillan   J.R.Orndorff
    F.H.Lee   E.J.McSweeney   A.L.Miller
    H.A.Blair   C.M.Newman   C.T.Rommel
                     C.P.VanGundy

    Group No. 126

Pittsburgh, Pa., April 14, 1955

306

Messrs.

R. W. Dean   J. A. DeGennaro
T. B. Taylor   J. H. Bingham
D. W. Brown   James Lewis
W. N. Judy   C. C. Davis
L. R. Freeland   F. P. Ryan
L. M. Schalk   J. Plunkett, Jr.
E. M. Yaeger   G. H. Gross
C. W. Grube

        Quote below letter received from Mr. A. B. Lawson dated April 8,1955
in connection with application of new lettering and marking on caboose cars,
which is self-explanatory:

        "The management has recently approved new lettering and marking
scheme for caboose cars, particularly to employ the use of large "B & O"
initials, such as now being applied to our box, gondola and hopper cars,
and in advance of general letter that will be issued we enclose the following prints:

    W-84651-A - Lettering and Marking, Classes I-5a, I-5b, I-5ba, I-12,
                I-17 and I-17a, (superseding prints W-60480 and W-82205).
    X-84671-A - Lettering and Marking, Classes I-13, I-16, (superseding
                print X-67644).
    W-84674-A - Lettering and Marking, Classes I-1, I-1a, I-4, I-5, I-5c,
                I-5d, I-9, I-10 (superseding print W-33265).
    Z-72582-D - 25" B&O Emblem.
    Y-84631-A - 16" B&O Stencil.
    Y-84653-A - 18" B&O Stencil.

        "The 18" stencil will be used on all cabooses except classes I-13,
I-16, I-17 and I-17a, where the 16" size will be used, due to limited clear-
ances over the bay window.

        "Prints were previously forwarded to Washington, Ind. covering
lettering and marking for the twelve new cabooses now under construction.

        "The above prints to be followed when cabooses are repainted in
the future."

        The new lettering and marking will be applied to the above class
caboose cars when they are repainted in your shop.

                                        W. C. Reister

Baltimore, Md., October 5, 1955.

Mr. G. F. Wiles
Mr. E. Stimson, Jr.
Mr. H. J. Burkley

Effective October 1st, 1955 we will inaugurate a scheduled production of repairs to caboose cars at Keyser, DuBois and Washington, Indiana. Sufficient forces have been allotted to each of these selected car shops in order to make possible an effective scheduled output of caboose cars.

At the present time we have been repairing caboose cars at miscellaneous car shops and in order to consolidate this work and in order to handle the situation more efficiently effective October 1st we will consolidate repairs to our caboose cars at the three stations specified.

I am attaching for the benefit of you gentlemen blank copy of proposed shopping schedule which will be put into effect at Keyser, DuBois and Washington, Ind. commencing with the month of October 1955.

Sufficient caboose cars have been transferred to these three selected shops to cover the proposed output for October 1955, but if additional transfers of bad order caboose cars will be necessary to complete the October schedule such transfers will be arranged through this office in cooperation with the General Managers.

Messrs. Schalk, Crockett and Gross will kindly arrange to fill in the proposed shopping schedule for October 1955, covering the intended output of caboose cars for the shop under their respective jurisdiction.

It is absolutely necessary that the schedule form be completed with the information shown to cover the caboose cars listed for shopping and for out-shopping in the month of October.

Arrangements have been made with the General Managers to notify this office a month in advance when additional caboose cars are to be withdrawn from service and which cars will require shopping attention. This information must be available in order to prepare schedule a month in advance, which will in turn enable us to inform the General Managers as to their allocation of caboose cars to be repaired and enable us to schedule such cars through the shops. When this information is available in this office we will arrange for scheduling at one of the three selected stations where such repairs will be made. In other words, it is the prerogative of this office to advise the various General Managers where bad order caboose cars are to be repaired.

Am sending to Messrs. Schalk, Crockett and Gross sufficient copies of these schedule blanks to enable them to fill in the data for October 1955. Three copies of the filled in schedule for October and for subsequent months when due should then be forwarded from DuBois, Keyser and Washington, Ind. direct to the respective Superintendent of Motive Power, who will approve or adjust, and forward two copies of form to this office for final processing. One copy of the filled in schedule form should be forwarded direct from each of the three shops to the Regional Master Car Builder for the information of that officer. After the schedules are finally approved and issued copy of same

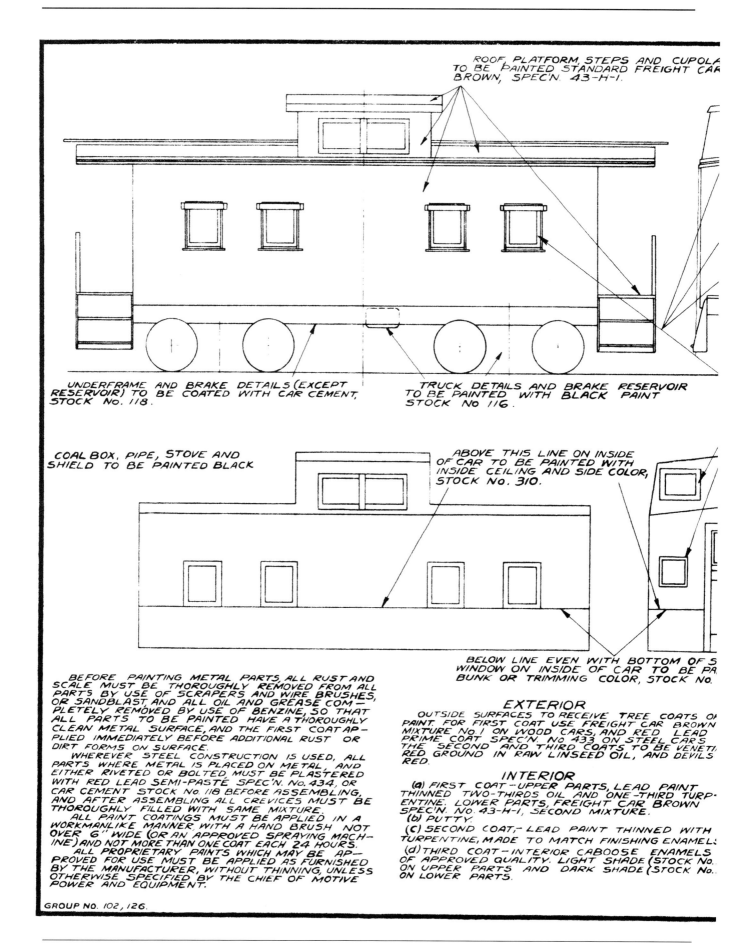

ROOF, PLATFORM, STEPS AND CUPOLA
TO BE PAINTED STANDARD FREIGHT CAR
BROWN, SPEC'N. 43-H-1.

UNDERFRAME AND BRAKE DETAILS (EXCEPT
RESERVOIR) TO BE COATED WITH CAR CEMENT,
STOCK No. 118.

TRUCK DETAILS AND BRAKE RESERVOIR
TO BE PAINTED WITH BLACK PAINT
STOCK No 116.

COAL BOX, PIPE, STOVE AND
SHIELD TO BE PAINTED BLACK

ABOVE THIS LINE ON INSIDE
OF CAR TO BE PAINTED WITH
INSIDE CEILING AND SIDE COLOR,
STOCK No. 310.

BELOW LINE EVEN WITH BOTTOM OF S
WINDOW ON INSIDE OF CAR TO BE PA
BUNK OR TRIMMING COLOR, STOCK No.

BEFORE PAINTING METAL PARTS, ALL RUST AND
SCALE MUST BE THOROUGHLY REMOVED FROM ALL
PARTS BY USE OF SCRAPERS AND WIRE BRUSHES,
OR SANDBLAST, AND ALL OIL AND GREASE COM-
PLETELY REMOVED BY USE OF BENZINE, SO THAT
ALL PARTS TO BE PAINTED HAVE A THOROUGHLY
CLEAN METAL SURFACE, AND THE FIRST COAT AP-
PLIED IMMEDIATELY BEFORE ADDITIONAL RUST OR
DIRT FORMS ON SURFACE.
    WHEREVER STEEL CONSTRUCTION IS USED, ALL
PARTS WHERE METAL IS PLACED ON METAL, AND
EITHER RIVETED OR BOLTED, MUST BE PLASTERED
WITH RED LEAD SEMI-PASTÉ SPEC'N. No. 434, OR
CAR CEMENT STOCK No. 118 BEFORE ASSEMBLING,
AND AFTER ASSEMBLING ALL CREVICES MUST BE
THOROUGHLY FILLED WITH SAME MIXTURE.
    ALL PAINT COATINGS MUST BE APPLIED IN A
WORKMANLIKE MANNER WITH A HAND BRUSH NOT
OVER 6" WIDE (OR AN APPROVED SPRAYING MACH-
INE) AND NOT MORE THAN ONE COAT EACH 24 HOURS.
    ALL PROPRIETARY PAINTS WHICH MAY BE AP-
PROVED FOR USE MUST BE APPLIED AS FURNISHED
BY THE MANUFACTURER, WITHOUT THINNING, UNLESS
OTHERWISE SPECIFIED BY THE CHIEF OF MOTIVE
POWER AND EQUIPMENT.

GROUP NO. 102, 126.

EXTERIOR
OUTSIDE SURFACES TO RECEIVE TREE COATS O
PAINT. FOR FIRST COAT USE FREIGHT CAR BROWN
MIXTURE No. 1 ON WOOD CARS, AND RED LEAD
PRIME COAT SPEC'N. No. 433 ON STEEL CARS
THE SECOND AND THIRD COATS TO BE VENETI
RED GROUND IN RAW LINSEED OIL, AND DEVILS
RED.

INTERIOR
(a) FIRST COAT - UPPER PARTS, LEAD PAINT
THINNED TWO-THIRDS OIL AND ONE-THIRD TURP-
ENTINE. LOWER PARTS, FREIGHT CAR BROWN
SPEC'N. No. 43-H-1, SECOND MIXTURE.
(b) PUTTY.
(c) SECOND COAT, - LEAD PAINT THINNED WITH
TURPENTINE, MADE TO MATCH FINISHING ENAMEL:
(d) THIRD COAT - INTERIOR CABOOSE ENAMELS
OF APPROVED QUALITY. LIGHT SHADE (STOCK No.
ON UPPER PARTS AND DARK SHADE (STOCK No.
ON LOWER PARTS.

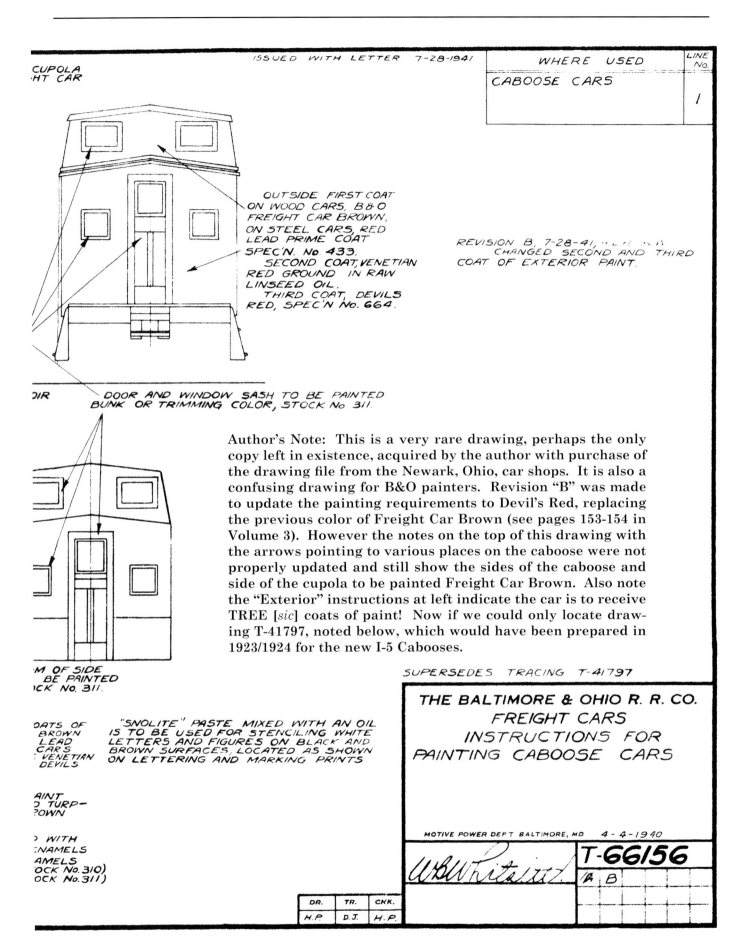

CUPOLA
HT CAR

ISSUED WITH LETTER 7-28-1941

WHERE USED
CABOOSE CARS

LINE No.

1

OUTSIDE FIRST COAT ON WOOD CARS, B&O FREIGHT CAR BROWN, ON STEEL CARS, RED LEAD PRIME COAT SPEC'N. No. 433.
SECOND COAT, VENETIAN RED GROUND IN RAW LINSEED OIL.
THIRD COAT, DEVILS RED, SPEC'N No. 664.

REVISION B, 7-28-41, ... CHANGED SECOND AND THIRD COAT OF EXTERIOR PAINT.

DOOR AND WINDOW SASH TO BE PAINTED BUNK OR TRIMMING COLOR, STOCK No 311.

Author's Note: This is a very rare drawing, perhaps the only copy left in existence, acquired by the author with purchase of the drawing file from the Newark, Ohio, car shops. It is also a confusing drawing for B&O painters. Revision "B" was made to update the painting requirements to Devil's Red, replacing the previous color of Freight Car Brown (see pages 153-154 in Volume 3). However the notes on the top of this drawing with the arrows pointing to various places on the caboose were not properly updated and still show the sides of the caboose and side of the cupola to be painted Freight Car Brown. Also note the "Exterior" instructions at left indicate the car is to receive TREE [sic] coats of paint! Now if we could only locate drawing T-41797, noted below, which would have been prepared in 1923/1924 for the new I-5 Cabooses.

M OF SIDE
BE PAINTED
CK No. 311.

OATS OF
BROWN
LEAD
CARS
VENETIAN
DEVILS

"SNOLITE" PASTE MIXED WITH AN OIL IS TO BE USED FOR STENCILING WHITE LETTERS AND FIGURES ON BLACK AND BROWN SURFACES, LOCATED AS SHOWN ON LETTERING AND MARKING PRINTS

AINT
TURP-
?OWN

WITH
NAMELS
AMELS
OCK No. 310)
OCK No. 311)

SUPERSEDES TRACING T-41797

THE BALTIMORE & OHIO R. R. CO.
FREIGHT CARS
INSTRUCTIONS FOR
PAINTING CABOOSE CARS

MOTIVE POWER DEPT BALTIMORE, MD   4-4-1940

T-66156

A B

DR.	TR.	CKK.
H.P.	D.J.	H.P.

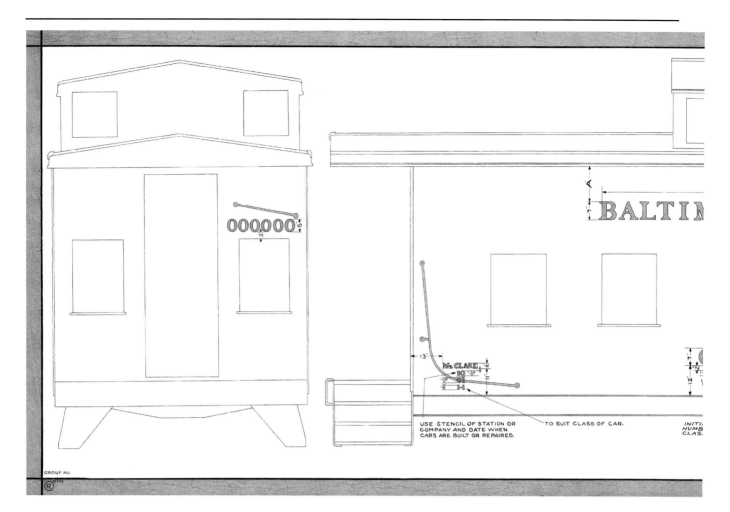

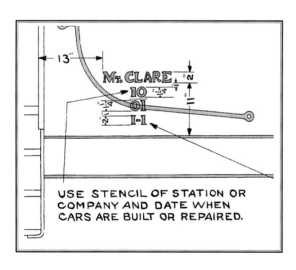

USE STENCIL OF STATION OR
COMPANY AND DATE WHEN
CARS ARE BUILT OR REPAIRED.

Drawing Z-72580 shown on this drawing as the larger circle is the 36" diameter "linking 13 Great States" emblem. It replaced the original Kuhler open-ampersand emblem which the draftsman had a difficult time removing from the drawing as it still shows faintly on the drawing. The good news is that both emblems show located the same 5" dimension below the Baltimore & Ohio lettering.

Wood Cupola
Paint & Lettering

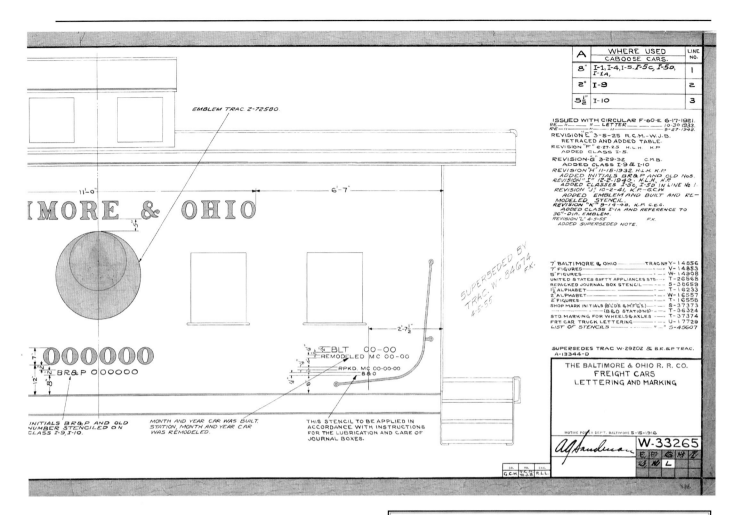

EMBLEM TRAC. Z-72580.

11'-0"

6'-7"

5"

BALTIMORE & OHIO

000000

BR&P 000000

2'-7½"

BLT 00-00
REMODELED MC 00-00

RPKD. MC 00-00-00
B&O

7"
2"
1"
12"
8"

INITIALS BR&P AND OLD
NUMBER STENCILED ON
CLASS I-9, I-10.

MONTH AND YEAR CAR WAS BUILT.
STATION, MONTH AND YEAR CAR
WAS REMODELED.

THIS STENCIL TO BE APPLIED IN
ACCORDANCE WITH INSTRUCTIONS
FOR THE LUBRICATION AND CARE OF
JOURNAL BOXES.

A	WHERE USED CABOOSE CARS.	LINE NO.
8"	I-1, I-4, I-5, I-5c, I-5D, I-1a,	1
2"	I-9	2
5½"	I-10	3

ISSUED WITH CIRCULAR F-60-E 6-17-1921.
RE-"——" LETTER———10-30-1933.
RE-"——"——9-27-1948.
REVISION "E" 3-5-25 R.C.M.-W.J.B.
RETRACED AND ADDED TABLE.
REVISION "F" 6-27-25 H.L.H. K.P.
ADDED CLASS I-5.
REVISION "G" 3-29-32 C.M.B.
ADDED CLASS I-9 & I-10
REVISION "H" 11-15-1932. H.L.H. K.P.
ADDED INITIALS BR&P AND OLD NoS.
REVISION "I" 12-2-1940. H.L.H. K.P.
ADDED CLASSES I-5c, I-5D IN LINE No 1.
REVISION "J" 10-2-41, K.P.-G.C.W.
ADDED EMBLEM AND BUILT AND RE-
MODELED STENCIL.
REVISION "K" 9-14-48, K.P. C.E.C.
ADDED CLASS I-1a AND REFERENCE TO
36"-DIA. EMBLEM.
REVISION "L" 4-5-55 F.K.
ADDED SUPERSEDED NOTE.

7" BALTIMORE & OHIO————TRAC No Y-14856
7" FIGURES————————"—V-14853
5" FIGURES————————"—W-14908
UNITED STATES SAFTY APPLIANCES STD.——"—T-26568
REPACKED JOURNAL BOX STENCIL——"—S-38659
1½" ALPHABET————————"—T-16233
2" ALPHABET————————"—W-16557
2" FIGURES————————"—T-16558
SHOP MARK INITIALS (BL'DS. & MFG's.)——"—S-37373
———————(B&O STATIONS)——"—T-36324
STD. MARKING FOR WHEELS & AXLES——"—T-37374
FRT. CAR TRUCK LETTERING——"—U-17729
LIST OF STENCILS————————"—S-45607

SUPERSEDES TRAC W-29202 & B.R.&P. TRAC.
A-13344-D

THE BALTIMORE & OHIO R. R. CO.
FREIGHT CARS
LETTERING AND MARKING

MOTIVE POWER DEPT. BALTIMORE 5-15-1916

W-33265

DR. TR. CHK.
G.C.H. G.C.H.W.J.B. R.L.L.

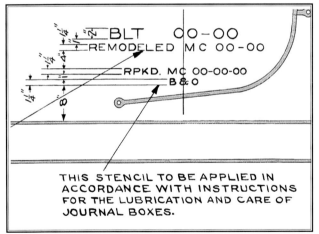

BLT 00-00
REMODELED MC 00-00

RPKD. MC 00-00-00
B&O

THIS STENCIL TO BE APPLIED IN
ACCORDANCE WITH INSTRUCTIONS
FOR THE LUBRICATION AND CARE OF
JOURNAL BOXES.

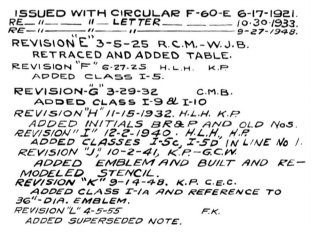

ISSUED WITH CIRCULAR F-60-E 6-17-1921.
RE-"——" LETTER———10-30-1933.
RE-"——"——9-27-1948.
REVISION "E" 3-5-25 R.C.M.-W.J.B.
RETRACED AND ADDED TABLE.
REVISION "F" 6-27-25 H.L.H. K.P.
ADDED CLASS I-5.

REVISION "G" 3-29-32 C.M.B.
ADDED CLASS I-9 & I-10
REVISION "H" 11-15-1932. H.L.H. K.P.
ADDED INITIALS BR&P AND OLD NoS.
REVISION "I" 12-2-1940. H.L.H. K.P.
ADDED CLASSES I-5c, I-5D IN LINE No 1.
REVISION "J" 10-2-41, K.P.-G.C.W.
ADDED EMBLEM AND BUILT AND RE-
MODELED STENCIL.
REVISION "K" 9-14-48. K.P. C.E.C.
ADDED CLASS I-1a AND REFERENCE TO
36"-DIA. EMBLEM.
REVISION "L" 4-5-55 F.K.
ADDED SUPERSEDED NOTE.

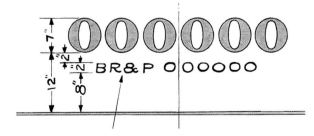

000000
BR&P 000000

Key parts of the above drawing have been enlarged to assure maximum readability for modelers and historians.

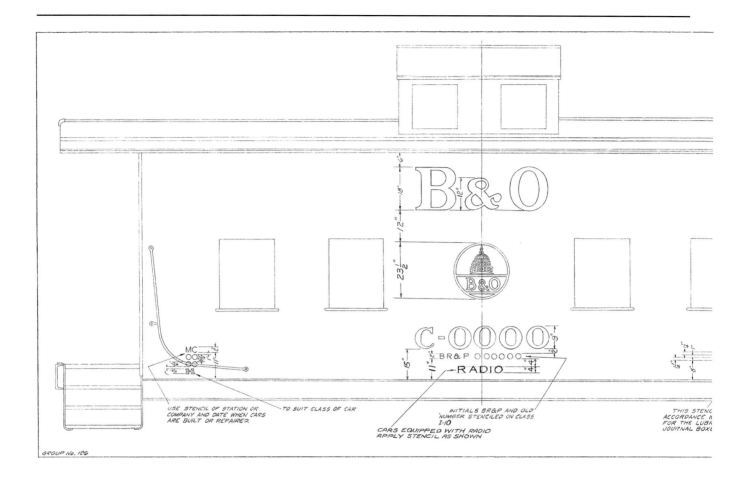

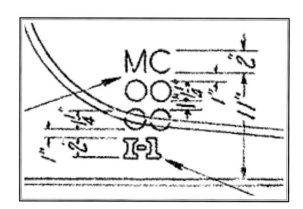

The enlarged view of the painting information above, is presented so that readers can clearly read the dimensions for the lettering and its spacing.

At right, the various revisions to this drawing provide a history of the lettering changes for these cars in very readable format.

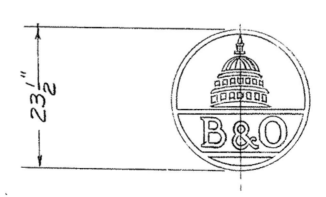

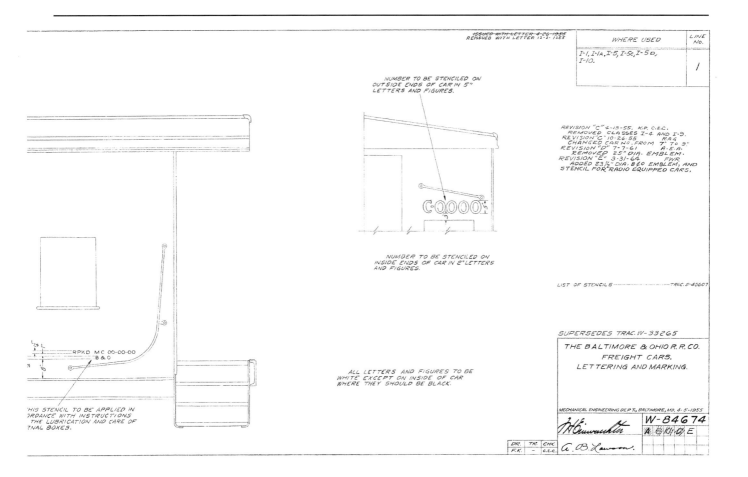

WHERE USED	LINE NO.
I-1, I-1A, I-5, I-5C, I-5D, I-10	1

NUMBER TO BE STENCILED ON
OUTSIDE ENDS OF CAR IN 5"
LETTERS AND FIGURES.

C-0-0000-F

NUMBER TO BE STENCILED ON
INSIDE ENDS OF CAR IN 2" LETTERS
AND FIGURES.

ALL LETTERS AND FIGURES TO BE
WHITE EXCEPT ON INSIDE OF CAR
WHERE THEY SHOULD BE BLACK.

REVISION "C" 4-13-55. K.P. C.E.C.
REMOVED CLASSES I-4 AND I-9.
REVISION "C" 10-26-55 R.A.G.
CHANGED CAR NO. FROM 7" TO 9"
REVISION "D" 7-7-61 A.E.A.
REMOVED 25" DIA. EMBLEM.
REVISION "E" 3-31-64 FWR
ADDED 23½" DIA. B&O EMBLEM, AND
STENCIL FOR RADIO EQUIPPED CARS.

LIST OF STENCILS ——————— TRAC. S-45607

SUPERSEDES TRAC. W-33265

THE BALTIMORE & OHIO R.R. CO.
FREIGHT CARS.
LETTERING AND MARKING.

MECHANICAL ENGINEERING DEP'T., BALTIMORE, MD. 4-5-1955

W-84674
A B C D E

RPKD MC 00-00-00
B & O

THIS STENCIL TO BE APPLIED IN
ORDANCE WITH INSTRUCTIONS
THE LUBRICATION AND CARE OF
RNAL BOXES.

DR. F.K.	TR. -	CHK. C.E.C.

B&O engineers were also prone to occasional errors. In the revision list above revision "B" was incorrectly listed as revision "C" resulting in two revisions "C".

REVISION "C" 4-13-55, K.P. C.E.C.
REMOVED CLASSES I-4 AND I-9.
REVISION "C" 10-26-55 R.A.G
CHANGED CAR NO. FROM 7" TO 9."
REVISION "D" 7-7-61 A.E.A.
REMOVED 25" DIA. EMBLEM.
REVISION "E" 3-31-64 FWR
ADDED 23½" DIA. B&O EMBLEM, AND
STENCIL FOR RADIO EQUIPPED CARS,

At right is reproduced a closeup view of the dimensions and formatting for the stencilling of journal box servicing.

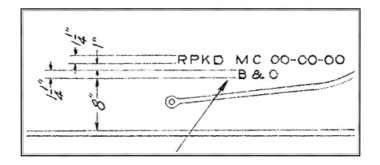

RPKD MC 00-00-00
B & O

I-1, I-1A, I-5, I-5C, I-5D, I-10
Paint & Lettering

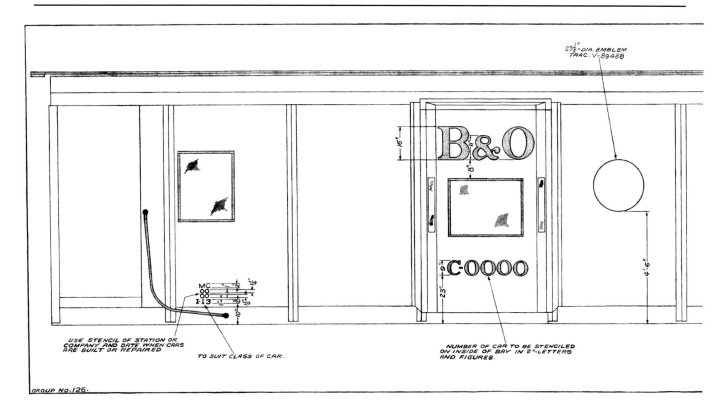

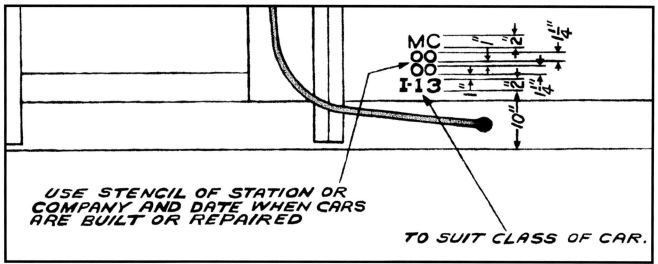

The enlarged view of the painting information above, is presented so that readers can clearly read the dimensions for the lettering and its spacing.

At right, the various revisions to this drawing provide a history of the lettering changes for these cars in very readable format.

I-13, I-16
Paint & Lettering

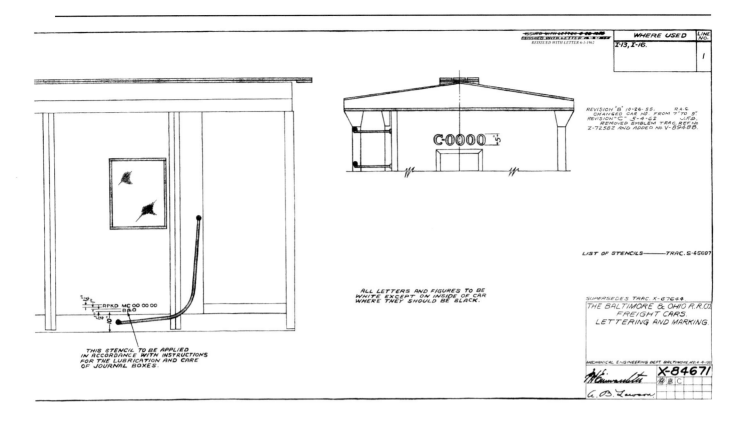

ALL LETTERS AND FIGURES TO BE
WHITE EXCEPT ON INSIDE OF CAR
WHERE THEY SHOULD BE BLACK.

LIST OF STENCILS——— TRAC. S-45607

SUPERSEDES TRAC. X-67644.

THE BALTIMORE & OHIO R.R.CO.
FREIGHT CARS.
LETTERING AND MARKING.

MECHANICAL ENGINEERING DEPT. BALTIMORE, MD. G-4-1935

X-84671

THIS STENCIL TO BE APPLIED
IN ACCORDANCE WITH INSTRUCTIONS
FOR THE LUBRICATION AND CARE
OF JOURNAL BOXES.

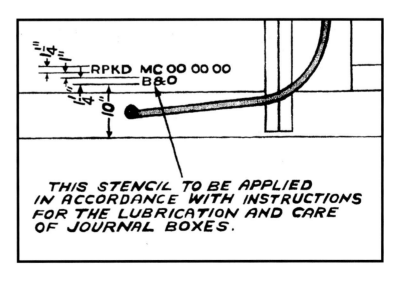

REVISION "B" 10-26-55.   R.A.G.
    CHANGED CAR NO. FROM 7" TO 9".
REVISION "C" 5-4-62   J.F.B.
    REMOVED EMBLEM TRAC. REF. No
Z-72582 AND ADDED No. V-89488.

Emblem V-89488, called for on this revision of the drawing, is the 23-1/2" diameter simplified B&O emblem.

At right is reproduced a closeup view of the dimensions and formatting for the stencilling of journal box servicing.

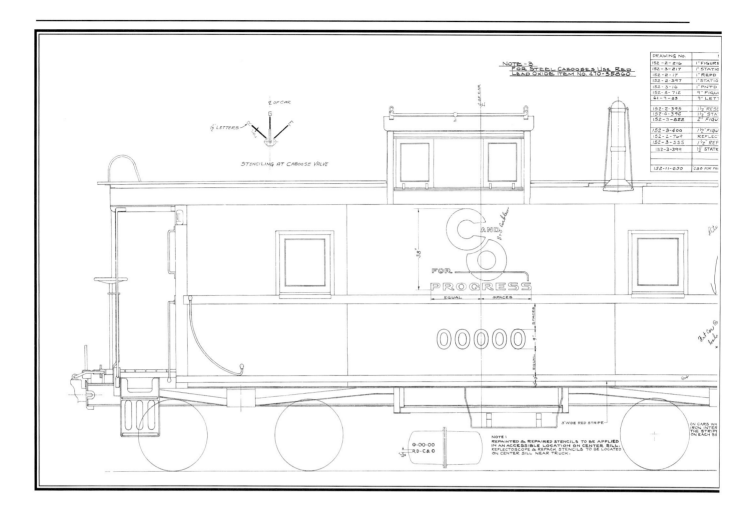

NOTE-3
FOR STEEL CABOOSES USE RED
LEAD OXIDE ITEM No. 470-35860

DRAWING No.	
152-2-216	1" FIGURES
152-3-217	1" STATIC
152-2-17	1" REPD
152-2-397	1" STATIC
152-3-16	1" PNTD
152-5-712	9" FIGU
61-9-83	9" LET'T
152-2-395	1½" RESE
152-4-396	1½" STA
152-3-822	2" FIGU
152-3-400	1½" FIGU
152-2-769	REFLEC
152-3-555	1½" REF
152-3-399	1½" STATIC
152-11-630	C&O FOR PR:

STENCILING AT CABOOSE VALVE

C AND O
B+O emblem
FOR
PROGRESS

00000

NOTE:
REPAINTED & REPAIRED STENCILS TO BE APPLIED
IN AN ACCESSIBLE LOCATION ON CENTER SILL.
REFLECTOSCOPE & REPACK STENCILS TO BE LOCATED
ON CENTER SILL NEAR TRUCK.

3" WIDE RED STRIPE

ON CARS WH
IRON INTER
THE STRIP
ON EACH SIL

0-00-00
RD-C&O

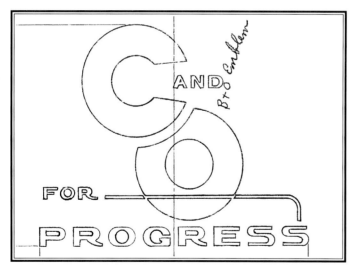

The author acquired this drawing with other drawings from the files of the closed Chillicothe shops. This was the actual drawing used by shop personnel to paint cabooses into the yellow C&O scheme in 1970 and 1971. No drawing for B&O cars was prepared for this scheme. Instead a C&O drawing was supplied to the Chillicothe shops and it was "marked up" to show instructions for the B&O carmen. We have cleaned up the drawing to remove the shop smudges and finger prints but the hand-written instructions have been retained. An example is the enlarged logo shown at left. Instructions were hand-written on the drawing indicating to replace the C&O emblem with a "B&O emblem".

1970-71 C&O Scheme
Paint & Lettering

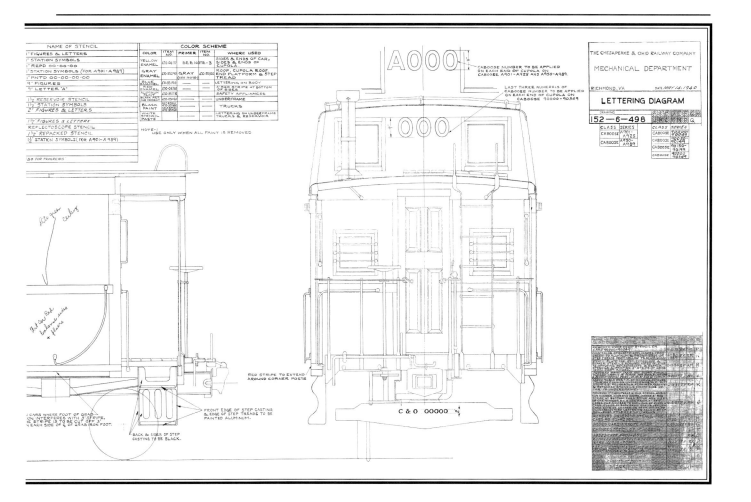

COLOR SCHEME				
COLOR	ITEM NO.	PRIMER	ITEM NO.	WHERE USED
YELLOW ENAMEL	470-04177	SEE NOTE-3		SIDES & ENDS OF CAR, SIDES & ENDS OF CUPOLA.
GRAY ENAMEL	470-35290	GRAY (SEE NOTE-1)	470-35320	ROOF, CUPOLA ROOF, END PLATFORM & STEP TREAD
BLUE ENAMEL	470-35190	—	—	LETTERING ON BODY
RED ENAMEL	470-04730	—	—	3" RED STRIPE AT BOTTOM OF SIDES
ALUMINUM PAINT	470-35030	—	—	SAFETY APPLIANCES
BLACK FRT. CAR CEMENT	470-03060	—	—	UNDERFRAME
BLACK PAINT	HOT SPRAY 470-35160 COLD SPRAY 470-35460	—	—	TRUCKS
WHITE STENCIL PASTE		—	—	LETTERING ON UNDERFRAME TRUCKS & RESERVOIR

The enlarged table above documents the colors of the lettering applied to the B&O cabooses painted at Chillicothe during the 1970-71 caboose program. As we have documented many times the lettering on these cars was Blue, not black. An exception to the above table was the color of the categories shown as Gray Enamel which were painted Aluminum on Chillicothe repaints.

As noted on the previous page, a number of handwritten comments were added to the above drawing to assist the Chillicothe painters. The word RED was written on the red side stripe and the interior colors were documented to the right of the right side window: LIGHT GREEN on the upper parts of the interior walls and ceiling and Frt. CAR RED below the windows on the sides and for the floor.

We have not cleaned up the list of drawing revisions shown at bottom right of the drawing as these apply to C&O cabooses in previous years and are documented in our C&O caboose books.

How do you paint a red stripe along the bottom of a wood-side caboose, not waste a lot of masking tape and do so quickly and efficiently? Use a long board on top and bottom, of course! The ingenuity of the carmen at the Chillicothe shops demonstrates that on this car, being painted on May 19, 1971. The boards were painted red to assure they would not be cut up for some other use.
Dwight Jones

The C-2138 last was painted at the Willard shops in August 1966 and is one of the Willard copycat I-5Dm versions with plywood covering. The painter has made a boo boo by stenciling the "8" backwards. Photographed at Willard on December 3, 1966, by Julian Barnard, Jr.

This I-5Dm car painted at DU 9-61 has the "B&O" too low on the sides and the "B" is painted upside down. Perhaps there was a new painter in training. The car was photographed at Dover, Ohio, on January 29, 1967.
J.W. Barnhard, Jr.

Baltimore, Md., July 31, 1942.

126 – Lettering and Marking – Stencilling Freight, Caboose, Camp, Work Cars,Etc. –

Messrs.

W.S.Eyerly	W.H.Longwell	E.B.Cox
H.M.Sherrard	W.B.Nolan	R.B.Fisher
C.W.Esch	G.H.Rosenberg	A.H.Keys
F.L.Hall	E.Stimson,Jr.	A.J.Larrick
F.M.Galloway	J.W.Schad	F.J.Crockett
L.R.Haase	C.H.Spence	H.A.Harris
I.L.Harper	W.E.Lehr	W.P.Hollen
W.F.Harris	J.S.Major	E.H.Meckstroth
J.P.Hines	W.A.Bender	G.O.Prosser

     Check shows that the lettering and marking on our Freight, Caboose, Camp, Work Cars, etc., is not being handled in a uniform manner at all stations.

     At some stations where the stencilling is done the spaces shielded by the bridges in some forms of lettering and stencils are not painted solid to complete the letters, figures, etc. This also applies to the B. & O. emblem adopted for our cars.

     It is very important that the stencil be painted solid where the figures and letters are 3" and over, as it would be difficult to hand paint the smaller stencils.

     Kindly arrange to handle with all concerned, so that our cars will be painted and stencilled in a uniform manner at all stations.

F.H.Einwaechter

APPROVED:

N.P.Galloway   *W.W.Litsitt.*

Cy. Messrs.

F.H.Becherer	C.M.House	H.J.Burkley
H.L.Holland	H.Rees	E.M.Scherch
E.J.McSweeney	F.A.Baldinger	W.W.Calder

Shop short cuts in not filling in the stencil tabs (bridges in B&O lingo) did not escape the ire of Baltimore officials, to the point that a neo-style letter was issued to address the situation. Caboose C-2295 was painted at Lima, Ohio, in September 1946, and is representative of a "Great States" emblem with the tabs not filled in. The other lettering, which has been filled in, likely had bridges made of wire which were automatically filled in during the stencilling process with no further touchup required. *Paul Dunn collection / collection of Dwight Jones*

The Baltimore and Ohio Railroad Company

MOTIVE POWER DEPARTMENT

BALTIMORE, MD., June 1, 1944.

SHOP BULLETIN No. 18-B
(Superseding Shop Bulletin No. 18-A)

PNEUMATIC PAINT SPRAY

The following prints, of latest revision, cover Pneumatic Paint Spray for use in painting trucks of Passenger Cars, and Locomotive Tenders; also, Steel Underframe and Body of Freight Cars, and general painting where a first class finish is not required:

T-30228—Pneumatic Paint Spray—Portable Hand Type for Small Work.

This spray to be manufactured at Mt. Clare.

T-63345—Pneumatic Paint Spray and Truck for Large and General Work.

The latter facility, when required, to be manufactured locally; stations not in a position to manufacture will arrange for manufacture at stations in a position to do the work.

Operators of Pneumatic Paint Sprays to be governed by instructions covering necessary precaution and protection per Shop Bulletin No. 152 of the latest revision.

A. K. Galloway
General Superintendent
Motive Power and Equipment

W. B. Whitsitt
Chief Engineer Motive Power & Equipment

Group Nos. 215, 228.

Stencils

On August 2, 1978, we brought out the Capitol Dome emblem stencils from the Chillicothe shops stencil room in order to take side-by-side photos. The 38" diameter emblem on the left was used to letter the cabooses painted in the C&O yellow scheme. The stencil on the right was used on the previous red scheme in the late 1960s. Wire bridges were used on both stencils which eliminated the need for any hand touchup of the bridge areas. *Dwight Jones*

This Chillicothe stencil shows how characters were assembled into a wood frame for application. *Dwight Jones*

This Chillicothe stencil featuring the 25" diameter 13 states emblem has bridges which must be touched up by hand after spraying or pouncing the stencil design on the caboose. Attaching a wood frame not only protects the stencil during storage and application but also guards against overspray when using the stencil. *Dwight Jones*

From the author's collection this is a photo of a piece of concrete imbedded with steel punchings salvaged from the floor of an I-5D caboose compared to a six inch ruler.

187

Washington Car Shop

1	Roundhouse
2	Store houses & Division Headquarters (until 1948)
3	Blacksmith Shop
4	Locomotive Shop
5	Coach Shop
6	Power House
7	Wood Shop
8	Bolt House
9	Paint Shop
10	Stencil Shop
11	Warehouse
12	Lumber Sheds
13	Carpenter's Shop
14	Material Storage
15	Transportation Yard

B&O Shops

Washington, Indiana

Photo from July 1926
Baltimore & Ohio Magazine

Both of the aerial views in this chapter look from west to east. In the view above the long narrow transportation yard shows at the right. The roundhouse area is out of view at the top of the image. Four long car shop tracks allow for assembly line construction and refurbishment of projects in the B&O's "Spot" repair/assembly system.

Ed Young (with input from Frank Dewey) researched and penned an extensive article on Washington, Indiana, and the shops there which appeared in the 1Q2012 Sentinel (B&ORRHS). Ed has graciously allowed us to use his information for this two-page synopsis of the shops.

This 1940s era aerial photo shows the roundhouse area located on the east end of the yard and part of the car shop buildings at lower right of the photo. Transportation caboose tracks show at the top left of the photo. Almost all of the cabooses are of the cupola style. *Two aerial photos courtesy of Ed Young*

The Washington shops constructed the 401 class I-5 cars and 75 class I-16 cabooses making their coverage very relevant to this book. During the 1950s the shops constructed the I-17 and I-17A cabooses. Ed Young has documented that the shops were moved to Washington in the late 1800s from other locations on the old Ohio & Mississippi.

Washington was a key B&O repair point for passenger cars, cabooses and freight equipment being the largest car shop complex on the western part of the system.

The shops at Washington were closed on December 27, 1965, just a few months after the closure of the shops at Keyser, West Virginia (May 1965). These closings likely were related to C&O cost reduction initiatives and consolidations. Newer equipment required less shop facilities for maintenance.

In 1966 a contract repair operation was using the shop complex; several other contract rail car repair companies have used it since and continue today. Ed Young reports that one building may eventually be converted into a railroad museum.

Shops: B&O Cabooses Built 1924-1943

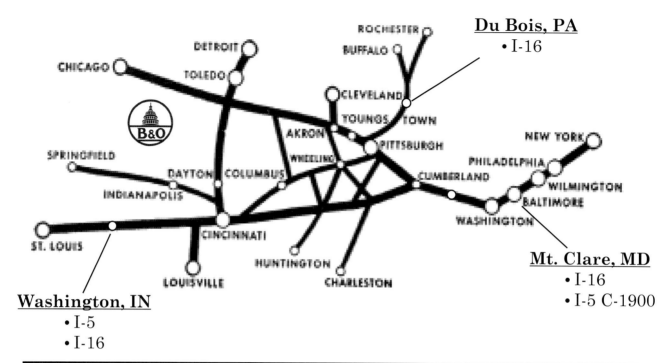

Du Bois, PA
- I-16

Mt. Clare, MD
- I-16
- I-5 C-1900

Washington, IN
- I-5
- I-16

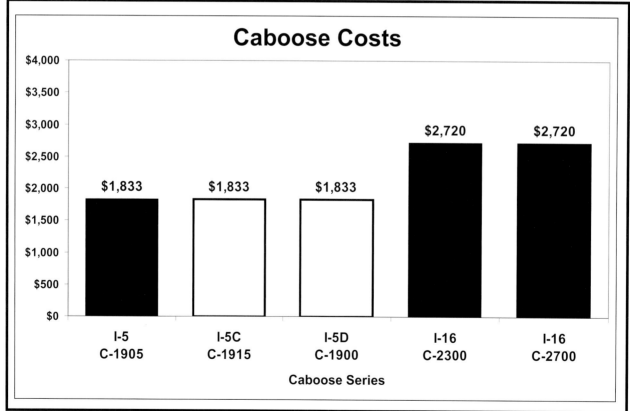

This chart graphically illustrates the average price per caboose for the listed car series. Data for this chart was derived from Chessie System Accounting Department records. Costs on this chart may not match AFE data, due to cost over runs and decisions to add betterments after completion of the original Authority For Expenditures. I-16 cars have the modification costs added to their initial book value. I-5 family cabooses did not show an increased book value when modified to I-5C or I-5D modifications.

CHAPTER 9

Caboose Trucks

This class I-5D caboose is equipped with Andrews trucks (note the "ANDREWS" name cast in the side frame under the elliptic springs. Carrying a 1928 cast date, we wonder how these trucks found their way under this B&O caboose since they carry Chicago and North Western markings! *Dwight Jones*

Class I-5 caboose C-2252 was equipped with trucks having Vulcan cast side frames on July 17, 1965, in this J. W. Barnard, Jr, photo taken at Willard, Ohio.

These 5-1/2" x 10" trucks from an I-5Dm caboose have so many coats of paint on them that some lettering is difficult to read, but not the 8-1947 cast date. B&O made a practice of upgrading caboose trucks by reclaiming side frames from dismantle freight cars. This view provides a good look at the round side bearings and the center pin. It was generally thought that paint on trucks could conceal defects such as cracks. *Dwight Jones*

C-375	***	Deforest Jct		
C-1419		Akron Jct	XN Yard Job	
C-1948		Haselton		Shop
C-1951		Deforest Jct	Dist Run #20	
C-1959		Deforest Jct		Extra Service
C-1961		Willard		Chillicothe Shop 6/15/70
C-1963		Willard		Extra Service
C-1967		Ohio Jct	Yard Mill Job	
C-1973	***	Willard		
C-1974		Unrichsville	Work Train	
C-1975		Deforest Jct	Dist Run #30 & #31	
C-2003		Akron Jct	Canton Locals	
C-2006		Willard		Shopped Garrett
C-2018		Willard	Defiance Turn	
C-2041	***	Willard		
C-2043		New Castle	Yard Hill Job	
C-2068		Garrett	Switcher Run	
C-2081		Garrett	Switcher Run	
C-2116		Massillon	Massillon-Holloway Loc #2	
C-2127		Cleveland	Peninsula Local	
C-2130		Haselton		Shop
C-2138		Deforest Jct	Dist Run #18	
C-2143		Cleveland		Extra Service
C-2161		Cleveland	Lester Local	
C-2181		Akron	Peanut Run	
C-2213		Willard	Defiance Turn	
C-2218		Willard		Extra Service
C-2230	***	Haselton		
C-2250		Willard		Chillicothe Shop
C-2262		Deforest Jct	Chardon Turn	
C-2264	***	Willard		
C-2270		Cleveland	Sterling Local	
C-2277		Haselton	Brier Hill Job	
C-2607		Deforest Jct	Akron Local	
C-2624		Akron	Air Port Job	
C-2629		Lorain	Elyria-Grafton Local	
C-2632		Cleveland	Newburg Local	
C-2638		Massillon	Massillon-Holloway Loc #1	
C-2662		Haselton	River Job	

*** - Cabooses dropped as of this report. Under authority for dismantling request
by Car Department.

E. A. Howard
Train Master

5-f
7-24-70

This 1970 document is a sample of the caboose reporting that local train-masters were required to submit to their division headquarters on a periodic basis. Thanks to Dave Ori for providing this copy which supplements the assignment location information provided earlier in this book. By the date of this 1970 report the local assigned cabooses were mostly from the I-5 family supplemented by a few I-10 cars off the Buffalo Division.

B&O Cabooses In Color!

Extensive coverage of caboose C-3051 was provided in volume 1 of this series where we pointed out that cabooses painted in the Chessie scheme at the Du Bois shops had their trucks cleaned but not painted. This March 1979 view of the C-3051 at Cincinnati shows trucks freshly painted black. We suspect this was done at the Raceland shops five months earlier when the steps were modified to comply with UTU requests. *collection of Dwight Jones*

The C-2063 was photographed at Frederick, Maryland, on August 20, 1951, fresh from the Mt. Clare shops in Baltimore. The body is Devil's Red, while the steps and end platform are Freight Car Brown. The platform end is black, the green is the earlier Olive Green and the trucks are unpainted. *collection of John R. King*

Baltimore and Ohio Magazine

November   1926

SAFETY
Above Everything Else

In John McMackin's Caboose

Photographed at Cumberland, Maryland, the C-2193 is in fresh paint wearing the 1945 lettering scheme. This is a good look at the Devil's Red paint contrasted with the Freight Car Brown, which has been applied to the end platform, steps, and apparently the entire cupola area, and roof, in accordance with drawing T-66156. A single marker wing or shield shows on this car. *William H. Shryock, collection of Dwight Jones*

This is another nice image showing the 1945 lettering scheme as well as the application of Devil's Red to the body and Freight Car Brown to the steps and end platforms. The Mount Clare shops last painted this class I-5 car, painting the window sash as well as the window frames Olive Green. As is the case with other C-2000-series cabooses, this car has the flat-stock type of ladder-to-roof handholds. *collection of John R. King*

On the previous page is a reproduction of the cover of *Baltimore and Ohio Magazine* for November 1926. This rendition may provide a clue to the interior color of cupola cabooses in this era and appears to show a light gray over olive green. On the bottom of the cover is the wording "In John McMackins Caboose". Conductor McMackin must have been quite the celebrity on the B&O. At this era he had a wood cupola caboose with many wall photos. He also was featured on page 48 of volume 3 in this series as he had been assigned wagon top bay-window caboose C-2502. He served as a tour guide for his caboose at the Wheeling Centennial in 1936 at which time he was referred to as the "famed conductor of the Cumberland Division".

The Willard shops last rehabilitated the C-1976, outshopping it as a copycat I-5Dm not long before this August 1965 image was made of the car in service at Dover, Ohio. Its copycat status is easy to spot with its full radius side grabirons and stem-winder brake wheel. *Edwin C. Kirstatter*

Class I-5D C-2130 is shown at Akron, Ohio, in fresh paint in July 1964, wearing the standard 1955 paint and lettering scheme. The car still exhibits the contour steps, wide at the top and narrow at the bottom, unusual for this late date. *Edwin C. Kirstatter*

A coal train with empties passed the Morgantown depot and local in this circa 1972 photo. GP9 6575 awaits its next run behind the caboose. Mounted on the end of the caboose, just under the platform roof, is an air horn. *collection of Dwight Jones*

At Morgantown, West Virginia, the local operated with a caboose on both ends (see volume 3, page 16). When the Cumberland shops last painted C-2056 (6-71) it was all red, but locals have repainted the left end white for better visibility when shoving caboose-first (note the sealed beam headlight). The cab was back in Cumberland two years later with smashed steps from a crossing accident. *collection of Dwight Jones*

The Cumberland shops last painted the C-2225 with unusual green window frames and window awnings as well as not-so-unusual, for the Cumberland shops, small "B&O" lettering. This I-5Dm car was photographed at Cumberland in February 1970. *George Berisso / collection of Dwight Jones*

Gassaway, West Virginia, was the location for the C-1922 when photographed in April 1971. The car has a new sectional metal roof, likely salvaged from a boxcar. The lettering scheme indicates it is one of the cars that graduated from the Du Bois shops during 1968/1969. The painters there have retained the green window sash but have abandoned the green doors. *George Berisso / collection of Dwight Jones*

Shown departing Grafton, West Virginia, for the west is C-2125 in this August 1966 photo by Jim Atkinson. A typical modeler question is "what color was the roof?" Perhaps this photo can provide some guidance. After a couple of years of service the color is that of "dust"! The trainman in the cupola is making good use of the wind shield.

This photo of the C-2079 exhibits several interesting characteristics, the most unusual being the reflector markers mounted to the end. The car also has a whistle mounted above the roof, rare Adlake electric marker lights, screens over the windows for the bug season, smokestack cap rotated in the wrong direction and the flat-stock type of ladder-to-roof handholds, a typical application for most of the C-2000-series cars. The "J" side grabirons, two side windows and power brake stand identify this car as an I-5Dm. *B&O Railroad Historical Society collection*

Veteran caboose photographer Paul Dunn captured the C-1915 fresh from the Du Bois paint shop in the spring of 1969 at Zanesville, Ohio. They are still applying green to the window sash but have apparently given up on the green end doors. *collection of Dwight Jones*

Under repair at the Chillicothe shops on July 20, 1970, is the C-2139. The car already had a covering of plywood from a previous shopping, needing only a couple of sheets replaced on the left side. This photo is cropped to show extra parts in the foreground including a step, smokestack, truck side frames and other smaller parts salvaged from other cabooses for possible future reuse. *Dwight Jones*

C-2141, one of six 1969-1970 repaints from the Brunswick shops in this scheme, is shown coming off the branch at Harpers Ferry, West Virginia, eastbound for Brunswick in early 1970. The car is equipped with a pair of battery-operated markers since it will be operating in Maryland on the other side of the Potomac River. Brunswick shop superintendent R. P. "Dick" Mullen was a B&O man through and through; no yellow C&O paint on his cabs! And green sash and doors survived to the very end. *collection of Dwight Jones*

You could easily tell where Terry Arbogast lived in Fairmont—he kept the brush cut on the east side of the river so he could see this view clearly from his house! In the fall of 1968 he recorded this view of seven red cabooses, including one in fresh paint from the Du Bois shops.

The C-2296 has an odd look to it, not only due to the spartan lettering but also because the cupola handholds, running boards, and ladder roof handholds all have been removed for safety. The car was photographed at Julietta, Indiana, on August 31, 1974, and likely was last painted at Moorefield Yard in Indianapolis. We suspect the car was also safety-enhanced at that same location. *Dwight Jones*

We are withholding B&OCT cars for a future volume. We present an exception here to make the point that black roofs were a Chicago Terminal characteristic typically not found on I-5 family B&O system cars during the color photography era. C-2122 exemplifies that in Chicago on October 26, 1966.
collection of Dwight Jones

The Chillicothe shops could make a veteran wood caboose look almost brand new with a few repairs and a fresh coat of paint. The C-1993 had just been painted when photographed on December 28, 1974. Car Forman Ora Sheets was always proud of the work his carmen did and he expected a top quality job with every small detail. At this shopping a power brake stand has been added. *Dwight Jones*

On August 11, 1970, C-1927 was under repair at the Chillicothe shops and being painted yellow. Many cars are undergoing work with just a few feet between them for access. *Dwight Jones*

C-2132 is just about ready to be released from the Chillicothe shops on July 20, 1970. C&O Signal Yellow with Enchantment Blue (not black) lettering spruces up this old car. The small home-built scaffold shows that the last step is to install the ACI plate. *Dwight Jones*

A painter on the roof and one by the right coupler do last minute touchup work to cab C-2084 at the Chillicothe shops on July 20, 1971. A third shop worker is transporting a ladder to the next work site. The craftsmen at Chillicothe took great pride in their work; cabooses looked as good as new when released from the shops.
Dwight Jones

Camera artist Terry Arbogast made this exposure on July 4, 1979, to capture the C-2227 with backlights from the Grafton, West Virginia, depot and town. If you look closely you can see the reflective properties of the colored stripes from the ACI plate on the caboose side, each different color coded stripe representing a digit or letter which, taken all together, identified the railroad name and car number when read by a lineside scanner.

Caboose C-2000 represents the oddball scheme applied to a few cabooses by the Cumberland, Maryland, shops in 1974/1975. The yellow scheme features black trim and lettering. Photographed at Benwood, West Virginia, on June 29, 1975, the similarly-painted cabs include C-1946, C-2127 and C-2210. Note the reflector markers displaying red to the rear and green on the opposite side. *Dwight Jones*

The craftsmen at the Chillicothe shops were called on again in the mid-1970s to rehab a few more wood cabs. About a dozen I-5 family cars were included. On May 18, 1975, the Chillicothe yard engine removes completed C-2283 and "Chessied" C-2928 from the shop area. *Dwight Jones*

On this page are shown cars wearing the representative Chessie schemes given to the I-5 family cars. At right, a product of the Grafton, West Virginia, shops, the C-2165 lost its "C" prefix during the repainting of April 1975. The car is shown at Benwood, West Virginia, May 20, 1978. *The Houser collection*

C-2175 is shown exhibiting the so-called "Walbridge Scheme" at Walbridge, Ohio, on April 29, 1978. The car is in "R"estricted service (note the "R" below the number) due to the car's age. Roof walks and the upper ladder sections have been removed. *Dwight Jones*

One of the more creative Chessie schemes was applied to the C-1975 by the carmen at Haselton (Youngstown), Ohio, during July of 1975. The car was kept locally in that area, being renumbered X-150 for non-revenue service after its caboose days were over.
Dwight Jones

Charles Mahan captured the C-2311 in fresh paint at Baltimore on January 28, 1950. The brightness of the fresh paint is in stark contrast to the weathered I-5 family caboose it is coupled to. This is the 1945 paint scheme with olive green window sash.

The C-2334 is shown wearing the I-16 lettering scheme adopted in 1955 which featured the "B&O" on the top of the side bay and the smaller version of the "Great States" emblem. This car last was painted at the Du Bois shops. It was wrecked at Fostoria, Ohio, in 1957, probably not long after this image was recorded. It was written up as scrap at Willard. *collection of Ed Kirstatter*

The C-2778 appears to be in the process of being stripped, possibly for use as a building. On the ground we can identify the sink and the two conductor desk seats. Plywood covers the doorway. The wheels are very rusty—an indication this car has not moved in quite some time. It was photographed at Springfield, Illinois, on November 11, 1962. The car was reported as destroyed by fire in 1972 at Ridgeley, Illinois (a Springfield suburb and likely this same spot). *Karl C. Henkels /collection of Dwight Jones*

Representative of the many I-16 cabooses that were converted for MofW service is the X-4196 photographed by John R. King at Grafton, West Virginia, in June of 1968. Two smokestacks suggest that there may be compartments in the car for workers. The silver color for certain non-revenue equipment was adopted by the B&O with the issuance of a letter dated February 8, 1960. Class I-16 cars were ideally suited for conversion to MofW cars due to their long length and interior equipment. Small lettering on this car indicates MAINTENANCE OF WAY, EMERGENCY CAMP.

Silver X-4198 is an I-16 conversion from caboose C-2784 completed at the Washington, Indiana, shops in 1962. This 1964 image, taken at an unknown location, also has caboose C-2194 bringing up the rear of the train. The caboose was assigned to the St. Louis Division in 1964. *David P. Oroszi collection*

The dark view of the C-2137 at right is the only color image that has surfaced of the rare early yellow scheme applied to this caboose likely as a test case. The car is shown adjacent to the B&O Museum, date unknown. See page 83.

The X-2773, showcasing its yellow corner triangle, is shown in April 1965 at an unknown location. Renumbered at Keyser in December 1955 from C-2710, this is the car that today resides at Cool Springs Park near Rowlesburg, West Virginia.

Jim Corbett collection

Quite the interesting paint scheme on X-2140 converted at Mount Clare in 1955 from caboose C-2374. Date and location unknown.

collection of Dwight Jones

Nearing the end of wood cabooses on the B&O, bad-order cars have accumulated at the Chillicothe shops on November 3, 1974. *Dwight Jones*

Acknowledgments

Veteran equipment historian Carl Shaver has helped us on all of our book projects, and was a help again on this one, as he reviewed the final draft and made suggestions for improvement, including editing suggestions.

The many fans who helped us on painting projects or loaned images for publication, include Terry Arbogast, Jim Atkinson, Charles Brown, Alex Campbell, Jim Corbett, Donald Davis, Jerry Doyle, Fred Fox, Charles Freed, Fran Giacoma, Art Gladstone, Ed Hladik, Ross Jack, David Jones, Len Kilian, Joseph Lavelle, John Lawrence, Dave Ori, James Parker, Bud Puskarich, Charlie Rogers, Dennis Schmidt, Brian Solomon, Richard Solomon, Linda, Chris and Randy Strogen, George Votava, Clyde Wagner, Jay Williams, Tim Wilson, Bob Withers, Charlie Winters, and Bob Withers.

We also pay tribute to the top B&O caboose gurus that we have worked with over the years, including Bud Abbott, Julian Barnard, Paul Dunn, and Ed Kirstatter. Ed also reviewed this book's manuscript for us. We appreciate his expertise and B&O knowledge.

Other subject matter experts who reviewed the manuscript include Dennis Fulton, Fred Heald, and David Jones. We appreciate their input and suggestions.

A special acknowledgment is given to Dave Oroszi of Dayton, Ohio. A photographer, author and historian, he maintains one of the largest railroad image collections in the entire U.S. His sharing of his resources is second to none.

Buffalo Division historian Brian DeVries deserves special recognition for his untiring efforts to save and share key records for B&O equipment and operations.

John P. Hankey allowed us to use his captions for the I-12 construction sequence. His B&O knowledge is tremendous.

From the B&O Railroad Historical Society, we thank Nick Fry, Richard Lind, Al McElvoy, Nick Powell, Mike Shylanski, Greg Smith, Michael Watnoski and Chris Winslow.

From the B&O Railroad Museum, we thank George Harwood, Ryan McPherson and Dave Shackelford.

We also thank the many CSX employees that we have met during our equipment searches and photography. Special thanks is due Joseph Brinker, Hank DeVries, Bucky Jones, Mike Montonera, Barry Totty, Len Whitehead and others that we have listed below.

During the years that our research was underway for this book, we talked to dozens of Chessie and CSX employees across all parts of the system. Almost to a person, all took time from their busy schedules to grant permissions, or answer questions, give permission for photos to be taken, allow documents to be copied, or at least provide a lead or two for additional information. Many of these people have since become cherished friends that we continue to work with on future projects. Certainly a big tip of the hat is due from all of us in the historical community to the following Chessie and CSX men and women: George Athanas, Matt Carson, Curtis Barr, Gary Brannock, Jim Burnette, Teddy Cain, Franklyn Carr, J.J. Cassidy, Brian Clark, Ric Cole, Don Daniels, Henry DeVries, Frank Dewey, Ron Drucker, John Eccleston, David Farley, Andy Foster, Danny Friedman, Carol Geben, Art Gladstone, Richard Godbey, H.J. Harbert, Randy Harrell, Bob Hastings, Crew Heimer, George Hendrien, Jeff Hensley, Bucky Jones, Chuck Jones, Bart Kohl, Lloyd Lewis, Frank LeMaster, Lew Lubarsky, Scott Marshall, Mike Martino, Charlie Mewshaw, Jack Mills, Kenny Morriss, Russ Peery, Billy Jack Peirce, Bob Perkins, Delse Piper, W.A. Reich, Dennis Richmond, John Riddle, Mark Rogers, Jim Sadler, John Shanahan, Ora Sheets, Maurice Short, Larry Smith, Alan Smith, Jack Spatig, Jim Spainhower, Steve Tackett, W. B. Vander Veer, Jerry Wess, Harry White and Al Wiles.

How to Contact Us

We are constantly looking for new material to help with our future projects. We have a number of them on deck, particularly regarding B&O cabooses. If you have material that can help, we certainly would like to hear from you. We are always looking for old photos, company records, drawings, company correspondence, old files, recollections, etc. You can contact us by using one of the methods listed in the block below.

Dwight Jones
536 Clairbrook Avenue
Columbus, Ohio 43228

614-870-7315

csxcabooses@msn.com

Publications from This Same Author

C&O/B&O Cabooses, Display and Private Owner Cars, Volume I, II, III, IV contain photo and history coverage of hundreds of C&O and B&O cabooses sold by the railroad and now on display in city parks, in backyards, in museums, etc. Additional sections cover moving a caboose, caboose trains operated by shortline and tourist railroads, and more. Softcover, with color covers. Available from the author, volume I =$15.95; volume II = $16.95; vol III = $17.95, vol IV = $18.95 + 4.00 S/H: Dwight Jones, 536 Clairbrook Avenue, Columbus, Ohio 43228.

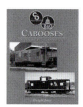   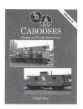

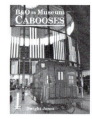 *B&O Railroad Museum Cabooses* is a compilation of the history of each of the many cabooses that have been added to the museum collection over the years or that have visited the museum. A total of 30 cabooses are included in the coverage which provides many behind-the-scene stories and photos showing cabooses being moved to the museum and cars being restored. The author is uniquely qualified to author this book as he has worked on almost every caboose at the museum including helping to acquire many of the cars. ($31.95 plus $5.00 shipping; Ohio residents include $2.08 state tax). Order from Dwight Jones.

Encyclopedia of B&O Cabooses, volumes 1-3 are the first complete and detailed histories of the B&O caboose fleet. Hardbound, 176-208 pages, these books are loaded with photos, detailed historical coverage, painting and lettering drawings, which are reproduced in such a manner as to have all data contained on them in readable format. Most impressive are the detailed rosters by individual caboose number giving full historical details for each caboose including retirement and disposition data as well as modification and paint dates. This series begins what likely will be a 5 volume set covering the history of all B&O cabooses. ($41.99-$46.99 plus $5.00 shipping; Ohio residents include applicable state sales tax). Order from Dwight Jones.

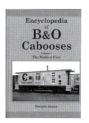 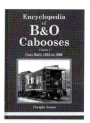 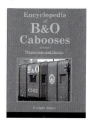

Other publications cover cabooses of C&O (wood and steel), Western Maryland, DT&I, and L&N.

Caboose Photos in This Publication by Page Number

Should one wish to locate photos of a specific caboose quickly, this listing can be consulted